FIVE VIEWS ON THE GOSPEL

Scot McKnight

Michael Horton

David A. deSilva

Julie Ma

Shively T. J. Smith

Michael F. Bird and Jason Maston, general editors
Stanley N. Gundry, series editor

ZONDERVAN ACADEMIC

Five Views on the Gospel
Copyright © 2025 by Michael F. Bird, Jason S. Maston, Scot McKnight, Michael Horton, David A. deSilva, Julie C. Ma, and Shively T. J. Smith

Published in Grand Rapids, Michigan, by Zondervan. Zondervan is a registered trademark of The Zondervan Corporation, L.L.C., a wholly owned subsidiary of HarperCollins Christian Publishing, Inc.

Requests for information should be addressed to customercare@harpercollins.com.

Zondervan titles may be purchased in bulk for educational, business, fundraising, or sales promotional use. For information, please email SpecialMarkets@Zondervan.com.

Library of Congress Cataloging-in-Publication Data

Names: McKnight, Scot, author.
Title: Five views on the gospel / Scot McKnight, Michael Horton, David A. deSilva, Julie C. Ma, Shively T. J. Smith, Michael F. Bird, and Jason Maston, general editors.
Description: Grand Rapids : Zondervan Academic, [2025] | Series: Counterpoints: Bible and theology | Includes index.
Identifiers: LCCN 2024043571 | ISBN 9780310128533 (softcover) | ISBN 9780310128540 (ebook) | ISBN 9780310128564 (audio)
Subjects: LCSH: Bible. Gospels--Commentaries. | BISAC: RELIGION / Biblical Studies / New Testament / General | RELIGION / Christianity / General
Classification: LCC BS2554.B54 F58 2025 | DDC 226/.052--dc23/eng/20250113
LC record available at https://lccn.loc.gov/2024043571

Unless otherwise noted, Scripture quotations are taken from The Holy Bible, New International Version®, NIV®. Copyright © 1973, 1978, 1984, 2011 by Biblica, Inc.® Used by permission of Zondervan. All rights reserved worldwide. www.Zondervan.com. The "NIV" and "New International Version" are trademarks registered in the United States Patent and Trademark Office by Biblica, Inc.®

Scripture quotations marked ESV are taken from the ESV® Bible (The Holy Bible, English Standard Version®). Copyright © 2001 by Crossway, a publishing ministry of Good News Publishers. Used by permission. All rights reserved.

Scripture quotations marked KJV are taken from the King James Version. Public domain.

Scripture quotations marked NRSV are taken from the New Revised Standard Version Bible. Copyright © 1989 National Council of the Churches of Christ in the United States of America. Used by permission. All rights reserved.

Scripture quotations marked NRSVue are taken from the New Revised Standard Version Updated Edition. Copyright © 2021 National Council of Churches of Christ in the United States of America. Used by permission. All rights reserved worldwide.

Any internet addresses (websites, blogs, etc.) and telephone numbers in this book are offered as a resource. They are not intended in any way to be or imply an endorsement by Zondervan, nor does Zondervan vouch for the content of these sites and numbers for the life of this book.

All rights reserved. No part of this publication may be reproduced, stored in a retrieval system, or transmitted in any form or by any means—electronic, mechanical, photocopy, recording, or any other—except for brief quotations in printed reviews, without the prior permission of the publisher.

Cover design: Tammy Johnson
Cover image: Public domain
Interior typesetting: Kait Lamphere

$PrintCode

This book models charitable dialogue while also exposing key differences among approaches. Its contributors reflect not only theological but also contextual and disciplinary diversity. I learned not only about the diverse frameworks but also more about Calvin, Wesley, and other historical theology. I found myself agreeing with much in each essay and hoping that such dialogue can help us synthesize the best insights of each, while keeping Jesus's identity and work at the center.

Craig S. Keener, F. M. and Ada Thompson Professor of Biblical Studies, Asbury Theological Seminary

"Gospel" is perhaps the most important word and concept in the Bible, but it nonetheless runs the risk of becoming a buzzword that is overused and underdefined. *Five Views on the Gospel* avoids this risk by bringing several scholars into conversation to discuss in detail what they believe the gospel is—and isn't. This book is warmly recommended for pastors, students, and scholars alike as they seek to better understand and explain the biblical gospel.

Brandon D. Smith, Chair of the Hobbs School of Theology & Ministry and Associate Professor of Theology & Ministry at Oklahoma Baptist University; cofounder of the Center for Baptist Renewal

Jesus said, "The time is fulfilled, and the kingdom of God is near. Repent and believe in the gospel" (Mark 1:15). What exactly is the "gospel"? "Gospel" is a term meaning "good news" in the original Greek. What exactly is the "good news" preached by Jesus and his apostles? If you were asked this question, how would you define "gospel"? The answer is not necessarily a simple one. For the New Testament authors often seem to define "gospel" somewhat differently. It should not surprise us, therefore, to observe differences in how five scholars in this volume present and defend their understanding of it. This volume is a wonderful contribution to the discussion and will be a valuable resource, not only for theologians and pastors but also for those of us who want to see lives powerfully transformed by the "gospel."

Michael Licona, Professor of New Testament Studies, Houston Christian University

For Christians, the gospel is a crucially important theological topic, well-deserving of extensive and penetrating discussion. Bird and Maston have brought key voices into conversation about the nature and implications of the main message of Jesus and the apostles. While disagreements are highlighted, this book isn't a competition between views; it's an opportunity for clarification, refinement, and for readers to ponder the width, height, and depth of the glory of the good news of the Messiah. This is one of my favorite volumes in Zondervan's Counterpoints series, and I highly recommend it to anyone interested in the gospel and its effects.

Nijay K. Gupta, Julius R. Mantey Professor of New Testament, Northern Seminary

This valuable resource brings together five articulations of the gospel, each with different yet mostly complementary framings and emphases. It challenges us to pay attention to aspects of the gospel that are found in Scripture but may not have as prominent a place in our own formulations and traditions.

Tim MacBride, Principal, Morling College, Australia

Drs. Bird and Maston have assembled a learned group of scholars with different definitions of the gospel to offer readers a clear, informed, and provocative dialogue about the gospel. The result is an accessible conversation about the most important question in the world: What is the gospel of Jesus Christ? As readers from different theological traditions turn each page, they might be moved to shout, "Amen!" while others might be provoked to declare, "Oh my!" Yet they will likewise walk away from this book, longing to know more about the gospel and about the Christ whom it announces as good news for Jews, for gentiles, and for the cosmos as they seek the most faithful way to preach and teach it to anyone with ears to hear.

Jarvis J. Williams, Professor of New Testament Interpretation, The Southern Baptist Theological Seminary

At first, the five contributors of this volume seem like strange bedfellows. Then, the editors invite us to sample their offerings over conversations. Engaging with biblical evidence and with each other, each contributor demonstrates how sin, salvation, the centrality of Christ, and discipleship are enacted within their tradition. A gospel feast for thought.

Jean K. Luah, Assistant Professor, Singapore Bible College

If all the "gospel-centered" ministries were listed in one spot, I suppose Microsoft Excel itself couldn't contain the list. Yet, to the surprise of some, there are different schools of thought on how to briefly describe what precisely the gospel is. The benefit of putting this discussion in a five-views book is that one can see interactions among the diverse outlooks. Readers may enter this book not knowing these discussions are occurring, or they might arrive leaning toward one perspective. Either way, after reading the book, they will have a better understanding of the starting points, why there are differences, and the main areas of emphasis. Possibly something we can all learn from this book is that the gospel is as deep and rich as it is simple and straightforward. Because the gospel is central to what Jesus and the apostles preached, this discussion is worth having, and this book does an admirable job of overviewing some of the different perspectives.

Patrick Schreiner, Associate Professor of New Testament and Biblical Theology, Midwestern Baptist Theological Seminary

This book is a theological treasure, offering deep, well-articulated perspectives on the gospel from a diverse range of voices. Each author presents a compelling and thoughtful argument, making it an invaluable resource for anyone seeking a richer understanding of the gospel's depth and breadth. As someone rooted in the Wesleyan tradition, I appreciated seeing my perspective well represented by Dr. deSilva, while also being challenged and enriched by views beyond my own. *Five Views of the Gospel* is a gift to the church, exemplifying how Christians can engage in meaningful, charitable dialogue even amid theological differences.

David Donnan, Global Methodist Elder
Host, The David Donnan Podcast

Books in the Counterpoints Series

Church Life

Evaluating the Church Growth Movement: Five Views
Exploring the Worship Spectrum: Six Views
Remarriage after Divorce in Today's Church: Three Views
Understanding Four Views on Baptism
Understanding Four Views on the Lord's Supper
Who Runs the Church?: Four Views on Church Government

Bible and Theology

Are Miraculous Gifts for Today? Four Views
Do Christians, Muslims, and Jews Worship the Same God? Four Views
Five Views of Christ in the Old Testament
Five Views on Apologetics
Five Views on Biblical Inerrancy
Five Views on Law and Gospel
Five Views on Sanctification
Five Views on the Church and Politics
Five Views on the Exodus
Five Views on the Extent of the Atonement
Four Views on Christian Spirituality
Four Views on Christianity and Philosophy
Four Views on Creation, Evolution, and Intelligent Design
Four Views on Divine Providence
Four Views on Eternal Security
Four Views on Heaven
Four Views on Hell
Four Views on Moving beyond the Bible to Theology
Four Views on Salvation in a Pluralistic World
Four Views on the Apostle Paul
Four Views on the Book of Revelation
Four Views on the Church's Mission
Four Views on the Historical Adam
Four Views on the Role of Works at the Final Judgment
Four Views on the Spectrum of Evangelicalism
Genesis: History, Fiction, or Neither?: Three Views on the Bible's Earliest Chapters
How Jewish Is Christianity?: Two Views on the Messianic Movement
Show Them No Mercy: Four Views on God and Canaanite Genocide
Three Views on Christianity and Science
Three Views on Creation and Evolution
Three Views on Eastern Orthodoxy and Evangelicalism
Three Views on the Millennium and Beyond
Three Views on the New Testament Use of the Old Testament
Three Views on the Rapture
Two Views on Homosexuality, the Bible, and the Church
Two Views on the Doctrine of the Trinity
Two Views on Women in Ministry

CONTENTS

Contributors 9
Abbreviations 13
Introduction: What Is the Gospel? 15
    MICHAEL F. BIRD

1. **THE KING JESUS GOSPEL** 25
    SCOT MCKNIGHT

              Responses
    MICHAEL HORTON 46
    DAVID A. DESILVA 51
    JULIE MA 55
    SHIVELY T. J. SMITH 57

2. **THE REFORMATION GOSPEL** 63
    MICHAEL HORTON

              Responses
    SCOT MCKNIGHT 86
    DAVID A. DESILVA 93
    JULIE MA 98
    SHIVELY T. J. SMITH 101

3. **THE WESLEYAN GOSPEL** 107
    DAVID A. DESILVA

              Responses
    SCOT MCKNIGHT 131
    MICHAEL HORTON 137
    JULIE MA 145
    SHIVELY T. J. SMITH 150

4. **THE PENTECOSTAL GOSPEL** 157
   JULIE MA

   Responses
   SCOT MCKNIGHT 176
   MICHAEL HORTON 182
   DAVID A. DESILVA 188
   SHIVELY T. J. SMITH 192

5. **A LIBERATION GOSPEL VIEW** 197
   SHIVELY T. J. SMITH

   Responses
   SCOT MCKNIGHT 215
   MICHAEL HORTON 222
   DAVID A. DESILVA 232
   JULIE MA 236

CONCLUSION 239
   JASON MASTON

For Further Reading 245
Scripture Index 246
Subject/Author Index 251

CONTRIBUTORS

Michael F. Bird (PhD, University of Queensland) is Deputy Principal, Director of Research, and Lecturer in New Testament at Ridley College in Melbourne, Australia. He is an Anglican priest and author of over thirty books, including *Evangelical Theology*, *Romans* (Story of God Bible Commentary), *Seven Things I Wish Christians Knew about the Bible*, and with N. T. Wright, *The New Testament in Its World* and *Jesus and the Powers*.

David A. deSilva (PhD, Emory University) is Trustees' Distinguished Professor of New Testament and Greek at Ashland Theological Seminary. He is the author of more than thirty books, including *An Introduction to the New Testament* (rev. ed., 2018), *Introducing the Apocrypha* (rev. ed., 2018), *Discovering Revelation* (2021), *Honor, Patronage, Kinship, and Purity* (rev. ed., 2022), and commentaries on Galatians, Ephesians, and Hebrews.

Michael S. Horton (PhD, Wycliffe Hall, Oxford and Coventry University) is the J. Gresham Machen Professor of Systematic Theology and Apologetics at Westminster Seminary California and founder and editor-in-chief of Sola Media, along with its productions, *White Horse Inn*, *Modern Reformation*, *Core Christianity*, and Theo Global.

Dr. Horton has written and edited more than forty books, including award-winning titles such as *Justification* (2 vols.) and *The Christian Faith*, as well as many popular titles, including *Ordinary: Sustainable Faith in a Radical, Restless World*; *Christless Christianity: The Alternative Gospel of the American Church*; and *Putting Amazing Back into Grace: Embracing the Heart of the Gospel*. His most recent book is *Shaman and Sage: The Roots of "Spiritual but Not Religious" in Antiquity*, the first of three volumes in his Divine Self series, an intellectual history of "spiritual but not religious" as a phenomenon in Western culture.

Julie C. Ma (PhD, Fuller Theological Seminary) is Professor of Missiology and Intercultural Studies at Oral Roberts University, Tulsa, Oklahoma. She previously served as a Korean missionary in the Philippines (1981–2006) and as Research Tutor of Missiology at Oxford Centre for Mission Studies, Oxford, UK. Her publications include *When the Spirit Meets the Spirits: Pentecostal Ministry Among the Kankana-ey Tribe in the Philippines* (Peter Lang, 2000), and *Mission Possible: Biblical Strategies in Reaching the Lost*, 2nd ed. (Oxford: Regnum, 2016), and numerous articles published in different journals. She has also contributed articles to collected works in different books and dictionaries/encyclopedias. She served as a general council member and executive committee member of Edinburgh 2010. She also served as the president of the Asian Pentecostal Society from 2008–2010.

Jason Maston (PhD, Durham University) is Associate Professor of Theology and Associate Dean, School of Christian Thought, at Houston Christian University. He is the author of *Divine and Human Agency in Second Temple Judaism and Paul* and has coedited several works, including the Reading in Context volumes (Zondervan Academic) and *Paul and the Apocalyptic Imagination*.

Scot McKnight (PhD, University of Nottingham) has been a professor of New Testament for more than four decades and is now a visiting professor of New Testament at both Houston Theological Seminary and Westminster Theological Centre (England). He is the author or editor of more than ninety books, including *The King Jesus Gospel*, *The Blue Parakeet*, *Pastor Paul*, and *Kingdom Conspiracy*.

Shively T. J. Smith (PhD, Emory University) is Associate Professor of New Testament at Boston University School of Theology and has spent over twenty years in the study of Bible, theology, and religion. In 2021 the General Board of Higher Education and Ministry of the United Methodist Church honored her with the exemplary teacher of the year award. Smith is also the author of two books, *Strangers to Family: Diaspora and 1 Peter's Invention of God's Household* and *Interpreting 2 Peter Through African American Women's Moral Writings*. She has also written numerous essays. She serves as editor for the SBL's Semeia

Monograph series and as associate editor of the New Testament for the *HarperCollins Study Bible*, 3rd edition. Smith is also a commissioner for the Association of Theological Schools (ATS) and serves as a board member for the National Council of Churches and Friendship Press Board of Translation Utilization, which oversees the use of the NRSV, RSV, and NRSVue. Smith has emerged as a sought-after scholar, teacher, preacher, and writer who is dedicated to the service of academic theological studies and ecumenical conversations in the public square.

ABBREVIATIONS

CR	*Corpus reformatorum*. Edited by C. G. Bretschneider, H. E. Bindseil, et al. 101 vols. Halis Sazonum (Hall): Schwetschke; et al., 1834–1963. Repr., New York: Johnson, 1964
LXX	The Greek Old Testament (Septuagint)
NCBC	New Cambridge Bible Commentary
NICNT	New International Commentary on the New Testament
NTS	*New Testament Studies*
SBLMS	Society of Biblical Literature Monograph Series
WJW	*The Works of John Wesley*. 14 vols. London: Wesleyan Conference Office, 1872. Repr., Grand Rapids: Zondervan, 1958
WUNT	Wissenschaftliche Untersuchungen zum Neuen Testament

INTRODUCTION: WHAT IS THE GOSPEL?

MICHAEL F. BIRD

What Is There to Debate?

Christianity became a global religion through many factors including colonization and migration, but above all through evangelization. Christianity is a missionary religion, and missionaries have gone out to places as remote as Iceland, Mongolia, Peru, and Zimbabwe, embedded themselves within Indigenous communities, and made forming international networks something of an artform since the days of the earliest church in Jerusalem. Although there are still several unreached people groups and still many places in the world where the free and unhindered promotion of religion is prohibited, nonetheless the gospel has spread from Jerusalem to the ends of the earth (Acts 1:8). This very day, there are Christians in Jerusalem, Jena, Jakarta, Jalal-Abad, and Jackson. That is the case because Christians, wherever and whenever they went, whether as migrants or merchants, as soldiers or slaves, as laity or clergy, both men and women, took with them the Christian message, the evangel, the gospel. They took it with them and rooted it in their own setting. They built churches, set up ministries, and did the work to which the gospel called them.

But what is the gospel? The gospel is something that every Christian should know, understand, and be able to articulate on the spot. We are baptized in the story of the gospel, and the Lord's Supper is a regular celebration of the gospel. We habitually read from books called "Gospels." We are told that we should support evangelism—that is, the active promotion of the gospel. Our churches sponsor missionaries and parachurch ministries whose primary business is the advancement of the gospel. There is even a broad Protestant coalition called

"Evangelicalism." The evangel, the gospel, is so ubiquitous that its content and concerns should be self-evident to all people of Christian faith.

And yet the topic of the gospel, what one might think is undebatable, is debated. Yes, we all agree that the gospel has something to do with God and Jesus, salvation, and faith, but after that it can get contentious and confusing. Theologians and pastors disagree on what the gospel is in essence, what to emphasize in the gospel, what problem the gospel is trying to rectify or remedy, how we should respond to the gospel, and what the implications of the gospel are for the church, mission, individual piety, and everyday life. No wonder there is an industry of books trying to clarify the substance of the gospel, its meaning, and entailments for contemporary audiences.

The complexity over defining the gospel is not merely a result of our unsanctified souls, a deficiency in religious education, or even a creeping worldliness in the church. Discussion over the gospel is generated by the very necessity of articulating it for diverse audiences. The gospel is not a mathematical formula. It is more like the performance of a dramatic story about God and his Son, and all performances have to be scripted, interpreted, translated, and communicated to audiences.

The first thing we must note is that there is a diverse testimony to the gospel in the biblical materials. If we compare some passages from the Gospel of Luke (Luke 4:16–31; 23:1–56), Paul's epistle to the Romans (Rom 1:2–4; 3:21–26; 5:1; 8:1–3), Peter's speech to the household of Cornelius (Acts 10:34–43), Paul's speech at the Athenian Areopagus (Acts 17:22–31), and the Petrine and Johannine letters (1 Pet 2:1–10; 1 John 1:5–2:2), we would find a cluster of commonalities as well as some individual iterations of the gospel. The question is whether we have a diverse witness to the one gospel or whether the New Testament conveys several different versions of the gospel.[1]

The second thing that should be borne in mind is that one must tailor the gospel to the audience one is preaching to because the audience might know nothing of Christianity, have misconceptions about Christianity, or even interpret Christian concepts through the lens of

---

1. James D. G. Dunn, "Methodology of Evangelism in the New Testament: Some Preliminary Reflections," in *New Testament Theology in Light of the Church's Witness: Essays in Honor of I. Howard Marshall*, ed. Jon C. Laansma, Grant Osborne, and Ray van Neste (Eugene, OR: Wipf & Stock, 2011), 25–40.

their resident social, cultural, and religious framework. I can tell you from experience that what John 3:16 means to me, a Christian theologian, is not what it means to a Buddhist shopkeeper in Thailand. A Muslim man in Eritrea might be affronted by John's reference to Jesus as God's "only begotten Son" (KJV). A science student at a Czechian university might think of John's Gospel as somewhere between myth and science fiction. The words, "God," "love," "sin," and "world" have different meanings in different contexts. In order to share the gospel with anyone, the gospel must be contextualized. On the one hand, the fact that the gospel is translatable into different languages and contexts is a strength. On the other hand, it presents a problem since there are some seven thousand languages in usage in the world today and a constant flux of cultures and contexts into which we have to speak the gospel. How do you speak the word of the gospel to a refugee family from Syria living in Idaho compared to speaking the gospel to a gay Gen-Z teenager with Pakistani parents working as a graphic artist in multicultural London? How does one live a life "worthy of the gospel" at the Waco Walmart, at a university in Nigeria, or in a retirement village in Swansea?

Third, our respective Christian traditions and Christian experiences will make us naturally gravitate toward certain ways of articulating the gospel or preferring some articulations over others. For those of us who live within a Christian tradition derived from the Latin West, we are naturally inclined to think of the gospel as the answer to the problem of sin and guilt and the solution as "righteousness," however "righteousness" is understood. For those of us who live within a Christian tradition derived from the Orthodox family of churches, we are naturally inclined to think of the gospel as the answer to the problem of death and condemnation and the solution as new life and participation "in the divine nature" (2 Pet 1:4). Consider also how the gospel might resonate differently with people who experience socioeconomic affluence or alienation, whether your ancestors were slaves or slave owners, or whether the dominant culture around you is secular, Islamic, or Christian. Whether consciously or unconsciously, our respective religious traditions, whether Catholic, Protestant, or Orthodox and our socioreligious location are going to shape the way we explain the good news that God "loves" us and that Christ died "for" our sins, because the meaning of "love" and "for" can be construed in several different ways.

As you can tell, there are many debates to be had because there is much to dissect, deliberate, and discuss concerning the gospel. The gospel matters. It is the center, boundary, and integrating point for Christian faith, the touchstone of authentic Christianity, and what drives the church's mission. If that is so, then getting the gospel right and wielding it rightly, will be a task of first importance. To that end, in this volume we are pursuing a multi-perspectival exploration of the gospel: its biblical foundations, its meaning, and its various entailments. We have assembled a fantastic and diverse collection of authors, each of whom have a deep love for God, an abiding faith in Christ, a commitment to advance the gospel, and a history of Christian service. They are at the top of their respective fields when it comes to scholarship, and they hail from diverse traditions and contexts. This book brings them all together to explain and explore the gospel both individually and as part of an ongoing conversation.

Obviously, we have not been able to incorporate every single perspective, tradition, and theology into this discussion. Accordingly, we did not solicit perspectives from Catholics, Greek Orthodox, Oriental Orthodox, or dozens of Protestant perspectives. But what we have included is, I think, a diverse sample of views that will speak to churches, mainly Protestant churches in the Anglophone world, and help them think evangelically about the gospel. The views included in this volume are:

King Jesus: A view of the gospel rooted in Scripture's storyline that places an emphasis on the identity of Jesus as Messiah and Lord.

Reformation: A view of the gospel indebted to the legacy of the Reformation that places emphasis on God's grace, justification by faith, and union with Christ.

Wesleyan: A view of the gospel that accents the free offer of grace and the transformative power of the Holy Spirit.

Pentecostal: A view of the gospel that focuses on Jesus and the Spirit as the power for faith, forgiveness, and freedom.

Liberation: A view of the gospel that centers on the holistic redeeming and liberating work of the gospel and how it addresses the entire human condition.

As part of the exploration of the gospel in this volume, we have asked the contributors to address several things to make these conversations happen.

First, the contributors were asked to write about the gospel with a view to explaining what the gospel means to them in light of their reading of Scripture, from the perspective of their religious tradition, and from the crucible of their own experiences. To that end, we have asked each contributor to do several things:

1. Provide a Twitter length opening definition and summary of the gospel.
2. Explain the proper context for understanding the gospel. Is it the Old Testament, first-century Judea, the Roman imperial cult, human sin and fallenness, the Reformation, the surrounding culture, the experience of oppression, or something else? Why do we need the gospel?
3. Identify the primary biblical texts that express the gospel and how it is to be understood.
4. Explain how people are meant to respond to the gospel and what benefits are promised to us in the gospel.
5. Answer the question, "What does it mean to live a life worthy of the gospel?"
6. Provide further thoughts on the content, meaning, and significance of the gospel as required.

This is the task the contributors were given, but this volume is more than stating what the gospel means for them; it included an additional task. The nature of Zondervan's Counterpoints series is that it does not allow authors to state their own position, then leave their perspective siloed and juxtaposed. Instead, it helpfully asks the contributors to enter into dialogue with each other. That is why the second task that each of the contributors was assigned was to write responses to each other in order to provide a mixture of mutual affirmation and critical interaction. This allows us to observe patterns of convergence as well as points of difference among the views. It makes for a beneficial exercise to see these learned biblical scholars and theologians wrestle with each other about the gospel.

A Summary of the Gospel Perspectives

Scot McKnight presents the **King Jesus Gospel** position. According to McKnight, the New Testament gospel is indebted to the storyline of Scripture, a story that climaxes in the revelation of Jesus the Messiah, the king, who rescues his people and makes them his royal subjects. What is more, the gospel is something that Jesus preached, it was a gospel about a kingdom, and a kingdom is a people ruled by a king. The context for understanding the gospel is the intrusion of evil into the world, the eschatological promises for redemption given in Scripture, and the empires of the ages that represent the sum of anti-God forces in our world. McKnight believes that the gospel calls for people to surrender to God in faith, embrace the lordship of Jesus, and live out the gospel story of healing and hope in our own everyday lives. The biblical texts that McKnight regards as paramount for understanding the gospel are Isaiah 40:3, Mark 1:15, Acts 2:36, 38, 13:38–39, and 1 Corinthians 15:3–5. The impact that the gospel makes is for believers to submit to Christ by adopting a pattern of life typified by Christoformity with cruciformity.

Next, Michael Horton expounds the **Reformation Gospel** position indicative of the Calvinistic and Westminster tradition. Horton takes as central Jesus's work as prophet, priest, and king, who imputes righteousness to believers, taking them from condemnation to righteousness. He closely coordinates the gospel with a forensic understanding of justification by faith. Viewed this way, the context of the gospel is the biblical narrative of plight and solution, with the plight construed as curse and condemnation, and the solution construed as righteousness and eternal life. The texts that Horton regards as the most salient for his case are Luke 18:9–16, Acts 15:8–11, and Romans 4:3–6, with manifold references to Romans and Galatians along the way. For Horton, the gospel demands faith, not a passive faith but a faith that yields holiness and obedience. To live a life worthy of the gospel means, under Horton's Reformed perspective, to ensure that faith operates in, through, and for love.

David A. deSilva articulates a **Wesleyan Gospel** that has currency in Methodist circles and various holiness movements influenced by John and Charles Wesley. For deSilva, the gospel is the story of how

God's grace undoes the penalty and power of sin and concurrently draws us into a life of holiness. The context for the gospel is the conviction that human beings have failed to worship God and need a change of heart to render to God the holy worship due to God as our Creator and Redeemer. Several texts are central in that articulation for deSilva, including John 3:3, Romans 6:1–11, 13:11, and Hebrews 12:14. He sees the gospel calling people to faith, the experience of new birth, a sense of assurance, with the Spirit given as a power toward perfection. Believing the gospel should result in intentional discipleship, a reliance on the Holy Spirit, divesting oneself of sin, and investing in a Christian community.

Julie Ma advocates for a **Pentecostal Gospel** shaped by her Asian heritage and ministry experience and resourced from the Pentecostal tradition. Ma contends that the gospel is principally concerned with the liberating work of the Holy Spirit. The gospel meets our need to escape marginalization and to receive blessings. Human beings are alienated from God and need to return to the abundant, precious blessings that God designed us to enjoy. What stands in the way is not only our sin but the sinful institutions and structures around us. Biblical texts that strike Ma as important include Luke 4:18–19, Acts 1:8, 2:1–12, and 1 Corinthians 12:7–9. The benefits that the gospel confers are empowerment for our own participation in the mission of God in our world. The result of our gospel-experience should be, argues Ma, a holistic spirituality where we seek to care for each other in body, mind, and spirit.

Shively T. J. Smith presents a **Liberation Gospel** in the tradition of African-American experience and religious testimony. For Smith, the fact that Jesus died a slave's death means that the gospel is concerned with liberation, both spiritual and social, to set people free from the forces of death and exploitation. The context for the gospel is the human experience of depravation caused by our own sinning and deprivation caused by the sinful behavior of others. Manifold texts speak about the human experience of illness, poverty, ethnic and racial discrimination, gender bias, social-class stratification, dispossession, disinheritance, and marginalization. Thus, for Smith, biblical texts that she finds important are stories like the good Samaritan from Luke 10:25–37 and others that speak about and emphasize human dignity and accompaniment as a necessity for resolving human misery, exploitation, and struggle.

The gospel, then, should drive persons toward caring for others and dismantling systems that harm people and even creation itself. Smith believes that when the gospel is practiced, it results in the witness of inclusion, equality, and freedom. An essential benefit of the liberation gospel, in Smith's mind, is championing our moral responsibility to each other.

How This Book Will Benefit You

Not long ago, the Anglican Church in North America (ACNA) put out its own catechism, which, in the second question, asks and answers the following:

> What is the Gospel?
> The Gospel is the good news that God loves the world and offers salvation from sin through his Son, Jesus Christ (Ps 103:1–13; Isa 53:4–5; John 3:16–17; 1 Cor 15:1–5).[2]

The ACNA catechism prioritized the gospel in its instruction to believers because the gospel obviously matters. All our contributors, whatever their disagreements on major or minor details, agree that the gospel matters. It mattered for church history, it matters still for our contemporary mission, and what we believe about the gospel permeates every aspect of Christian thought and practice.

The apostle Paul expounded the gospel to the Corinthians because it was something of "first importance" (1 Cor 15:3). In the second century, the church father Irenaeus, a chief opponent of many heresies, declared the gospel "handed down to us in the scriptures, to be the ground and pillar of our faith."[3] In many ways, Irenaeus is similar to Calvin who said that "The Spirit, promised to us, has not the task of inventing new and unheard-of-revelations, or of forging a new kind of doctrine, to lead us away from the received doctrine of the gospel, but of sealing our minds with the very doctrine which is commended by the gospel."[4] The gospel

---

2. James I. Packer et al., *To Be a Christian: An Anglican Catechism* (Wheaton, IL: Crossway, 2020), 23. Also available at https://anglicanchurch.net/wp-content/uploads/2020/06/To-Be-a-Christian.pdf.
3. Irenaeus, *Against Heresies* 3.1.1.
4. Calvin, *Institutes*, 1.9.1.

is what Irenaeus believed he was defending and what Calvin believed he was recovering during the Reformation.

But what is at stake is more than doctrine, dogmatic beliefs about God, about Jesus, and about salvation. There are manifold implications that follow on from what we make of the gospel. The gospel is more than doctrine, because the gospel creates a type of gospel living, gospel spirituality, gospel mission, and gospel-centered communities. This is why the apostle Paul called on the Philippians to live a life "worthy of the gospel" (Phil 1:27) and for the Corinthians to exercise "obedience" that accompanies their "confession of the gospel" (2 Cor 9:13). Concerning the Christian life, the third-century church father Origen exhorted readers, "Guided by God through Jesus Christ, let us walk in the great and life-giving way of the gospel, in hope that we may now traverse it until we reach its end."[5] We find something similar in the seventeenth century with John Wesley, who expressed in a letter his belief that the gospel is both proclamation and a pattern of life: "Go on in the work where to God has called you, and He will do all things well. I hope our preachers preach and live the gospel—I am."[6]

Contemporary theologians have restated the same thing for ethics and pastoral ministry. According to theologian Oliver O'Donovan: "The foundations of Christian ethics must be evangelical foundations; or, to put it more simply, Christian ethics must arise from the Gospel of Jesus Christ. Otherwise it could not be Christian ethics."[7] In terms of pastoral ministry, Derek Tidball writes: "Pastoral work is simply bringing to full flower the bud of the gospel," and, "The gospel determines everything about the pastor—his motives, authority, methods, and character are all governed by the good news of Jesus Christ."[8]

One might allege that being gospel centered is a fad, a good marketing gimmick, because attaching the word "gospel" to something is just a trendy way of arguing that it is important. But the gospel is important for

---

5. Origen, *Comm. John* 32.1.1, cited in Francis Watson, *Gospel Writing: A Canonical Perspective* (Grand Rapids: Eerdmans, 2014), 516.
6. John Wesley, "To George Merryweather," Dec. 20, 1766. Cited in John Telford, ed., *The Letters of John Wesley*, 8 vols. (London: Epworth, 1960), 5:34.
7. Oliver O'Donovan, *Resurrection and the Moral Order: An Outline for Evangelical Ethics* (Leicester, UK: Inter-Varsity Press, 1986), 11.
8. Derek Tidball, *Skillful Shepherds: Explorations in Pastoral Theology* (Leicester, UK: Apollos, 1997), 100, 120.

determining the identity of Jesus, the human predicament, the meaning of salvation, understanding our mission in the world, and above all for grasping the glorious and majestic nature of God. According to the late John Webster:

> The best evangelical theological work emerges from the delight in the Christian gospel, for the gospel announces a reality which is in itself luminous, persuasive, and infinitely satisfying. That reality is Jesus Christ as he gives himself to be an object for creaturely knowledge, love, and praise. To think evangelically about this one is to think in his presence, under the instruction of his Word and Spirit, and in the fellowship of the saints. And it is to do so with cheerful confidence that his own witness to himself is unimaginably more potent than any theological attempts to run to his defense.[9]

The aim of this book is not to problematize the gospel, not to make the gospel opaque or obtuse by inundating readers with a myriad of perspectives or by burying them in scholarly details. Quite the opposite. The objective of this book is to help readers appreciate the richness and depth of the gospel, to grasp the different ways the gospel can be proclaimed and applied, to notice diverse scriptural witness to the gospel, to exhort the churches to attain clarity and conviction about the gospel, and to consider the ministry of the gospel as a task that the entire church, both lay people and clergy, have responsibility to undertake. The gospel requires knowing, teaching, preaching, guarding, going, giving, living, and loving in the name of our Lord Jesus Christ.

Accordingly, the objective we are pursuing is that readers may come away from this book knowing God better (see Eph 1:17) by wrestling with the manifold wisdom of God as it is given to us in the gospel, so that we might better delight in the gospel, live a life worthy of it, and carry it with us in our life, work, and service.

---

9. John Webster, "Jesus Christ," in *The Cambridge Companion to Evangelical Theology*, ed. T. Larsen and D. Treier (Cambridge: Cambridge University Press, 2007), 60.

CHAPTER ONE: THE KING JESUS GOSPEL

SCOT MCKNIGHT

On any given day, on any social media, one will discover the word *gospel* being used for what one thinks is most important: from love to God to salvation in Christ to justification by faith to Jesus himself to the story of Israel to justice to social justice to peace to one's political party. Americans, living as they do in what one might call a post-Christian nation, are acclimated to framing their best idea as the gospel. It is the Christian's deepest claim and most important belief. Yet it is surprising how diverse the claims are when using the word. Listen, if you will, to the mainline, to the evangelical, to the Christian nationalist, to the progressive, to the social, racial, and economic justice warriors—listen to the preacher and prophets and pamphleteers of our age—and the gospel arises with the force of demanding claims. To call something "gospel" is to make the ultimate claim.

The Billy Graham gospel illustrates our point. Though similar gospel presentations preceded him, it was Graham who perfected what many today would call the gospel of personal salvation:[1] God loves you and has a wonderful plan for your life; though created in God's image, you were actually born in Adam's sin and stand eternally guilty before God, which means eternal punishment in hell after death; but God

---

1. Scot McKnight, *The King Jesus Gospel: The Original Good News Revisited*, 2nd ed. (Grand Rapids: Zondervan, 2015), 75–93.

loves you and sent his Son, Jesus Christ, to die for you on the cross where he absorbed the punishment for sin on your behalf; if you turn to Jesus and trust him for your salvation you will be delivered from eternal punishment and experience eternity in heaven, in the presence of God and the saints. I have in another context called this the "soterian" gospel, the gospel of salvation (*sōtēria* is the Greek word for "salvation").[2] This understanding of the gospel is framed by an individual's need for salvation and how personal redemption can be found through faith in Christ. This gospel for Billy Graham, and now his son Franklin, is the beginning and end of all discussions. It is their ultimate message with an eternal claim on the entire world.

Yet, I have many friends who would frame the gospel in other terms. If one frames the gospel as justification by faith, the framework is slightly different than the above, which frames it as personal salvation. If one frames it as reconciliation, the problem changes because the solution changes. If one frames it in more systemic terms—not just personal—or more cosmic terms—that is, in terms of evil or injustice, again changing the solution changes the problem the gospel resolves. The solution, in other words, determines the problem. We can reverse it: the problem determines the solution. What term frames the gospel is always the solution, so I prefer to think that our gospeling is more about a solution determining the precise problem than the problem determining

---

2. For this chapter I am indebted to my earlier book on this topic. See McKnight, *King Jesus Gospel*. It is not possible in this short chapter to document the literature deserving mention, but I have provided some indication of scholarship. Of particular delight to me in writing this essay was the discovery of a book at the recommendation of my friend, Brad Nassif, who suggested I read Theodore G. Stylianopoulos, *The Apostolic Gospel* (Brookline, MA: Holy Cross Orthodox Press, 2016). He sees the primary content of the gospel to be Christology and the secondary, as it were, to be the benefits or blessings of the gospel, a distinction I have maintained for some time now, and his third theme is the demand or the response to the gospel. See also Bradley Nassif, "What is the Gospel in Eastern Orthodoxy?," in *Living the Gospel of Jesus Christ: Orthodox and Evangelical Approaches to Discipleship and Christian Formation*, ed. Mark Oxbrow and Tim Grass (Oxford: Regnum, 2021), 9–20. I have long benefited from approaches similar to mine by N. T. Wright, *What Saint Paul Really Said: Was Paul of Tarsus the Real Founder of Christianity?* (Grand Rapids: Eerdmans, 1997), 39–62; Michael J. Gorman, *Apostle of the Crucified Lord: A Theological Introduction to Paul and His Letters*, 2nd ed. (Grand Rapids: Eerdmans, 2016), 120–39; Matthew W. Bates, *The Hermeneutics of the Apostolic Proclamation: The Center of Paul's Method of Scriptural Interpretation* (Waco, TX: Baylor University Press, 2012). Gorman's thesis that the gospel is good news *about* Jesus and good news *for* us gets it just right (p. 124), as he too distinguishes the content of the gospel from its benefits.

the solution.[3] The two (problem and solution) are not, however, independent, but they correlate with one another into a harmonic perception of the gospel, into an ultimate claim on life.

Because gospel is so central to the Christian faith—it is in fact *the* Christian faith—theologians are summoned to the table to define it. I offer my "tweet" definition of *gospel* and then a brief explanation before turning to some questions about gospel and gospeling.

Gospel Tweet

The *gospel* is the announcement or proclamation of Jesus as the long-awaited Messiah of Israel's hope who through his life, death, burial, resurrection, and ascension conquers sin and death—personal, systemic—in order to unleash the redemption of God—that is, the kingdom of God, for the transformation of humans and systems.

In an even shorter tweet, the gospel is the story about Jesus.

In one word, Jesus.

Gospel Explanation

For there to be a "gospel" there must be a context, a story, a narrative that gives rise to a solution called the gospel. As stated above, in hermeneutical terms, it is the solution that often determines the problem. If the solution is Jesus, and I will demonstrate this (I hope) to everyone's satisfaction in the next section, a need for Jesus must be also shown. I assume that conclusion—namely, that *Jesus's coming is the solution* to a problem, and that means we need to seek for a problem for which Jesus is the solution. The solution Jesus offers to the Galileans and Judeans of his day was the *kingdom*, which could be translated the "empire" of God. More than one hundred times this word is found in the Synoptic Gospels, even if it is rendered into "life" and "eternal life" in the Fourth Gospel. If Jesus's embodiment and announcement of the kingdom are the solution, we need to find the problem in the aching desire for and expectation of God's kingdom breaking into the world.

---

3. For discussions of plight and solution, see E. P. Sanders, *Paul and Palestinian Judaism: A Comparison of Patterns of Religion*, repr. ed. (Philadelphia: Fortress, 2017); and Douglas A. Campbell, *The Deliverance of God: An Apocalyptic Rereading of Justification in Paul* (Grand Rapids: Eerdmans, 2013).

The standard soterian model thinks the problem is the sin of Genesis 3 because the solution is the atonement of Romans 3, and one could reverse that sentence if one prefers. Without denying the importance of the themes of sin, salvation, and atonement in Christ, we need to recognize that Paul's solution is Paul's and should not be imposed on Jesus. Jesus announced kingdom because kingdom was the expectation, so I begin with Jesus.

First, Jesus's kingdom is the kingdom *of God*, or as Matthew prefers, the kingdom *of heaven*. This is an immediate piece of polemics: a kingdom of God, or of heaven, as Jonathan Pennington has demonstrated, transcends and thus stands over against a kingdom of humans, of men, of human kings.[4]

Second, to call the kingdom that Jesus inaugurates the kingdom *of God* is to undo a temporary accommodation. To use "of God" with "kingdom" makes us think of that oft ignored transition in the work of 1 Samuel 8 where God's people desire a kingdom like that found among other nations. Prior to this, God was the sole king, but after the appointment of Saul and then David as kings, God—this is to me the best term—*accommodates* to Israel's desire. Yet it is not the best of God's plan for humans in God's world. The plot of the Bible for those who think kingdom is the solution is theocracy moving to monarchy and then to its fulfillment in Christocracy.[5]

Third, this plot toward Christocracy in the divine plan reveals fundamental categories of both problem and solution. If Jesus brings kingdom and if he is the king in this kingdom, then the *problem* was human subjects not living under the world's true king and the *solution* is humans living under Jesus as lord and king—that is, as Messiah. I have now entered into the narrative of what we often call *sin*, though I don't think we need to obsess about that specific term, as *rebellion, disobedience, transgression, idolatry*, and others work just as well—especially the biggest term of all: *evil*.[6] In the sweep of the Bible from Genesis to

---

4. Jonathan T. Pennington, *Heaven and Earth in the Gospel of Matthew* (Grand Rapids: Baker Academic, 2009); Scot McKnight, *Kingdom Conspiracy: Returning to the Radical Mission of the Local Church* (Grand Rapids: Brazos, 2014).

5. McKnight, *Kingdom Conspiracy*, 29–33.

6. James D. G. Dunn, *The Theology of Paul the Apostle* (Grand Rapids: Eerdmans, 1998), 79–127. On sin as agent and as systemic, see Matthew Croasmun, *The Emergence of Sin: The Cosmic Tyrant in Romans* (New York: Oxford University Press, 2017).

Revelation, sin is personal/individual, corporate, cosmic-spiritual, and cosmic-systemic, and any gospel that does not deal death blows to the comprehensiveness of sin is inadequate. Rejection and repudiation of God's lordship and the lordship of Jesus are core meanings of sin.

Christocracy is the core of the gospel, as it is a declaration about Jesus and, in fact, is a declaration by Jesus himself. Put differently, the gospel is a message about Jesus and his identity in the plan of God. Eastern Orthodox scholar Theodore Stylianopoulos, after sketching some prominent voices defining the gospel, summarizes it in these terms:

> The essence of the gospel is the Christology, or perhaps better the "Christ-devotion"—the experiential understanding and prayerful celebration of who Christ is and the significance of his saving work as lived and believed by the apostolic community of faith.[7]

Notice his wording: *the Christology . . . who Christ is . . . and the significance of his saving work.* To carry through with this, even Jesus must preach that gospel if we want to say he preached the gospel. Did he preach himself? The answer to that question is an affirmative also to each of these sub-questions: Did he make himself the center of God's plan? Did he have an egocentricity about his message? Did he call people to follow himself? Yes, yes, yes. That's gospeling.

A test I have for assessing any articulation of the gospel is this: Did Jesus preach what this person says is the gospel? I ask this of the Bridge Diagram. Of the Four Spiritual Laws. And of every gospel I hear. I do not mean some aren't cobbling together verses from the Bible to form their version of the gospel, for that happens often. No, what I mean is simple: Did Jesus explicitly preach the gospel someone claims is the gospel? If Jesus didn't preach it, I ask why someone thinks they've improved Jesus's own gospel. I ask why anyone who thinks Jesus is the Lord would also think Jesus *didn't* preach their gospel? This assessment is not being heavy-handed but rather springs from my disturbances over what some claim to be the gospel.

---

7. Stylianopoulos, *Apostolic Gospel*, 16.

Fourth, this king and his kingdom should not be reduced to personal redemption, but it also should not minimize it either. The word *kingdom* entails five elements if we comprehend kingdom as something intelligible to first-century Galileans and if we approach kingdom on the basis of evidence in the Jewish Scriptures (the Old Testament).[8] (1) For there to be a kingdom, there must be a king. In that world that king was the God of Israel, who is now revealed in Jesus of Nazareth. For there to be a kingdom, (2) there must be a rule by that God and by Jesus. Unlike the rule of the Roman emperors, the rule of this king is both by way of redemption and by governance. The prototypical redemptive act of God in the Bible is the exodus liberation that is embodied in the death, burial, resurrection, and ascension of Jesus. But this God governs in this kingdom as well, and hence the Hebrew term *Adonai* is applied to Jesus as *Kyrios*. The redeeming agent becomes the Lord of the kingdom. For there to be a kingdom, there (3) must be a people whom this God has redeemed and over whom this God governs. The people of this God in the Bible is Israel as fulfilled in Jesus as the church. For there to be a kingdom, there must be (4) an ethic or law through which the redeeming, governing God of the kingdom reveals life for those in the kingdom. Again, this is the law of Moses as fulfilled in the teachings of Jesus (e.g., Matt 5:17–48) and then articulated in fresh ways by the apostles as life in the Spirit. Finally, for there to be a kingdom, there must be (5) a land, a territory, or a location. Kingdoms are not abstractions and purely spiritual realities, a view that has too often been the attraction of Christians who seemingly have little sympathy for the Old Testament or Judaism. Recently Dale Allison has demonstrated that kingdom and territory must be connected if we want to talk about the meaning of kingdom for Jesus.[9] The word "kingdom" in the Old Testament over and over and over refers to a territory, and that's how Josephus uses the term too. In the Old Testament that territory is the land, but the land promise in the New Testament (and I recognize we are treading here on somewhat contested terrain) is both the physical land and the embodied, mobile location of followers of Jesus taking up space in various locations across the Roman Empire. For instance, Matthew 5:13

---

8. McKnight, *Kingdom Conspiracy*. I rely on this study throughout my essay.
9. Dale C. Allison Jr., *Constructing Jesus: Memory, Imagination, and History* (Grand Rapids: Baker Academic, 2013), 164–204.

should be translated, "You are the salt of the *land*." That land promise is not extinguished, for even in Revelation the final vision is of a "New Jerusalem" (see Rev 21–22). Space matters. The temple is the heart of the land promise, and in the New Testament the people of Jesus are the (mobile) temple of God (e.g., 1 Cor 3:16–17; 6:19; Eph 2:21–22; Rev 3:12).

If Jesus is the king and the people of God are the people of his kingdom, then the ethic of Jesus is the way of life for kingdom people. The ethic of Jesus, as is the case for the entire New Testament ethic, is an ethic of relations with others and is not reducible to personal piety and individual spiritual formation, regardless of how singularly important those are for personal discipleship to Jesus. Hence, the ethic of Jesus becomes systemic. An ethic practiced by a people forms itself into a living agent, and that living agent acts upon the people in some manner to remind the people how to live as kingdom people. Since that ethic-as-living-agent is about the kingdom, that systemic impact as such becomes a kingdom constraint.[10] The ethic of Jesus for the kingdom people, then, is a systemic order of kingdom living.

This leads now to a more expansive articulation of the gospel, beginning with brief words about the context.

Context

At issue in any discussion of the gospel today is whether Jesus and the apostles are responding to the Roman empire's routine "good news" declarations about the emperor, a military victory, or the Pax Romana.[11] Did they derive their use of gospel from the Old Testament texts, as, say, is found in LXX 2 Samuel 4:10; 18:20, 22, 25, 27 and Jeremiah 20:15—where it means news—or in the more Jesus-sounding Psalms (40:9 [39:10 LXX]; 68:11 [67:12]; 96:2 [95:2])—where it is about public announcements of the saving work of God—or in the even more early Christian-evoking lines from the prophets (Isa 40:9; 52:7; 61:1; Joel 2:32 [3:5 LXX]; Nah 1:15 [2:1])? In his so-called inaugural sermon in Nazareth from Isaiah 61, words are put on the lips of Jesus that lead most to think his usage, at least, derives especially from Isaiah (cf. Luke

---
10. Croasmun, *Emergence of Sin*.
11. Adrian Goldsworthy, *Pax Romana: War, Peace and Conquest in the Roman World* (New Haven: Yale University Press, 2016).

4:16–30, esp. vv. 18–19). That Qumran has texts (4Q521; 11Q13) that sound the same lends credibility to a Jewish origin for the Christian usage of gospel. Were the authors of the New Testament using a "hidden transcript"—saying "gospel" but meaning subversion of Rome and the imperial cult? Can we even detect such double-layered speech? Were they swiping Rome's term and so participating in social resistance, dissidence, and foot-dragging?[12] To the point, then, too, is that Paul's language of gospel, prominent as it is, had audiences who at least would have known Rome's use of "gospel" as empire announcements, and one has to wonder if Paul didn't make use of that context when he turned to this term. Unless Paul was profoundly naive to usage, we must conclude that when Paul said "gospel" and tied it to Jesus as Lord, his audience would have said "Caesar is not." Which doesn't make it so much a conscious anti-imperialism as it expresses the inevitable conflict when two lords are on the stage.

How to adjudicate? The topic has become political at times, so much so that one wonders if it is not present politics determining what one chooses to pull out of the ancient world for framing the discussion. If one thinks Jesus used the term "gospel," as I do, then we at least begin with the conclusion that Jesus drew from Isaiah and the Jewish tradition to express his eschatology and gospel: the day promised and predicted has now come to pass. But there is no reason to force an either-or decision. Paul's usage had relevance in the context of the Roman Empire, and that relevance entailed some level of resistance. I'm dubious that Paul's intentional, overriding agenda was to subvert the Roman Empire and its imperial claims or even the imperial cult. To be sure, the claim that Jesus was Lord entailed subversion at some level, but forming the entailment

---

12. Discussion is intense. Compare G. N. Stanton, *Jesus and Gospel* (Cambridge: Cambridge University Press, 2004), 9–62; Scot McKnight and Joseph B. Modica, eds., *Jesus Is Lord, Caesar Is Not: Evaluating Empire in New Testament Studies* (Downers Grove, IL: IVP Academic, 2013). See also Christoph Heilig, "Methodological Considerations for the Search for Counter-Imperial 'Echoes' in Pauline Literature," in *Reactions to Empire: Proceedings of Sacred Texts in Their Socio-Political Contexts*, ed. John A. Dunne and Dan Batovici, WUNT 2/372 (Tübingen: Mohr Siebeck, 2014), 73–92; Christoph Heilig, *Hidden Criticism? The Methodology and Plausibility of the Search for a Counter-Imperial Subtext in Paul*, WUNT 2/392 (Tübingen: Mohr Siebeck, 2015); Laura Robinson, "Hidden Transcripts? The Supposedly Self-Censoring Paul and Rome as Surveillance State in Modern Pauline Scholarship," *NTS* 67.1 (2021): 55–72. For a broader work, see Drew J. Strait, *Hidden Criticism of the Angry Tyrant in Early Judaism and the Acts of the Apostles* (Lanham, MD: Lexington Books/Fortress Academic; 2019).

into the vanguard of the Pauline gospel makes subversion of the emperor too prominent. What Drew Strait has made clear is that one cannot separate religion from politics in the empire: one's politics entailed the imperial cult, and the imperial cult was fundamentally political.[13] The tension in the Apocalypse of John, then, is not simply the temptation or practice of idolatry but that participation in the Roman cult was simultaneously denial of the lordship of Jesus. Thus, any gospel claim in the first century that had some publicity was both eschatology rooted in the Jewish Scriptures and at the same time a call for believers to turn from the gospel of the empire.

The Texts

Which texts are we to bring into play if we want to form what can be called a "biblically grounded" gospel? How do we frame a theology of the gospel in a way that is both biblically shaped (the primacy of Scripture) and also recognizes the great tradition of the church?[14] Here one's personal preferences must become conscious enough to let the texts of Scripture challenge our thinking. As stated in the introduction to this chapter, the gospel is defined most of the time by our favorite ideas (Jesus, justification, justice), but if we want to catch the inspiring vision of Jesus as his disciples heard it, we must do our best to get back to his world and hear this term "gospel" as Jesus and the first followers used it. We have to search for texts where gospel is defined as explicitly as possible, even if the results challenge our cherished ideas.

First, the summary statement of the evangelist Mark defines gospel. He opens with "the beginning of the gospel about Jesus the Messiah, the Son of God" (Mark 1:1, my trans.), and this is articulated by Mark to be the fulfillment of Isaiah 40:3. Here the gospel is the announcement of the arrival of God's agent of redemption. It's about a person. Then we turn to Mark's own summary of the message of Jesus at Mark 1:15:

> "The time has come," he said. "The kingdom of God has come near. Repent and believe the good news!"

---

13. Strait, *Hidden Criticism*.
14. Scot McKnight, *Five Things Biblical Scholars Wish Theologians Knew* (Downers Grove, IL: IVP Academic, 2021).

Jesus summons his audience (Galileans are in view) to turn in repentance and to trust in the "gospel" or "good news," which in this context is surely the good news of the arrival or inauguration of the kingdom of God (cf. 1:14).[15] Jesus is the agent and announcer of that kingdom's arrival. If our five-point articulation of kingdom is at all correct, the gospel for Mark's Gospel is a message about Jesus as the bearer of good news—that is, the dawn of the kingdom in and through him. When Jesus articulates ethics for his followers in Mark 8, he connects the paradigm of his life as the embodiment of the gospel itself: "whoever loses their life for *me* and for *the gospel* will save it" (8:35, emphases added). Jesus and the gospel are inseparable.

Second, we need to observe that "gospel" becomes a *genre* by the end of the second century CE because the entire text of each of the Gospels—Matthew, Mark, Luke, John—is the gospel itself. I could perhaps rephrase this. One might say "gospel" is not genre, that the genre of each of the Gospels is biography, but that the biography of Jesus is the gospel. Which leads to the twisty sentence that the gospel is a biography as the biography of Jesus is the gospel.[16] The title to each paragraph of each of the four Gospels should begin with the word "Jesus," which should then be followed by a verb about what he says or does. The myopic concern of the Gospel writers is exclusively Jesus: he is the subject of each paragraph and by far the most sentences. Gospel as genre (or biography as genre) then articulates that the gospel is the story about Jesus.[17] That the church entitled each of these books as "The Gospel according to..." ought to have taught us that the gospel itself is on display.

Third, the gospel is preached by the apostles in the book of Acts seven, perhaps eight, times: 2:14–39; 3:12–26; 4:8–12; 10:34–43 with 11:4–18; 13:16–41; 14:15–17; 17:22–31 and perhaps one could add Stephen in 7:2–53. What we can observe to those who read such sermons is that these gospeling events are framed by Israel's story (not our

---

15. George Eldon Ladd, *The Presence of the Future: The Eschatology of Biblical Realism* (Grand Rapids: Eerdmans, 1974); N. T. Wright, *Jesus and the Victory of God*, Christian Origins and the Question of God 2 (Minneapolis, MN: Fortress, 1996); Scot McKnight, *A New Vision for Israel: The Teachings of Jesus in National Context* (Grand Rapids: Eerdmans, 1999).

16. See Richard Burridge, *What Are the Gospels? A Comparison with Graeco-Roman Biography*, 3rd ed. (Waco, TX: Baylor University Press, 2020).

17. Helen K. Bond, *The First Biography of Jesus: Genre and Meaning in Mark's Gospel* (Grand Rapids: Eerdmans, 2020).

personal salvation), the apostles tell the whole story of Jesus, they frequently summed the gospel in language about Jesus's identity (e.g., Acts 2:36: Lord and Messiah), they learned to adapt the gospel to new audiences (e.g., Acts 17:24–31), only after these points of substance did they call their hearers to respond in repentance, faith, and baptism (2:38–39; 3:19–21; 10:43; 13:38–39), and they also issued forth statements about the benefits of turning their lives over to Jesus as king (2:38; 13:38–39).

Fourth, it is worth pausing to read carefully the following verses in Acts that summarize the gospel down to a word or two. Our first two passages speak about the gospel that is *about Jesus*, and that's it.

> **Acts 8:35:** Then Philip began with that very passage of Scripture and told him **the good news about Jesus**.

> **Acts 11:20:** Some of them, however, men from Cyprus and Cyrene, went to Antioch and began to speak to Greeks also, telling them **the good news about the Lord Jesus**.

In Athens, Paul adds the resurrection to Jesus:

> **Acts 17:18:** A group of Epicurean and Stoic philosophers began to debate with him. Some of them asked, "What is this babbler trying to say?" Others remarked, "He seems to be advocating foreign gods." They said this because Paul was preaching the good news **about Jesus and the resurrection**.

In other places we find Jesus as the Messiah. Notice below that gospeling is the attempt to convince fellow Jews that Jesus was in fact Israel's long-awaited Messiah:

> **Acts 18:5:** When Silas and Timothy came from Macedonia, Paul devoted himself exclusively to preaching, testifying to the Jews **that Jesus was the Messiah**.

> **Acts 18:28:** For he vigorously refuted his Jewish opponents in public debate, proving from the Scriptures that **Jesus was the Messiah**.

Gospeling for the apostles was as it was with Jesus: healings and exorcisms were the power of the gospel at work. The apostle did such "in the name of Jesus":

> **Acts 19:13:** Some Jews who went around driving out evil spirits tried to invoke **the name of the Lord Jesus** over those who were demon-possessed. They would say, "**In the name of the Jesus** whom Paul preaches, I command you to come out."

> **Acts 20:20–21:** You know that I have not hesitated to preach anything that would be helpful to you but have taught you publicly and from house to house. I have declared to both Jews and Greeks that they must turn to God in repentance and have faith in our Lord Jesus.

And in Rome the gospel is about the kingdom of God, as Paul sought to persuade them about Jesus. Kingdom and Jesus are all but identical content in gospeling:

> **Acts 28:23:** They arranged to meet Paul on a certain day, and came in even larger numbers to the place where he was staying. He witnessed to them from morning till evening, **explaining about the kingdom of God**, and from the Law of Moses and from the Prophets **he tried to persuade them about Jesus**.

> **Acts 28:31:** He proclaimed **the kingdom of God and taught about the Lord Jesus Christ**—with all boldness and without hindrance!

The gospel sermons of Acts, it is now clear, were gospeling sermons that sought to persuade people about the identity of Jesus of Galilee as the true Messiah and Lord. When the gospel was reduced to its basic terms, *those terms were identity terms about Jesus.*

A momentary summary: To gospel is to tell people about Jesus in the context of the story of Israel and, in particular, to announce that the long-awaited Messiah/king and his kingdom have been launched through the life, death, burial, resurrection, and ascension of Jesus.

Fifth, we turn now to two texts that *explicitly state* what the gospel is, and they must be cited in full.

> Now, brothers and sisters, I want to remind you of the gospel I preached to you, which you received and on which you have taken your stand. By this gospel you are saved, if you hold firmly to the word I preached to you. Otherwise, you have believed in vain.
>
> For what I received I passed on to you as of first importance: that Christ died for our sins according to the Scriptures, that he was buried, that he was raised on the third day according to the Scriptures, and that he appeared to Cephas, and then to the Twelve. After that, he appeared to more than five hundred of the brothers and sisters at the same time, most of whom are still living, though some have fallen asleep. Then he appeared to James, then to all the apostles, and last of all he appeared to me also, as to one abnormally born. (1 Cor 15:1–8)

The opening paragraph here makes abundantly clear that just as Jews passed on their traditions, Paul is passing on the traditional gospel. That gospel is then explicated in lines about the life of Jesus in the second paragraph: the life of Jesus (implied), his death, his burial, his resurrection, and his appearances. If we continue through verse 28, we get his ascension (cf. Luke 24:50–53; Acts 1:9–11; perhaps 7:59–60; 1 Cor 15:24–25; Col 3:1; Heb 1:8; 4:14–16; 1 Pet 3:21–22; Rev 1:13; 4:2, 9–10; 5:6, 13)[18] and his return and the completion of the work by handing all things over to the Father. The gospel in 1 Corinthians 15 is (1) about Jesus, (2) it fulfills anticipations and promises in the story of Israel, and (3) it brings forgiveness of sins. What frames this gospel is the story of Jesus—the gospel in these lines tells facts about the life of Jesus. This summary suits the gospel sermons of Acts very well. The gospel for the apostles—this is the apostolic gospel tradition—is the story of Jesus fulfilling the story of Israel.

---

18. Douglas B. Farrow, *Ascension Theology* (New York: T&T Clark, 2011); Patrick Schreiner, *The Ascension of Christ: Recovering a Neglected Doctrine*, ed. Michael Bird (Bellingham, WA: Lexham, 2020).

We next turn to 2 Timothy, ignoring the authorship debate and taking the text as canonical and realizing at the same time that there's nothing here inconsistent with 1 Corinthians 15:1–8:

> Remember Jesus Christ, raised from the dead, descended from David. This is my gospel, for which I am suffering even to the point of being chained like a criminal. But God's word is not chained. Therefore I endure everything for the sake of the elect, that they too may obtain the salvation that is in Christ Jesus, with eternal glory.
>
> Here is a trustworthy saying:
>
> If we died with him,
>   we will also live with him;
> if we endure,
>   we will also reign with him.
> If we disown him,
>   he will also disown us;
> if we are faithless,
>   he remains faithful,
>   for he cannot disown himself. (2 Tim 2:8–13)

Our focus is on the opening line ending with "this is my gospel," which could be translated more literally as "consistent with" or "according to" my gospel. Those lines are the standard by which Paul measures the gospel. "This is" perhaps is too narrow, but it is too narrow only by a smidge—the facts of Jesus are to remember him as the Messiah, to affirm his resurrection, and to frame his story as one connected to King David. The ethic of the Christian in the "trustworthy saying" is nothing less than Christoformity or cruciformity.[19] Once again, the gospel's substance determines the substance of the Christian life, and

---

19. Michael J. Gorman, *Cruciformity: Paul's Narrative Spirituality of the Cross* (Grand Rapids: Eerdmans, 2001); idem, *Inhabiting the Cruciform God: Kenosis, Justification, and Theosis in Paul's Narrative Soteriology* (Grand Rapids: Eerdmans, 2009); idem, *Becoming the Gospel: Paul, Participation, and Mission* (Grand Rapids: Eerdmans, 2015); Scot McKnight, *Pastor Paul: Nurturing a Culture of Christoformity in the Church*, Theological Explorations for the Church Catholic (Grand Rapids: Brazos, 2019).

that substance is all about Jesus. The message in the gospel is a message *about* Jesus, not us, even if it is also *for* us.

A final point, one that I have wanted to put on the table sooner but believe this is the best location. The gospel about Jesus is a message that he has come *for all*. As the gospel message began to be proclaimed in synagogues outside the land of Israel, the authorities in Jerusalem were put on immediate notice that gentiles were coming into the church (Acts 8–28). Gentiles had always been welcome to the synagogue and were accepted as proselytes upon circumcision and submission to Torah, especially as practiced in Judaism of the time and location, but what was occurring in the Pauline mission churches alarmed the Christian leaders in Jerusalem, led by James. They were alarmed because these gentiles were not being required to embrace the Torah, and what concerned them were expressions of Torah observance like Sabbath, food laws, and circumcision. The Galatian Jewish believers seemed to have considered such believers as merely Godfearers instead of full converts. Paul dug into his Scriptures to find the blessing of Abraham going to the nations on the basis of faith alone (Gen 12; 15; Gal 3:6–9), to find the terminal fulfillment of Torah in the age of faith in Christ (Gal 3:15–25), and he found satisfaction in converts to Jesus being baptized. This baptism united Jewish and gentile believers, slave and free believers, and men and women believers (3:28). The theme of *for all* shapes the entire mission of Paul, most especially his letters to the Galatians and Romans. Everywhere Paul went he met the same criticism, yet everywhere Paul went he continued to respond and develop his theological response to the inclusion of all in Christ on the basis of faith alone, apart from the "works of the law."[20]

Response and Benefits

The substance of the gospel determines the response. In other words, the message itself shapes how one responds. If the substance is Jesus is

---

20. Again, a nest of interpretive hornets is disturbed by this sentence. I appeal to Dunn, *Theology of Paul the Apostle*; idem, *The New Perspective on Paul*, rev. ed. (Grand Rapids: Eerdmans, 2008); Matthew J. Thomas, *Paul's "Works of the Law" in the Perspective of Second Century Reception*, WUNT 2/468 (Tübingen: Mohr Siebeck, 2018); Scot McKnight, *Reading Romans Backwards: A Gospel of Peace in the Midst of Empire* (Waco, TX: Baylor University Press, 2019).

Lord, the proper response is turning to him as Lord. If the substance is Jesus is Messiah, the proper response is to embrace and indwell in that story. If the substance is Jesus is Savior, the proper response is to accept him as Savior. If the substance is Jesus brings peace or justice, the proper response is to live that peace and justice. If he is all those, the response is intensified.

How is one to respond to the gospel? Let me press toward a single but complex word: the required and proper response to the gospel about Jesus is *surrender* to God in Christ through the power of the Spirit. There are at least four dimensions to surrender: repentance, trust, embodiment of the gospel itself in baptism, all issuing into daily allegiance to Jesus. When Peter preached at Pentecost and the people asked what they should do, the answer was "repent and be baptized" (Acts 2:38). But repentance, deriving as it does mostly from the prophets of Israel and their message to turn, is not a term that must be used or that is reified into a system of salvation. Rather, it expresses what surrender is all about: one surrenders control over one's life and gives in to God in Christ. If we add to this the call to believe/trust (Acts 10:43; 11:17; 13:38–39), the proper response to the gospel is to turn away from sin, to turn one's life over to Jesus as king, to believe in him in the sense of trusting and becoming allegiant to the king,[21] and to be baptized. Each of these is Christoform in orientation: one turns from sin in order to turn to the new in Christ; one trusts and becomes allegiant in order to walk in the way of Christ; and one is baptized in order to enter into his very death and resurrection. The response is all about him, and it concerns all of us.[22]

What does one get? It's not like we need ask, "What's in it for me?" or strut with "sell me on this gospel message." One doesn't "get" so much as one enters into the circle of Christ—to be "in Christ"—and in Christ there is the abundant life of God at work in healing and forgiving and restoring and reconciling and justifying and redeeming and transforming us into the likeness of Christ (2 Cor 3:18). All these benefits come to

---

21. Matthew W. Bates, *Salvation by Allegiance Alone: Rethinking Faith, Works, and the Gospel of Jesus the King* (Grand Rapids: Baker Academic, 2017); idem, *Gospel Allegiance: What Faith in Jesus Misses for Salvation in Christ* (Grand Rapids: Brazos, 2019).
22. McKnight, *New Vision for Israel*, 164–76.

us so that we will be fit for the presence of God[23] in the New Jerusalem. The benefits of the gospel abound in the New Testament texts, so I turn to some of these. The Christian theology of salvation dominates the subject matter of theology itself, and assuming a widespread knowledge of our favorite terms of redemption, I will not explicate the benefits of salvation as much as we might like. I appeal to the development of this central theme in the secondary literature.[24]

God's gracious gift of forgiveness of sins is almost a non sequitur in Acts 2 if one is not reading closely. Connections must become clear: it is Pentecost, and this Pentecost fulfills the anticipated days of Joel 2, which is about the Spirit coming upon all, about the judgment of God against systemic rejection of God (the cosmic wonders indicate this) by crucifying Jesus, about the sterling character and acts of Jesus that were rejected by the audience who had voiced criticisms of the believers, and about Peter prophetically turning against that audience—but despite their murder of Jesus, God vindicated Jesus as Israel's Messiah by raising him from the dead (as David had prophesied), by welcoming him to the throne room of God, and by Jesus sending the Holy Spirit who just created this event at Pentecost. This Jesus is Israel's Messiah.

Their response is a question: What are we to do in light of what we have done in rejecting the Messiah? Peter's answer is "repent and be baptized, every one of you" (Acts 2:38). They sinned in complicity in the murder of Jesus, but that sin can be forgiven if they turn from it and turn to Jesus to participate in his death and resurrection. Sins to be repented of and forgiven in the New Testament are mostly particular—as we see with John the Baptist in Luke 3:10–14, where the very question asked at Pentecost was asked of the Baptist (What should we do to respond?). Forgiveness is not talked about much in the Gospels: Matthew 26:28; Mark 1:4; Luke 1:77; 3:3; 4:19; 24:47. It occurs only a few times in Acts: 2:38; 5:31; 10:43; 13:38; 26:18. These references, and others could be added, show that this is not the dominating benefit,[25] but it expresses the heart of the benefits of the gospel. It comes to all who surrender

---

23. Hans Boersma, *Seeing God: The Beatific Vision in Christian Tradition* (Grand Rapids: Eerdmans, 2018).
24. Michael F. Bird, *Evangelical Theology: A Biblical and Systematic Introduction*, 2nd ed. (Grand Rapids: Zondervan, 2020), 551–661.
25. It is not common even in Paul: cf. Rom 4:7 (citing an OT text); Eph 1:7; Col 1:14.

because in Christ there is forgiveness. Put differently, forgiveness is but one way of expressing the benefits for those who surrender. Paul prefers justification (e.g., Acts 13:38–39) and reconciliation (e.g., Rom 5:11; 11:15; 2 Cor 5:18–19),[26] while the benefits in Acts focus more on the outpouring and gift of the Holy Spirit (Acts 2:38–39; 10:44–47; 11:16–18). One of the most prominent terms in the Jesus traditions is "save," and the term does not distinguish healing from some kind of spiritual redemption (e.g., Matt 1:21; 8:25; 9:21–22; 10:22; 14:30; 16:25; 19:25; 24:13, 22; 27:40, 42, 49 and parallels). These come to the one surrendering by virtue of the life, crucifixion, burial, and resurrection of Jesus. Such expressiveness does not diminish any of these terms but instead reveals that these terms are expressions of a larger reality that cannot be narrowed to a single term. One term that, because it is not often used, can stun us into thinking more holistically is that the singular benefit of the gospel is *healing*.[27]

One larger theme should surround all discussions about benefits: the intent of God in saving a person is to transform the person into Christlikeness (2 Cor 3:18) so they will be fit for life in the kingdom of God. To the degree that this kingdom has been inaugurated in Christ, or in life in the Spirit in the here and now, to that same degree those who are in Christ should be in the process of transformation.[28] Heaven, as it is so often chatted up, is not simply for individuals in some ecstatic state of personal worship and blessed joy but is a world of love and goodness and justice and peace. The Bible's narrative shape or story is one leading to New Jerusalem, a vision for a utopian society as earthly as it is heavenly (of heaven come down to earth), not one leading simply to a person's eternal destiny in some far-off heaven. The final state of the Christian

---

26. Ralph P. Martin, *Reconciliation: A Study of Paul's Theology*, New Foundations Theological Library (Atlanta: John Knox Press, 1981); Michael F. Bird, *The Saving Righteousness of God: Studies on Paul, Justification, and the New Perspective*, Paternoster Biblical Monographs (Bletchley, Milton Keynes: Paternoster/Authentic Media, 2007); N. T. Wright, *Paul and the Faithfulness of God*, 2 vols., Christian Origins and the Question of God 4 (Minneapolis: Fortress, 2013), 2:1473–1520.

27. Graham H. Twelftree, *The Gospel According to Paul: A Reappraisal* (Eugene, OR: Wipf & Stock, 2019). Twelftree at times exaggerates benefit at the expense of Christology and message. See, too, the two-part essay by Jon Ruthven, "'This Is My Covenant with Them': Isaiah 59.19–21 as the Programmatic Prophecy of the New Covenant in the Acts of the Apostles," *Journal of Pentecostal Studies* 17 (2008): 32–47, 219–237.

28. David A. deSilva, *Transformation: The Heart of Paul's Gospel* (Bellingham, WA: Lexham, 2014).

vision is as social as it is spiritual, and as a social reality it fulfills the divine vision for how humans are to relate to God and to one another, as well as to creation itself.[29]

What is noticeable about the gospeling of the New Testament is that the benefits one gains in Christ do not frame the gospel as if it is a "do this and you will get this" affair. Rather, the gospel is about Jesus, people are summoned to surrender to Jesus, and when they get attached to Jesus, the goodness of God's redemption is theirs. What they "get" is Jesus, and in Christ are all the blessings (Eph 1:3). Sinclair Ferguson, not a normal running mate of mine, warned of the danger of separating the benefits (justification, etc.) from Christ himself, and today we can often experience a gospel in which the benefits are separated by overwhelming Christ—the person, the biography, and union with him.[30]

I put it this way: we announce first a Christology, and only after Christology do we announce soteriology. First, Christology; second, soteriology. It is not either-or but first and second. If we permit benefits to frame the gospel itself, then we turn Jesus into a means. If we put Christology first, then Jesus becomes the subject and substance of the gospel, and the salvation comes in him.

A Life Worthy of the Gospel

If the substance of the gospel is Jesus is Lord, Jesus is king, Jesus is Messiah, then the life to be lived is a life of submitting to him, of self-denial and of life-long Christoformity/cruciformity. I appeal to three texts as instances of a gospel-shaped life.

First, the Sermon on the Mount is singularly "egocentric." A close reading of the text exalts Jesus as the new Moses[31] in a manner that at least fits with the aftershock expressed by those who heard him (Matt 7:28–29). That Sermon considers kingdom people to be those who are customarily marginalized (5:3–12) and summons them to a kingdom way of life, a new Torah, based on the teachings of Jesus.

---

29. Often emphasized by N. T. Wright, *Surprised by Hope: Rethinking Heaven, the Resurrection, and the Mission of the Church* (New York: HarperOne, 2008).
30. I am grateful to my friend David G. Moore for pointing me to this from Ferguson. See Sinclair Ferguson, *The Whole Christ: Legalism, Antinomianism, and Gospel Assurance—Why the Marrow Controversy Still Matters* (Wheaton, IL: Crossway, 2016), 44.
31. Dale Allison, *The New Moses: A Matthean Typology* (Minneapolis: Fortress, 1993).

The discipleship passages that follow the Sermon on the Mount reflect the same Christocentricity. The essence of them is to follow Jesus in the path of the cross (e.g., 8:18–22; 16:21–28). Christology determines discipleship. The ethic of the Christian community is not an abstract ethic forged on the basis of abstract reflections on virtue ethics but is instead the concrete way of life embodied in Jesus.

Which is why, second, the apostle Paul appeals to the early Christian hymn in Philippians 2:6–11 as the paradigm of life for the Philippians, and this passage is worked out in detail in the paradigm-forming work of Michael Gorman.[32] Jesus as "example" must simultaneously be understood as life in the Spirit: what gives a human in Christ the power to live the Christoform life is the Spirit (Rom 8:1–4; Gal 5:22–26). All of this, too, happens because of the efficaciousness of grace itself.[33]

Third, in a passage mentioned already, we need to see how Paul not only frames the gospel but how a gospel life is lived:

> Remember Jesus Christ, raised from the dead, descended from David. This is my gospel, for which I am suffering even to the point of being chained like a criminal. . . .
>
> Here is a trustworthy saying:
>
> If we died with him,
>   we will also live with him;
> if we endure,
>   we will also reign with him.
> If we disown him,
>   he will also disown us;
> if we are faithless,
>   he remains faithful,
>   for he cannot disown himself. (2 Tim 2:8–13)

The Christocentricity comes to the fore again: the gospel is about Jesus, the substance of the gospel is Jesus, and the life lived in consort with the gospel is a Christocentric, Christoform, cruciform life. Those

---

32. Gorman, *Inhabiting the Cruciform God*.
33. John M. G. Barclay, *Paul and the Gift* (Grand Rapids: Eerdmans, 2015).

who live that life are those who will experience the eternal benefits of the gospel.

And the impact of humans swept into the kingdom vision of Jesus the king is a life that becomes systemic and socially impacting, as kingdom people embody a kingdom life in a world shaped by too much evil. The goal of the gospel is the kingdom of God.

Final Reflections

My own teaching, preaching, and writing about the King Jesus gospel has taught me that any rearrangement of the frame for talking about the gospel creates a learning anxiety that many would prefer not to be present. So, to retain their semblance of comfort they think the soterian gospel has got to be right because of the comfort it brings. My contention is that one need not surrender the comfort of a secure relationship with a God who loves us to embrace the center of the gospel in Christology. I contend that we look more carefully at explicit gospel passages where we discover that the reason the church called the first four books of the New Testament the "gospel" was because they told the story of Jesus, and that story of Jesus is itself the gospel.

First Christology, then soteriology. Not one without the other but in that order.

We evangelize or gospel whenever we mention Jesus, whenever we state his identity, and whenever we put his vision into play. The central question of evangelism then is this one:

Who do you think Jesus is?

RESPONSE TO SCOT MCKNIGHT

MICHAEL HORTON

"A test I have for assessing any articulation of the gospel is this: Did Jesus preach what this person says is the gospel?" (p. 29). I love Scot McKnight's criterion. It's not a red-letter edition or canon-within-a-canon approach, at least as far as I can see. If Jesus is the king and is ushering in his kingdom, then the nucleus of everything unpacked by the apostles must be there. As he taught them in the upper room, "But the [other] Advocate, the Holy Spirit, whom the Father will send in my name, will teach you all things and will remind you of everything I have said to you" (John 14:26).[1] This is the redemptive-historical foundation of the inspiration of the New Testament. They will not only preach Christ but will remember everything he said and did that's relevant to the case. Like the central character in a novel, he may not appear in every scene, but the whole Bible leads to Jesus and from him.

McKnight is obsessed with the concrete and particular, grounding the gospel in what Jesus actually said and did. Today, Jesus has become a wax nose—a mascot for whatever side of the polarized cultural and political divide one prefers. We need to come to the biblical narrative not first of all to find answers to our questions but to be given better questions. Jesus will tell us who he is and why he has come, regardless of whether we find it helpful, meaningful, informative, empowering, or whatever else.

Especially illuminating, I thought, was McKnight's nuanced wrestling with the often polarizing debate over whether Jesus should be

---

1. *Paraklētos* is definitely *not* "Helper," a poor rendering initiated by Origen because he wanted to distinguish him from Christ. But Jesus says "another Advocate" (John 14:16), and the same title is used of Jesus in 1 John 2:1.

understood as challenging Caesar's imperial claims. "Unless Paul was profoundly naive to usage," McKnight says, "we must conclude that when Paul said 'gospel' and tied it to Jesus as Lord his audience would have said, 'Caesar is not'" (p. 32). Yes, indeed, and that is how Romans certainly heard him and his disciples. It's also the way the Sanhedrin heard him in its self-preservation politics with the empire: "They cried out, 'Away with him, away with him, crucify him!' Pilate said to them, 'Shall I crucify your King?' The chief priests answered, 'We have no king but Caesar'" (John 19:15 ESV). This sentence must have caused many religious leaders to shudder if they had understood Jesus's statement, "'Render to Caesar the things that are Caesar's, and to God the things that are God's.' And they marveled at him" (Mark 12:17 ESV). At the same time, McKnight registers, "I'm dubious that Paul's intentional, overriding agenda was to subvert the Roman Empire and its imperial claims or even the imperial cult" (p. 32).

One could not separate politics from religion in the Roman Empire. Nor, I would add, could one separate politics from religion in Jesus's empire. The question is whether the purpose *right now* was to overthrow the Romans, turn the Roman Empire into Christ's kingdom, or a similar utopia, and Jesus's answer is clear: "My kingdom is not of this world" (John 18:36). It is a large-scale revolution, but only if one thinks that defeating Satan, death, and hell are more important than driving out the Romans or turning the empire into a nominally Christian society. McKnight turns to the Apocalypse, where the choice is between "taking the mark" (pinching incense to Caesar) and martyrdom. It *is* political in the most extreme terms, but it was not a call to build a just society. Rather, it was the call to attach oneself to the true king who will one day topple all Caesars in their pride. It is "the *gospel* of the empire" that they must repent of, which is a lesson to us today in the United States and the West generally. But we must turn from all such pseudo-gospels of *this regime*, even the ones that we understand to be more just and righteous.

McKnight thinks "Jesus and the gospel are inseparable" (p. 34). All of the passages on the kingdom are "proclaiming Jesus." That's the message of the kingdom. "The message in the gospel is a message *about* Jesus, not us, even if it is also *for* us." "The gospel about Jesus is a message that he has come for *all*" (p. 39). Hence, tension between Jew-gentile missions.

Under his section "Response and Benefits," I have some ambivalence with McKnight's presentation. Yes, there are many responses, including "surrender." But faith is *not* surrender. Maybe repentance is: throwing up one's hands before the law and saying, "I'm convicted and sentenced, guilty as charged." But we are not justified by allegiance but by trust in the only one who can save us despite our lack of allegiance. He cites Matthew W. Bates's work at this point.[2] I have interacted with Bates's paradigm.[3] It seems to me to lead to a massive confusion of law and gospel. Lutheran and Reformed churches have emphasized that faith does many things indeed. "It's a busy thing," as Luther said.[4] Faith works, serves, loves, speaks, and so forth. But in the event of justification, it isn't busy at all but rests in Christ. All of these other "busy" things I have no trouble with—after all, they're all over the pages of Scripture. In the act of being justified, faith merely receives a gift.

This is a very counterintuitive moment in McKnight's presentation, because the whole emphasis of "What is the gospel?" has been *on Christ*. But now it is *my allegiance* that is front and center. The response is not to throw up our hands, accept the law's verdict, but then in faith embrace Christ's imputed righteousness. Rather it is to "surrender to God in Christ through the power of the Spirit" (p. 40). Some of the same concerns I express in relation to the "Wesleyan Gospel" are relevant here. "There are at least four dimensions to surrender: repentance, trust, embodiment of the gospel itself in baptism, all issuing into daily allegiance to Jesus. . . . the proper response to the gospel is to turn away from sin, to turn one's life over to Jesus as king, to believe in him in the sense of trusting and becoming allegiant to the king, and to be baptized" (p. 40). It is true that there are *many* responses to the gospel announcement. However, faith is the instrumental cause of justification. And faith is not anything other than *trusting someone else—Christ—to do the job*!

I don't know why McKnight wants to downplay forgiveness. Even after citing many references to Jesus's own preaching of forgiveness of

---

2. Bates, *Salvation by Allegiance Alone*; idem, *Gospel Allegiance*.
3. Michael Horton, *Justification*, vol. 2, New Studies in Dogmatics (Grand Rapids: Zondervan, 2018), 386–87, 390–92, 412–13.
4. "Preface to the Epistle of St. Paul to the Romans" in *Luther's Works*, ed. Theodore Buchmann, vol. 35, Word & Sacrament I (Philadelphia: Fortress, 1960), 370–71.

sins, he says, "forgiveness is but one way of expressing the benefits for those who surrender." "Paul prefers justification (e.g., Acts 13:38–39) and reconciliation (e.g., Rom 5:11; 11:15; 2 Cor 5:18–19), while the benefits in Acts focus more on the outpouring and gifts of the Holy Spirit (Acts 2:38–39; 10:44–47; 11:16–18)" (p. 42).

It is important, I think, to distinguish genres at this point. The Gospels and Acts should be seen as one continuing narrative of the acts of God in first-century Judea to Rome, while the epistles unpack significance; in all those passages cited, forgiveness, reconciliation, and justification are *the message*. The outpouring of the Spirit, again, is the narrative of a new redemptive-historical event. But what does Peter preach? The other apostles in Acts? They all preached the forgiveness of sins, justification, full acceptance regardless of whether they were Jew or gentile.

McKnight concludes, "I put it this way: we announce first a Christology and only after Christology do we announce soteriology" (p. 43). "The central question of evangelism then is this one: Who do you think Jesus is?" (p. 45). I could not agree more.

I find myself in the greatest sympathy with McKnight's essay. The gospel is not *about* us, but it is *for* us, as McKnight argues. Nothing that happens *to* us is itself the gospel; rather, it is the impact of the gospel. The gospel is the proclamation of a person and what he achieved long ago in a minor Middle Eastern province of the Roman Empire. We are not the good news but are its beneficiaries and heralds. We also live in the light of the gospel (e.g., Rom 12:1–2; Phil 1:27; Col 3:12–14). The gospel creates its own community, a shining city on a hill (Matt 5:14). A notable sign that the kingdom has come is that "the poor have good news preached to them" (Luke 7:22 ESV). However, the poor and oppressed, no less than the individual bound by sin's guilt and dominion, are not at any point the subject of God's redeeming work but always the recipient. There is genuine transformation as a result of this regenerating, justifying, adopting, and sanctifying grace of God in Christ, but the gospel itself is that "*in Christ God* was reconciling the world to himself, not counting their trespasses against them, and entrusting to us the message of reconciliation" (2 Cor 5:19 ESV). Our own experience, good works, or individual or collective identity cannot be the gospel but rather is its fruit.

If anyone could relate the inner transformation Jesus effected in their lives, surely it would have been those who spent those momentous three years at his side. We might wish that Peter had related his transformative experience from denying Jesus three times to proclaiming the gospel boldly on the temple steps at a high feast. But for the apostles, "witness" and "testimony" meant relating what Jesus said and did, especially his resurrection. Paul speaks of his experience more than the other apostles, but always pointing away from himself to Christ. Considering his own continuing struggle with sin, he despairs—until he looks to Christ, in whom "there is therefore now no condemnation" (Rom 8:1 ESV).

The same can be said of believers collectively. If Jesus's identity is primarily that of a community organizer, can he be said to have succeeded? His preaching offended not only the religious elites but also the common people—even his own disciples (e.g., John 6). Many who hailed him as the Messiah on Palm Sunday cried, "Crucify him!" on Good Friday. Abandoned by his fearful disciples, Jesus alone hung on the cross, bearing the sin of the world. If it was his purpose to have transformed Judea or the Roman Empire into a just society, Albert Schweitzer's verdict seems justified: he failed to bring in the kingdom of God. Even John the Baptist seems to have felt this when he sent his disciples to ask Jesus, "'Are you the one who is to come, or shall we look for another?' And Jesus answered them, 'Go and tell John what you hear and see: the blind receive their sight and the lame walk, lepers are cleansed and the deaf hear, and the dead are raised up, and the poor have good news preached to them. And blessed is the one who is not offended by me'" (Matt 11:3–6 ESV).

Not only is the gospel about Christ, I would add, but Christ gives himself to us in its proclamation. In fact, Christ himself is the speaker through the lips of our fellow sinners as they herald the good news. Lutheran and Reformed traditions designate the preaching of the gospel "the sacramental word." As Paul preaches in Romans 10, Christ himself is present in the preached gospel. More than this, he is the preacher, even through the lips of a sinner. The gospel—good news—is a unique speech-act that, in the power of the Spirit, creates the reality of which it speaks. In preaching this gospel, Christ not only offers an invitation to receive himself with all his benefits but bestows them.

RESPONSE TO SCOT MCKNIGHT

DAVID A. DESILVA

I will admit it. When I first saw the lineup for the views on the gospel that would be represented in this book, I was surprised to find space being allocated to "the King Jesus Gospel," while none was being given to much older—and far more widely subscribed to—perspectives such as the Roman Catholic or Eastern Orthodox views on the gospel. However, after reading Scot McKnight's essay, I am persuaded of the editors' wisdom in giving this view place here alongside more standard "denominational" articulations of the gospel. This articulation of the gospel has such intrinsic value that it merits not merely to be examined but to be promoted. I want to say that it is "fresh," but not in the sense of being innovative (which would really not be a virtue when it comes to giving expression to that which had its most perfect expression in the first century CE). Rather, it is "fresh" in the sense of giving fresh expression to a gospel that has been overlooked for so long but, once it is given a hearing, seems almost self-evidently correct and worthy of a central place henceforth in conversations about the good news of God both announced and enacted in Jesus Christ.

McKnight and I agree that the "soterian" view of the gospel is inadequate both in terms of the many-layered problem that has beset humanity in its alienation from God and of the many-layered solution that God has provided in Christ through the Holy Spirit. We have been "selling" this gospel too long, as McKnight rightly notes, as the quick and easy way to get into heaven. He is correct that by permitting "benefits to frame the gospel itself, then we turn Jesus into a means" (p. 43). I am reminded of the hymn:

> My God, I love thee not because I hope for heaven thereby,
> nor yet for fear that, loving not, I might forever die.[1]

If our motivation for discipleship is ultimately self-centered, have we really been *converted*—have we *turned* toward God, or are we still the *homo incurvatus in se*, the person curved in on himself or herself, ultimately self-absorbed and self-serving rather than God-absorbed and other-serving?

I am impressed with the manner in which this view of the gospel is able to find its roots in Jesus's own proclamation of the good news of the kingdom of God (e.g., Mark 1:15), as well as by the way this view of the gospel makes room not only for Jesus's statements about the redemptive effects of his death as a ransom (Matt 20:28; Mark 10:45)—hence, for atonement and reconciliation—but also for Jesus's statements about the absolute necessity of obeying him if we are to enjoy the redemptive benefits of his death and a restored relationship with our Lord, escaping eschatological ruin (Matt 7:21–27; Luke 6:46–49). It does seem more straightforwardly true to the New Testament witness to think of the "gospel" in terms of what God has done in Christ (hence McKnight's emphasis on the content of the sermons in Acts or Paul's summaries of the gospel he received and handed on in 1 Cor 15:1–8) and the ramifications of God's acts in Christ for human beings called to give their allegiance and, therewith, their obedience to this Christ, than to think of the so-called Romans Road as "the" gospel (I say "so-called" because I regard this to be a gross truncation of the gospel Paul himself proclaimed—on which see further below).

Of course, as the representative of the Wesleyan gospel in this volume, I am delighted to find "the transformation of humans and systems" (p. 27) as the result of Jesus's saving action and God's redemptive work make it into McKnight's tweet, suggesting their core importance for his view of the gospel. I note with appreciation the place that this also makes for the liberation gospel's emphasis on the need to deconstruct and rebuild the *systems* that perpetuate harm rather than simply continue to bind up the wounds of the harmed. Indeed, a lived obedience to Jesus

---

1. "My God, I Love Thee, Not Because," attributed to St. Francis Xavier, trans. Edward Caswall, 1849. Text online at https://hymnary.org/text/my_god_i_love_thee_not_because.

as king—a commitment to put into practice his prescriptions for life-in-community, a commitment to make the "kingdom of God" real in all the spaces that we ourselves inhabit through our collective obedience as a community—has always been the surest way to transform human experience amid the kingdoms of this world.

I can get entirely behind the idea that a gospel ultimately about the reign of God and God's Messiah requires, in response, "surrender to God in Christ through the power of the Spirit" manifested, among other things, in "daily allegiance" (which I would take to include daily *obedience*) "to Jesus" (p. 40). Again, any articulation of a gospel that does not make room for the *requirement* of obedience, of a life brought ever more into alignment with the Creator's wishes for that life, is, in my view, a defective gospel, an inadequate solution to the fundamental human problem of the *mis*alignment of our lives vis-à-vis the purposes of the One who gave us our lives.

I appreciate also McKnight's awareness of the goal of such alignment—of our growing in righteousness and holiness, of Christ's life taking shape in our lives—being to make us "fit for the presence of God in the New Jerusalem" (p. 41). It is good news indeed that God has set in motion all that is necessary to equip us for eternity in the presence of the Holy One through the transformation of our hearts and lives. This is not about "works" or "synergism" or any of the usual bugbears conjured when the notion of living a new life is foregrounded in soteriology: it remains about God's gracious provision, a grace that we dare not receive in vain or set aside.

If I were to quibble (and I can only *quibble* in regard to this invigorating essay), it would be with what appears to be too quick an identification of the "standard soterian model" with "Paul's solution," with its emphasis on "the themes of sin, salvation, and atonement." I find Paul's assessment of both the problem of human existence and the extent of the remedy that God has provided in Christ to be far fuller and richer than this, reaching beyond atonement and reconciliation to the restoration of a proper, consistent response of grateful obedience that ought always to have characterized humanity's stance before its Creator (and now, Redeemer). The emphasis on the work of the Holy Spirit especially, and on the conformity of the believer's life to the mind, heart, and actions of Christ that pervades Paul's extant writings (whether this be expressed in terms of "newness of life," "the new person," "Christ formed in you") shows that Paul believed God to be at work saving us from what we *had* become for what we *could* and *would* become as we submit to the leading of, and receive the empowerment of, the Spirit to this end.[2] In other words, I find McKnight to stand in agreement with Paul when he claims that "the *problem* was human subjects not living under the world's true king" (p. 28, though Paul would speak about this in terms of the honor and obedience due the Creator God in Rom 1:18–32) and that "the *solution* is humans living under Jesus as Lord and king—that is, as Messiah" (p. 28, which Paul speaks about in terms of presenting our embodied lives as instruments for righteous action [Rom 6:12–14, 17–23] and, perhaps even more impressively, living no longer for ourselves but for the one who died and was raised on our behalf [2 Cor 5:15]).

Perhaps by way of refinement rather than disagreement, I think it important to foreground the experience of the Holy Spirit—clearly, in the context of Paul's ministry, an *intersubjective* rather than a purely *subjective* experience—in Paul's thinking as he contended with the rival teachers in Galatia. This experience was the starting point *from which* "Paul dug into his Scriptures to find the blessing of Abraham going to the nations on the basis of faith alone" (p. 39), and indeed Paul understood the Holy Spirit itself to *be* this blessing (according to some interpretations of Gal 3:13–14 at least). The experience was the catalyst that created the opportunity to account for it scripturally.

Quibbles aside, McKnight has foregrounded precisely what I find so clearly emphasized in Paul and underrepresented in too many presentations of the gospel: the "Christocentric, Christoform, cruciform life" is the one that "will experience the eternal benefits of the gospel" (p. 45).

---

2. This is a constant theme in my commentaries on Paul: *The Letter to the Galatians*, NICNT (Grand Rapids: Eerdmans, 2018); *Ephesians*, NCBC (Cambridge: Cambridge University Press, 2022). See also my *Transformation: The Heart of Paul's Gospel* (Bellingham, WA: Lexham, 2014).

RESPONSE TO SCOT MCKNIGHT

JULIE MA

Scot McKnight's King Jesus gospel is something that is both familiar and foreign to me. It is familiar in many aspects of what McKnight says about Jesus as king and Lord, familiar too in concerns it raises, even if I—as an Asian missiologist rather than a Western biblical scholar—am not familiar with much of its scholarly background and reasoning in secondary literature.

McKnight begins with a discussion of the old-time evangelical message of Billy Graham. What McKnight finds deficient, mostly, is what it lacks (identity of Jesus), and more so in what it emphasizes (saving benefits to an individual). Billy Graham himself preached in Asia, specifically in Taipei, Hong Kong, Singapore, Tokyo, Seoul, and elsewhere, always to large crowds. But with McKnight, I do wonder if his message was appropriately geared toward the diverse forms of Asian people and Asian Christianity or whether it was something of an American import, like a McDonald's with a crucifix. As an Asian Christian leader, I am sensitive to mission work being more contextual and informed than it perhaps was in the early days of the Billy Graham Association. So I'm naturally inclined to accept McKnight's critique of the American industrial, evangelical gospel. Beyond that I have several other observations.

First, McKnight is correct to connect the gospel to the kingdom of God. Yet I would want to stress that the kingdom of God is not just the climax of a scriptural story; rather, the primary concept of the kingdom of God in the New Testament focuses largely on the rulership of Jesus Christ as launching the kingdom. McKnight is big on Jesus as king, but as a Pentecostal I am aware that Jesus is no king without his subjects experiencing his kingly power, a power that he bestows on us like a king granting favors and disbursing titles.

Second, is it really true that the gospel is the story of Jesus's life? At one level, the incarnation is the most spectacular instance of cultural identification in the history of humankind. The Son of God did not stay in the safe abode of heaven, remote from the sin, pain, and tragedy of the world. Instead, he entered our world. He took on our nature, lived our life, endured our temptations, experienced our sorrows, bore our sins, and died our death. It was the total identification of life without any loss of his own identity. In becoming one of us, he neither ceases to be himself in becoming a man nor ceases to be God. But the life of Jesus is lived *for us*, for our redemption, sanctification, and new creation. The "who" and "for us" should not be separated. Even if McKnight wants to make sure the "who" is not neglected, the "for" is what makes the good news good to Pentecostals.

Third, McKnight is impressive and even inspiring when he talks about responses and benefits of the gospel. He emphasizes one thing in particular: surrender to God. I want to agree, with the qualification that our surrender or submission occurs in Christ through the power of the Spirit. Accordingly, submission takes on a particular shape: surrender is to turn away from sin, to give one's life over to Jesus as king, to believe in him in the sense of trusting and being allegiant to the king, to believe in him in the sense of believing and trusting, and to be baptized (Acts 10:43; 11:17; 13:38–39). Each of these is oriented in a Christocentric way: one repents of sin in order to turn to the new life in Christ; one trusts and pledges allegiance in order to follow Christ; and one gets baptized in order to participate in his suffering and resurrection. The reaction is all about him, and it affects us all. So submission is not just to a confession of Jesus, a recognition of Jesus's status, it is surrendering oneself into God's power, to throw oneself on his mercy, as well as to open oneself up to an infusion of divine enablement.

McKnight's gospel is great, because the kingship of Jesus is great, but there is one thing he needs: power! The gospel is power unto salvation, power for the powerless, power for the hopeless, the power of God's love and the love that works so powerfully in us.

RESPONSE TO SCOT MCKNIGHT

SHIVELY T. J. SMITH

With stylistic beauty and probing insight, Scot McKnight weaves an interpretive skein rich with biblical references and theological acuity. I found myself collecting fresh gems about the multidimensional meaning of the gospel in each reading of McKnight's view. He facilitates the interweaving of biblical threads that relate issues of biblical content to context by taking up matters such as the imagery of kingdom to the matter of Christology, which gives way to soteriology and even to the fundamental question of Christ's identity. Moreover, his essay supplies a reintroduction that extends the noun form of the word gospel into a verb, "gospeling." The moment McKnight couples gospel with gospeling, my interest was piqued, and questions formed: "What are the features of Jesus's gospel activity captured in the New Testament? And how does this gospel shape the orientation of believers who follow Jesus's model?"

I did not have to wait long for McKnight's response. His gospel tweet named the essential ingredient with two final lines, "In an even shorter tweet, the gospel is the story about Jesus. In one word, Jesus" (p. 27). I appreciate the clear distance McKnight places between Paul's construction of the gospel and Jesus as its embodiment and archetype of gospeling activity. Scott makes the point clear, saying, "Without denying the importance of the themes of sin, salvation, and atonement in Christ, we must recognize that Paul's solution is Paul's and should not be imposed on Jesus. Jesus announced kingdom because kingdom was the expectation, so I begin with Jesus" (p. 28). From a liberation-gospel view, Jesus's embodied proclamation is distinct from Paul's description of Jesus's messianic significance, though they speak back to each other. Indeed, McKnight's one tweet preference resonates: Jesus is the starting place for gospel understanding.

McKnight releases the gospel message from a static announcement and centuries-old story rehearsed repeatedly in our churches, faith communities, or even in the theaters of popular culture and civic forums. Gospel meaning expands in McKnight's essay from proclamation to an active solution interacting at the level of "a context, a story, a narrative" (p. 27). The beginning of the gospel story about Jesus, be it at his birth as rehearsed by Matthew and Luke or in Jesus's adulthood ministry as encountered in the Gospels of Mark and John (after John's prologue, of course), is no small matter in understanding McKnight's construction of the King Jesus Gospel. It is the setting upon which the common gospel phrase "kingdom of God" (or "heaven") is understood.

From whence did this Jesus come, and what circumstances shaded his perspective? The Gospels unanimously place Jesus outside the authorities of Israel's religious, political, and economic hubs—namely, Jerusalem, the temple, and Rome. The distance in terms of beginnings is further amplified compared to his cousin, John the Baptist (as described in Luke 1). His origin story, beginning with his father and mother, Zechariah and Elizabeth, initiates within the sanctuary of the temple where the very presence of God dwelled (Luke 1:8–23). The Gospel casts the iconic site of Jewish authority, peoplehood, and faith as the foreground for John's ministry.

In contrast, Jesus's lineage is tied to David in the Gospel of Matthew as early as its first verse. At the same time, Jesus's origin story in the Gospel of Luke locates him unequivocally as rising from the peasantry ranks of the Greco-Roman caste system operative at birth. Jesus is far from the ranks of imperial Rome, signified by "the reign of Tiberius Caesar" and Jesus's antagonists, Pilate, governor of Judea, and Herod, ruler of Galilee (Luke 3:1–2). Jesus is not born among the priesthood authorities of Annas and Caiaphas. While Jesus's birth and ministry are set outside power in contested space, his status as king is known by those powerful actors (Mark 15:2, 26; Luke 23:2; John 1:49; 18:33), though its form and purpose is misunderstood (Matt 27:29, 37, 42; Luke 23:37; John 6:15).

Reducing the gospel to a single-word tweet appears obvious and accurate enough. Of course, the gospel of Christ is "in one word, Jesus." But embedded within this matter-of-fact simplicity is the challenge—potentially even the danger of such a view. Jesus, as the single-word answer to the question of what the gospel is, risks objectification. Merely saying Jesus as an answer to a gospel view detaches him from his social and historical underpinnings. These are the ingredients and conditions under which Jesus was "enfleshed" and the gospel first proclaimed by him (Mark 1:14–15) and about him (1 Cor 15:1–10). To unfasten Jesus from the facts of his historical location misses his gospel message's target audience and intention in its first sounding.

For example, which Jesus appears in the gospel reader's imagination like a signpost when she encounters his name? Does one imagine and digest the gospel stories as about a reigning triumphant Jesus? Should Jesus and kingship be a primary starting point for gospel understanding? Or does one imagine the conditions and locations from which Jesus, the Christ, emerges? What is Christhood born from the edges of Judaism when pigeons are the best Jesus's parents can offer to sacrificially honor the birth of their son and Savior of the world (Luke 2:24)? That moment resonates with millions of parents yearly who give birth to their beloved children, bearing the pain that they—through no fault of their own—only have "pigeons" to give in recognition of the gift of life granted to them and the world in the form of child-bearing and child-rearing. What is the content of the gospel message about Jesus when it is understood to be cast in the body and craft of a tradesperson comfortable among other working tradespeople like builders, carpenters, and fishermen (Matt 13:55; Mark 1:16–17; 6:3), as opposed to one belonging to the religious and political arm of locales traversed across Galilee and Judea?

Howard Washington Thurman cautions against an objectification that seems to think merely naming Jesus "in a word" as the gospel captures his meaning and significance. It bears asking whose Jesus is captured by simply dropping his name. There is a foreboding danger in such simplicity. The dominant interpretive trend, often determined by European and US American triumphal histories, risks imposing the meaning of the gospel upon those whose view is understood from their histories of enslavement, apartheid, otherness, and second-class access. Thurman pens a gospel view of Jesus that leads with a context outside kingship ambitions and privileges shaped by the discourses of colonialism in the twentieth and twenty-first centuries. It functions as a shading screen for any contextualization of Jesus Christ in the ancient world one might do today. He says, "It is necessary to examine the religion of

Jesus against the background of his age and people and to inquire into the content of his teaching concerning the disinherited and the underprivileged."[1] Even the gospel view of King Jesus requires reckoning with the anatomy of the relationship between Jesus's people, his location as one among the large Jewish peasantry and working class, the political privileges and powers available to Jewish people of means and titles, and the Romans.

McKnight's essay masterfully calibrates our understanding of the kingdom Jesus preached by offering four historically and biblically informed meanings at work in the biblical script (e.g., Mark 1:14). His treatment culminates in a description of the "ethic of Jesus," which orders "the way of life for kingdom people" (p. 31). Such a perspective fuels the move from theocracy and monarchy to "fulfillment in Christocracy" (p. 28). Scott describes Christocracy as "the core of the gospel" in the form of "a declaration about Jesus," which stems from the declaration made *by* Jesus (p. 29). In this way, the core gospel message *now* depends on the message Jesus declared *then*. It is both a message and an activity. It is an active proclamation of salvation that travels, interrogates, disrupts, and resets the lives of Jesus's followers in the ancient past and the emerging present.

Another gem in McKnight's essay that I appreciate is how he clarifies the meaning of Jesus's kingdom-of-God idea as more than an abstract heavenly location. God's kingdom penetrates the earth. By making the point clear, McKnight renders the gospel as spatially oriented. It is not merely spiritual and otherworldly. Gospel is socially tangible. Our relational practices and how they create or destroy kinships texture the quality of the "gospeling" endeavor this view advances. From the conflict between Jesus and his family (Matt 12:46–50) to Judas's kiss of betrayal in Gethsemane (Matt 26:48–54), as well as the mother-son relationship Jesus puts in motion between Mary and the Beloved Disciple at the crucifixion (John 19:25–27)—gospel kingdom language fosters kinships that are both familiar and new. It is a challenge to put forward a notion of kingship to communities who have experienced overlordship that belittles their land ties, terrorizes their communities, displaces their people, and destroys families. What happens when those living in the

---

1. Howard Thurman, *Jesus and the Disinherited* (1949; repr., Boston: Beacon, 1996), 5.

view of the King Jesus gospel are so immersed in that positionality that they inadvertently diminish an imperative of the confession that Jesus is Christ and Lord, who is "God with" and "among us" (Matt 1:23; 28:20; John 1:14–18), restoring families and creating unimagined new social and fraternal ties?

Reading the King Jesus gospel view, one story continued to press upon me. In the exchange between Jesus and the Syrophoenician woman, cultural biases are on display that might make such a view unpalatable (Matt 15:21–28; Mark 7:24–30). The preexisting tension between Israelite and non-Israelite (Matt 15:22; Mark 7:27; cf. Matt 1:3, 5), Israel and Canaan (Deut 7:1), and even male and female interact in the story. This is a difficult text to situate within the King Jesus gospel view when read from those on the underside of society, who are most readily addressed and engaged as "other" or at least are different from the comfortable norms of society. Jesus's gospel message up to that point, especially in Mark's version, had been singular in focus and location as a proclamation intended for the salvation of Israel. The Syrophoenician woman's encounter disrupts that gospel trajectory. Initially, Jesus's cultural sensibility seems to get in the way when he likens Israel to the Lord's children and the woman to a puppy or a more docile version of scavenger pack animals, saying, "Let the children be fed first, for it is not right to take the children's bread and throw it to the dogs" (Mark 7:27; cf. Matt 15:26). One wonders if it was Jesus who got in the way at that moment, or if it was the social caste that pitted Jew against non-Jew, male against female, the haves against the have-nots.

Social constructions of insiders and outsiders act as speed bumps in the "gospel" model displayed in the exchange between Jesus and the woman as they face the question of whether her daughter will be healed. It also sensitizes us to the multiple significances of this story as a gospel message that asserts power, sovereignty, and salvation. After rehearsing readings of the Syrophoenician woman story that consider the historical perspectives of Japanese, Botswanan, US Indigenous-American, and Irish-American biblical scholarship, Kwok Pui-Lan asserts such variety makes a demand on every gospel view. "These diverse interpretations of the Syrophoenician woman's story illustrate how reading with other people can radically expand our imagination. . . . Sensitivity to contextual and cross-cultural interpretation helps us to live in a pluralistic world in which people have different worldviews and assumptions."[2] The King Jesus view makes space for such an exchange to occur, although it does not take up that task directly.

The contemporary task of gospeling, as McKnight puts forward, is as much about the peoplehood and location in antiquity and presently as it is about the content of Jesus's message found in Scripture. The "where" and "who" of the King Jesus view cannot be detached. It is by keeping them together that matters of triumphalism, colonialism, and even human proclivities toward lording over other human beings guided by the unanalyzed prejudices of race, gender, class, xenophobia, nationalism, and even regionalism might be checked. To go with Jesus to the margins and the fringes—those most historically targeted for exploitation, subservience, and erasure—is to hear the sounding of the gospel from the context in which it was forged and intended. We find the gospel message among them, not above them. In that place, the King Jesus view takes on a new sound and meaning recognizable in the African-American spiritual that responds to Christian practices of othering through faithful declaration: "Ride on king Jesus / No man can a-hinder me / Ride on king Jesus, ride on. // No man can a-hinder me / No man can a-hinder me."[3]

---

[2]. Kwok Pui-Lan, "Reading the Christian New Testament in the Contemporary World," in *The New Testament: Fortress Commentary on the Bible*, ed. Margaret Aymer, Cynthia Briggs Kittredge, and David A. Sanchez (Minneapolis: Fortress, 2014), 10.

[3]. "Ride on King Jesus," in *African American Heritage Hymnal*, ed. Delores Carpenter (Chicago: GIA, 2001), 225; Howard Thurman, *Deep River: The Negro Spiritual Speaks of Life and Death* (Richmond: Friend United Press, 1990), 20–21.

CHAPTER TWO: THE REFORMATION GOSPEL

MICHAEL HORTON

The good news is summarized well by the "new song" of Revelation 5:9–10:

> Worthy are you to take the scroll
> and to open its seals,
> for you were slain, and by your blood you ransomed people
> for God
> from every tribe and language and people and nation,
> and you have made them a kingdom and priests to our God,
> and they shall reign on the earth.[1]

Packed into this laconic hymn are the person and work of Christ as prophet, priest, and king, a catholic ecclesiology, and the future consummation of the kingdom. My tweet-version of this gospel would be from Romans 4:25: he "was delivered up for our trespasses and raised for our justification."

My chapter is designated "The Reformation Gospel," with the same reluctant acquiescence that the Reformers themselves would have expressed. In the first place, they believed they were recovering the apostolic gospel, not coining a new one. But, secondly, those familiar

---

1. All scriptural references for my essay are from the English Standard Version (ESV).

with the writings of Luther, Bucer, Melanchthon, Calvin, Vermigli, and other Reformers, as well as those of Lutheran and Reformed orthodoxy, are aware that the "Reformation Gospel" is not reduced to justification. Especially in the Reformed tradition ever since Calvin, the work of Christ has been treated under the integrative rubric of prophet, priest, and king.

The Reformers did not reduce the gospel to the crucifixion. The Son's assumption of our humanity is not a mere prerequisite of his redemptive work but the first crucial aspect of it. His saving work began even at his conception, says Calvin: "In short, from the time when he took on the form of a servant, he began to pay the price of liberation in order to redeem us."[2] The resurrection secured not only justification but participation in Christ's holiness and future glorification. The ascension ensures that just as our head has been exalted beyond the reach of sin and mortality, so will his body. In fact, the ascension is a particular emphasis in Reformed theology. Notice how Calvin binds every blessing "for us" to the various moments in Christ's work:

> We see that our whole salvation and all its parts are comprehended in Christ. We should therefore take care not to derive the least portion of it from anywhere else. If we seek salvation, we are taught by the very name of Jesus that it is "of him." If we seek any other gifts of the Spirit, they will be found in his anointing. If we seek strength, it lies in his dominion; if purity, in his conception; if gentleness, it appears in his birth. For by his birth he was made like us in all respects that he might learn to feel our pain. If we see redemption, it lies in his passion; if acquittal, in his condemnation; if remission of the curse, in his cross; if satisfaction, in his sacrifice; if purification, in his blood; if reconciliation, in his descent into hell; if mortification of the flesh, in his tomb; if newness of life, in his resurrection; if immortality, in the same; if inheritance of the Heavenly Kingdom, in his entrance into heaven; if protection, if security, if abundant supply of all blessings, in his Kingdom; if untroubled expectation of judgment, in

---

2. John Calvin, *Institutes of the Christian Religion*, ed. John T. McNeill, trans. Ford Lewis Battles, 2 vols., Library of Christian Classics 20–21 (Philadelphia: Westminster, 1960), 2.16.5.

the power given him to judge. In short, since rich store of every kind of good abounds in him, let us drink our fill from this fountain, and from no other.[3]

By contrast, alternatives to the so-called Reformation Gospel are reductionistic in their view of the plight and solution. It is argued that the real issue is not condemnation versus justification but rather death versus immortality, bondage versus victory over the powers, Israel's exile versus gentile inclusion in restoration, rebellion versus faithfulness, anarchy versus a kingdom, Caesar's regime versus Jesus's, social injustice versus human flourishing, and so forth. However, according to the Reformers' interpretation of the gospel, all of these pieces of the puzzle have their important place. Only if justification is true can there be freedom from the guilt that sanctions death and the harassment of evil powers; a settled basis on which adopted heirs are liberated from bondage and pursue righteousness in the certain hope of glorification. Unlike Roman Catholic and Eastern Orthodox theology, the Reformers affirmed justification as the basis for sanctification and deification.

Plight and Solution

The curse resulting from the fall is all-encompassing. The breach of humans with God (both judicial and relational) bled into blame-shifting toward one another. The earth, crying out against human violence and death, yields its produce grudgingly, groaning for release from its involuntary captivity. And, launching the story behind all stories in the Bible, the war of the serpent's surrogates (evident as soon as Cain) and the woman's offspring (Abel) ensues. No longer holy, endowed with a holy calling, living in a holy land with God in peace and safety, the royal family lives "east of Eden." At the same time, God issues a surprising announcement of a promised redemption and institutes a regime of common grace as space for this gracious pledge to be realized in history. Electing Abram and Sarah out of sheer grace as the parents of a chosen nation, the promise continues with a typological family (ethnic descendants) and ultimately the unilateral and unconditional announcement of

---

3. Calvin, *Institutes*, 2.16.19.

a single offspring in whom all peoples will find a sufficient mediator. From Sarah's fallow womb the promised offspring of Eve appears.

Reformation theology has always been eager to affirm that the nature created by God remains good yet corrupted; depravity is total in its *extensiveness* (heart, intellect, will, and body), not in *intensiveness* (as if the image of God could be eradicated). There is no safe landing for Christ when he comes in gracious redemption. No part of the world or the human self welcomes him apart from the new birth. Yet, as expounded by the Calvinist Isaac Watts in the hymn, "Joy to the World," the remedy is "so far as the curse is found." It is therefore reductive to define the gospel simply as the solution to one of these problems.

Christ himself *is* the solution to the extensiveness of the curse. In fact, he is the incarnate gospel. Jesus said that he was the unifying feature of Holy Scripture (Luke 24:27; John 5:39). Irenaeus said that Scripture's coherence lies in "Christ, the mosaic," in which each piece has its particular redemptive-historical place. The Protestant Reformers and their confessional heirs said that the scope of Scripture is Christ as he is clothed in his gospel. There are of course other topics, genres, supporting actors, and subplots, but all are subservient to this single message that grows clearer as the story unfolds. Thus, as I'm sure my colleagues would agree, there cannot be many gospels but only one, albeit with many facets. The good news is as encompassing as the bad news. In fact, it is even more so, since it announces not a mere return to a pristine condition but to a consummated condition that has never been experienced by any mortal except for our exalted brother, Jesus (1 Cor 2:9; Heb 2:8–9). All of this means that our tweet-summaries of the gospel might differ but without any contradiction, depending on which facet and genre comes first to mind.

Expounded in narrative, poetry, apocalyptic, wisdom, and didactic literature, this unfolding drama has given rise to distinct disciplines for its interpretation, including biblical studies, biblical theology, and systematic theology. This is the proper order of interpretation, as the varied biblical texts evidence a coherent historical plot whose implications can be articulated with logical interconnections. Like a topographical map, biblical theology displays the peaks and valleys along with the streams that flow into the mighty river that leads to Christ. More like a street map, systematic theology exhibits the inner connections of all the blessings that we have in Christ. Some of the tensions in defining the gospel no doubt turn on whether one privileges the former (e.g., the story of Israel) or the latter (e.g., the "plan of salvation"). However, these should be seen as integrally related. The drama is the source of the doctrine, which leads to doxology and discipleship. From the drama we learn, for example, that Christ was crucified, buried, and raised on the third day in accordance with the Scriptures (1 Cor 15:3–4). Yet it is the doctrine that announces its significance for us: "who was delivered up *for our trespasses* and raised *for our justification*" (Rom 4:25). I suppose that if I had to summarize the gospel in a tweet, I could not find a better one than this. We may enter the gospel mansion by many doors, but only with the confidence that justification secures before a holy God can these other entrances be safe passages rather than a bewildering and fearful maze.

Just as there are many narrative subplots supporting one unfolding drama, there are many doctrines that indicate the lavish grace that the Father has displayed toward us in Christ and by his Spirit. However, apart from the justification of the ungodly, even the most majestic facets become condemning law for me as a sinner. The sovereign God who elects, showing mercy to whom he will, can only be terrifying apart from the assurance that I am justified through faith in Christ alone. Christ's return in glory can only be an anxious prospect when I am told by Jesus himself that he will separate the sheep from the goats in final judgment. What good news could it be to me that the Spirit gradually conforms me to Christ's image when I know that this good work begun in me will not be perfect in this life? Apart from the certainty that I am already declared righteous before God, that the throne of judgment has become for me a throne of grace, sanctification threatens with the ominous declaration that without holiness no one will see the Lord (Heb 12:14).

A mere cross-centered theology cannot account sufficiently for the salvific import of the Word's assumption of our nature, while the incarnation by itself does not remove the obstacle to fellowship with God. The resurrection not only proves Jesus's divinity but is a further moment of his saving work. Moreover, the ascension of Christ is not merely an exclamation point to the resurrection but is another stage in his accomplishment of redemption. Through all of these events in

Christ's life, those who are united to him are forgiven, justified, sanctified, and glorified.

Consequently, the gospel cannot be reduced to justification. Yet apart from this fact—our guilt imputed to Christ and his righteousness imputed to us—there is no good news. When the justified hear the rest of the good news, they rejoice, but when these other blessings are meant to replace the problem of objective guilt before God, they become another gospel altogether. Christ is victor over the evil powers, to be sure, but the ground of his triumph was canceling the legal record of debt by nailing it to the cross (Col 2:14–15). Jesus came to destroy death, but how? Death is not ultimately in the hands of Satan and his minions but is a legal sentence imposed by God for our treason. "The sting of death is sin, and the power of sin is the law" (1 Cor 15:56). When the charges are canceled, so is the sentence—the devil has no legal grounds to keep us in the grave (v. 57).

Context

In their superb guidance, the editors have asked us to identify the main *context* of the gospel as we understand it: "Is it the Old Testament, first-century Judea, the Roman imperial cult, human sin and fallenness, the Reformation, the surrounding culture, or experience of oppression?" (p. 19). Again, I find myself wanting to answer: "yes." Like all Christian doctrines, justification has a reception history. However, it is a context, not a norm.

It is in the Old Testament where we come to know God's character as well as his promises, the righteousness that condemns as well as the righteousness that is given to those who deserve wrath. It is in the law where we encounter the vast complex of sacerdotal actions that point to "the Lamb of God, who takes away the sin of the world" (John 1:29). The promise of the redeemer-seed is traced through the patriarchal narratives and flowers brightly in the prophets. We meet "the righteous one, my servant" who will "make many to be accounted righteous, and he shall bear their iniquities," who "bore the sin of many, and makes intercession for the transgressors" (Isa 53:11–12).

It is first-century Judea where the promise is fulfilled—and misunderstood by the religious leaders and even by the disciples until Pentecost. Second Temple Judaism is therefore a *context*, but not a *norm* for what we should expect the gospel to be (contra Sanders, Dunn, and Wright). Jesus criticized sharply the rabbinical teaching of his day, accusing the Pharisees not only of misunderstanding but of refusing his mission as the fulfillment of everything promised by the prophets. The disciples themselves did not understand the plot—"the *exodus* he was to accomplish in Jerusalem" (Luke 9:31, my trans.)—until after the resurrection and Pentecost (Luke 24:13–53). Even at the ascension, the disciples were wondering whether Jesus would now restore the old-covenant theocracy, which Jesus answered by directing their attention to the Great Commission (Acts 1:6–8; cf. Matt 28:18–20). Second Temple Judaism is the setting, illuminating the sort of kingdom and deliverance that was expected in the first century. It is the immediate context. However, the ultimate context is the history of promise from Genesis 3:15 to Malachi 4:1–6, both of which set forth the day of the Lord as the plight and a gift of righteous standing in Christ as God's solution. Had first-century Judaism understood that plotline well enough, there would have been no conflict between Jesus and the Pharisees or Paul and the legalists. Moreover, as Jon Levenson points out, the Judaism that emerged after the destruction of the temple in 70 CE was not in continuity with the Hebrew Scriptures but reconstructed its faith to accord with the realities of no land, priesthood, or sacrifices.[4]

The Roman imperial cult, with its titles of "Savior" and "Lord" applied to Caesar, is also integral to the context of Jesus's announcement that "all authority in heaven and on earth" has been given to him, which grounds the Great Commission (Matt 28:18–20). Given its many facets, it is not surprising that one aspect of the good news will be especially cherished by oppressed and marginalized groups in society. And yet this cannot be the normative context for interpreting the message. Jesus himself claimed to be the king of a realm that is "not of this world" (John 18:36). The *fall* occurred before the calling of Abram and Sarah, the election of Israel, and the exile. Like Hamlet's play-within-a-play, the history of Israel is the subplot of universal sin and redemption. Human sin and fallenness are the universal context, with Israel finding itself "like Adam," having "broken the covenant" (Hos 6:7).

---

4. Jon Levenson, *Sinai and Zion: An Entry into the Jewish Bible* (San Francisco: HarperSanFrancisco, 1985), 65–155.

The least likely candidate for a "context" is the Reformation. Many scholars have made much of the uniqueness of this context—the macabre medievalism that led Luther to introspective subjectivity, a "merit-badge" system that the Reformers rejected but still presupposed, and so forth. The historical theology here rests on very shaky ground, but that is not my concern here.[5] Regardless, no more than our contemporary culture can the Reformation be the context for what the gospel means, and none of the Reformers would have thought otherwise.

Of course, that did not mean, for them or for us today, that certain emphases and reflections were not provoked by a quite different context. However, I am convinced that the existential crisis experienced by the Reformers was quite similar to that expressed by biblical witnesses. "How shall it be known that I have found favor in your sight, I and your people?" (Exod 33:16). "But how can a man be in the right before God?" (Job 9:2). "Good Teacher, what must I do to inherit eternal life?" (Luke 18:18). These are not the questions of a tortured conscience in the sixteenth century but of every human being, inflected in these passages by the specific story of Israel. It was not only the people of Israel who knew that they were guilty and that sacrifices were required; substitutes, animal and human, were offered in myriad ancient civilizations.

There is one gospel, but many aspects of the curse that it addresses; many contexts, but one universal plight and solution, which is why the gentile mission made any sense. It is instructive that Celsus and other early critics not only identified "Christ and him crucified" and the resurrection of the dead as the heart of the Christian message but considered it of one piece with the "earth-bound" mentality of Jews. Celsus finds particularly offensive the teaching of salvation by grace.[6] Respectable societies invite the wise, the good, and the righteous to join them, he writes.

> But the call to membership in the cult of Christ is this: Whoever is a sinner, whoever is unwise, whoever is childish—yea, whoever is a wretch—his is the kingdom of God.... I mean—what other

---

5. I offer a historical development of the doctrine in *Justification*, vol. 1, New Studies in Dogmatics (Grand Rapids: Zondervan Academic, 2018).
6. Celsus, *On the True Doctrine*, trans. R. Joseph Hoffmann (New York: Oxford University Press, 1987), 58.

cult actually invites robbers to become members! Their excuse for all of it is that their god was sent to call sinners: well, fair enough. But what about the righteous? How do they account for the fact that their appeal is to the lowest sort of person? Why was their Christ not sent to those who had not sinned—Is it any disgrace not to have sinned?[7]

There is considerable continuity, but the talmudic rabbis had also interpreted the Scriptures in a way that ran completely against the grain of the biblical narratives, such as the "merit" of Abraham and Jacob.[8] As Paul reminds them in Romans 4, a cursory reading of the patriarchal narratives would disallow such a doctrine.

It is in the Old Testament where we find the gospel first announced (Gen 3:15) and revealed with increasing clarity in the Abrahamic covenant, the Davidic covenant, and the new covenant foretold by the prophets. There is *eschatological* continuity of one covenant of grace alongside *covenantal* discontinuity. The one promise of God's unilateral rescue of fallen humanity in Christ is foreshadowed typologically in the temporary and conditional covenant sworn by the people at Sinai. Yet, "like Adam, they transgressed my covenant" (Hos 6:7); Israel, too, turns out to fail in its messianic mission.

The primary context, then, is the history of the covenant of grace, with distinct lines of law and promise. The contrast between law and promise becomes legible already in Genesis 3. Yet right where the sanctions of the covenant sworn by Adam are expected to be executed, God deconsecrates the land and evicts the royal family precisely in order to preserve their life. From his own merciful heart, Yahweh pledges that he will provide a redeemer, and it is this covenant of promise that keeps history moving forward despite human rebellion. These covenants can be easily distinguished. In a covenant of law Yahweh imposes the terms, with conditions and sanctions of life or death, there is a human mediator, and the human partner swears the oath. A covenant of promise, however, is sworn by God alone, who is himself the mediator, and he assumes the burden entirely for its fulfillment.

---

7. Celsus, *On the True Doctrine*, 74.
8. I engage various positions on this point in *Justification*, vol. 2, New Studies in Dogmatics (Grand Rapids: Zondervan Academic, 2018), esp. 17–150.

Like Genesis 3:15, the Abrahamic covenant is a unilateral divine oath. God makes all of the promises and confirms it by "passing between the pieces" in a theophany; Abraham makes no promises but is the recipient who believes God's oath and is justified (Gen 15). Obligations follow but are not conditions of inheriting the promise. Delivering Abraham's descendants from Egypt to fulfill his promise of an earthly nation and land, God endures the faithlessness and rebellion of his people. He will give them the land now occupied by idolaters and thus fulfill his promise.

At Mount Sinai, though, Yahweh as the great king (suzerain) imposes the terms for the nation to remain in his holy land and flourish under his protection. The Sinai covenant differed from the Abrahamic in several obvious respects:

1. *The vassal swears the oath.* God imposes the marriage contract, but it is the people who say, "All that the Lord has spoken we will do," confirmed by Moses splashing blood on the people as testimony that they bear the burden of fulfilling their pledge (Exod 24:7–8).
2. *Moses is the mediator.*
3. *The promises are temporal, conditional, and typological.* While God's promise in Genesis 3:15 and Genesis 15 includes everlasting life and justification before God at the last day, there is nothing in the Sinai law that promises more than a long and happy life with God in his earthly land. As Paul argues in Galatians, the Mosaic law was never a means of justification (Gal 3:21–22). The promises are conditioned upon the swearer's fulfillment of the commands. God will cleanse the land and divide it between his twelve tribes. God will give them rest. But if Israel violates the covenant to serve foreign gods, God will drive the nation out of his land to serve foreign nations. The promises are typological: an earthly land and nation, physical descendants of Abraham, priestly sacrifices and tabernacle/temple—all pointing to Christ as the reality in whom they are fulfilled.

This contrast of law and gospel does not divide Old from New Testaments, however. The covenant of grace established in Genesis 3:15 and with Abraham and his "seed" (Christ) is the larger narrative, with the national covenant as a typological drama, something like Hamlet's play-within-a-play. The gospel is embedded even in the Sinai code itself. After commanding the people to circumcise their own hearts, God foretells their history of disobedience and promises that he will one day circumcise the hearts of his people (Deut 30:6). The Davidic covenant is a further guarantee of God's unilateral promise to establish his own Son—and David's heir—on the everlasting throne (2 Sam 7).

The contrast between law and gospel is exhibited in the New Testament. John the Baptist's ministry is contrasted with that of Jesus's in such terms. Jesus compares John's urgent call to repentance in light of the coming judgment to a dirge and his own ministry to a joyful feast. Matthew's version of this episode concludes with Christ's call, "Come to me, all who labor and are heavy laden, and I will give you rest" (Matt 11:28–30). Luke's version concludes with Jesus forgiving a sinner: "And he said to her, 'Your sins are forgiven.' Then those who were at table with him began to say among themselves, 'Who is this, who even forgives sins?' And he said to the woman, 'Your faith has saved you; go in peace'" (Luke 7:48–50). Similarly, the Fourth Gospel attests, "For the law was given through Moses; grace and truth came through Jesus Christ" (John 1:17).

The law-gospel contrast is too pervasive in the Pauline letters to cover with any adequacy in this space, but a few examples may suffice. The same argument appears in several places. The conclusion to the argument of Romans 1–3 is that everyone is condemned by God's righteous judgment according to works but that Jew and gentile alike "are justified by his grace as a gift, through the redemption that is in Christ Jesus" (Rom 3:24). Romans 4 demonstrates that Abraham—who lived before the law—was justified apart from it, through faith alone.

Romans 5 begins with an aorist-indicative declaration, "Therefore, since we have been justified by faith [*dikaiōthentes*], we have peace with God through our Lord Jesus Christ" (v. 1). Thus, justification is not a moral process or a belonging to the people of God. Rather, it is a legal verdict of the final judgment that is rendered in the present through faith—on the basis of which we belong to God's people and grow in sanctification. The chapter continues by contrasting the condemnation (*katakrima*) we all inherit through Adam's covenantal headship with justification (*dikaiōma*) in Christ (5:16, 18). The contrast throughout is between works and faith, reward and gift, the law and Christ, not merely between some works (marks of Jewish identity) and others (love, allegiance, full surrender, etc.).

Again, contrasting the way of the law and the way of the gospel in chapter 10, Paul concludes, "So faith comes from hearing, and hearing through the word of Christ" (Rom 10:17). The gospel is an announcement that God has fulfilled his pledge, not an instruction for fulfilling our own. In Philippians 3 also the contrast is total: all of "my own" righteousness being counted refuse "in order that I may gain Christ and be found in him, not having a righteousness of my own that comes from the law, but that which comes through faith in Christ, the righteousness from God that depends on faith" (Phil 3:8b–9).

The lodestar for the law-gospel contrast is Galatians, where the Sinai covenant is distinguished clearly from the Abrahamic. Paul emphasizes that justification comes not by *doing* "works of the law" but "by hearing with faith—just as Abraham 'believed God, and it was counted to him as righteousness'" (Gal 3:5–6). Paul continues:

> Know then that it is those of faith who are the sons of Abraham. And the Scripture, foreseeing that God would justify the Gentiles by faith, preached the gospel beforehand to Abraham, saying, "In you shall all the nations be blessed." So then, those who are of faith are blessed along with Abraham, the man of faith.
>
> For all who rely on works of the law are under a curse; for it is written, "Cursed be everyone who does not abide by all things written in the Book of the Law, and do them." Now it is evident that no one is justified before God by the law, for "The righteous shall live by faith." But the law is not of faith, rather "The one who does them shall live by them." Christ redeemed us from the curse of the law by becoming a curse for us . . . so that in Christ Jesus the blessing of Abraham might come to the Gentiles, so that we might receive the promised Spirit through faith. (Gal 3:7–14)

The contrast could not be clearer: "but the law is not of faith," Paul says, because faith is believing God's oath. The difference is between "*Do* this and you will *live*" and *receiving* life as a *free gift* through faith.

The promise God made to Abraham with respect to justification was concerning a single offspring, "who is Christ" (Gal 3:16). "This is what I mean: the law, which came 430 years afterward, does not annul a covenant previously ratified by God, so as to make the promise void. For if the inheritance comes by the law, it no longer comes by promise; but God gave it to Abraham by a promise" (vv. 17–18). Finally, in chapter 4 the law-gospel contrast is drawn allegorically in correlation with Hagar and Sarah, with it said explicitly that "these women are two covenants," which correspond (shockingly no doubt to his audience) to Sinai and the heavenly Jerusalem (4:23–26).

The writer to the Hebrews also contrasts these two covenants sharply. The old covenant was temporary, conditional, and typological. The people swore the oath, and Moses is the mediator. Moses's entire ministry was a "copy"—like a movie trailer. This the writer contrasts with the Abrahamic covenant fulfilled in Christ:

> For when God made a promise to Abraham, since he had no one greater by whom to swear, he swore by himself, saying, 'Surely I will bless you and multiply you.' And thus Abraham, having patiently waited, obtained the promise. For people swear by something greater than themselves, and in all their disputes an oath is final for confirmation. So when God desired to show more convincingly to the heirs of the promise the unchangeable character of his purpose, he guaranteed it with an oath, so that by two unchangeable things, in which it is impossible for God to lie, we who have fled for refuge might have strong encouragement to hold fast to the hope set before us. (Heb 6:13–18)

Continuing in chapter 8, we read, "But as it is, Christ has obtained a ministry that is as much more excellent than the old as the covenant he mediates is better, since it is enacted on better promises. For if that first covenant had been faultless, there would have been no occasion to look for a second" (Heb 8:6–7). After quoting Jeremiah 31, the writer concludes, "In speaking of a new covenant, he makes the first one obsolete" (8:8–13).

Understandably, Jeremiah 31 is a primary text in these New Testament passages. It prophesies that the new covenant will not be "like the covenant" of Sinai, which "they broke" (Jer 31:32). Rather, in the new covenant God makes all the promises, including a new heart that delights to know and follow the Lord (vv. 33–34a) and "I will forgive their iniquity, and I will remember their sin no more" (v. 34b). Interestingly, when the Sinai covenant is in view, Jeremiah as God's covenant attorney pronounces condemnation. In contrast with God passing between the parts in Abraham's vision (Gen 15), Yahweh declares, "And the men who transgressed my covenant and did not keep the terms of the covenant that they made before me, I will make them like the calf that they cut in two and passed between its parts" (Jer 34:18). Recapitulating Adam's fall, the nation of Israel, living in exile, had only to believe the Abrahamic promise and be saved.

By his incarnation and entire life of obedience as the covenant servant, Jesus fulfilled the law not only for himself but for all whom he represents. In the upper room, on the night of his betrayal, Jesus instituted the Lord's Supper. "And he took bread, and when he had given thanks, he broke it and gave it to them, saying, 'This is my body, which is given for you.'. . . 'This cup that is poured out for you is the new covenant in my blood'" (Luke 22:19–20). Instead of splashing blood on the people in accordance with their oath, the incarnate God gave them his body and blood and passed between the pieces at Golgotha. *Therefore*, the Jew-gentile division is broken down in his body (Eph 2:13–15). Because all are justified through faith alone in Christ alone by grace alone, "There is neither Jew nor Greek, there is neither slave nor free, there is no male and female, for you are all one in Christ Jesus. And if you are Christ's, then you are Abraham's offspring, heirs according to promise" (Gal 3:28–29).

Texts

From the Gospels, I will select the parable of the publican and the Pharisee, although all of the parables in one way or another indict the religious leaders and welcome sinners. Yet here, Jesus especially contrasts his message with the piety of Second Temple Judaism. Let us focus on Luke's account:

> He also told this parable to some who trusted in themselves that they were righteous, and treated others with contempt: "Two

men went up into the temple to pray, one a Pharisee and the other a tax collector. The Pharisee, standing by himself, prayed thus: 'God, I thank you that I am not like other men, extortioners, unjust, adulterers, or even like this tax collector. I fast twice a week; I give tithes of all that I get.' But the tax collector, standing far off, would not even lift up his eyes to heaven, but beat his breast, saying, 'God, be merciful to me, a sinner!' I tell you, this man went down to his house justified, rather than the other. For everyone who exalts himself will be humbled, but the one who humbles himself will be exalted." (Luke 18:9–14)

First, it is significant that Jesus's parable is provoked by his recognition that "some . . . trusted in themselves that they were righteous." What is wrong with that? Even the fact that they "treated others with contempt" may have had some rationale if the people were transgressing God's law. Given the terms of the old-covenant theocracy, their righteousness was the basis for remaining in the land. Did the prophets not urge the nation again and again to return to the Lord and renew the oath that they made, so that the land would once again flourish with righteousness and peace? However, the Pharisees had confused the Sinai covenant (their oath to keep the law and thus live long in the land with God as their king) with the Abrahamic covenant (God's unilateral promise of grace in Christ). Moreover, they were not actually righteous but preferred their own rules to God's law. They were hypocrites, as Jesus charges repeatedly.

Second, the context of the parable is completely intra-Jewish, with no hint yet of gentile inclusion. Nor does it have anything to do with imperial Rome. Throughout the parables—and the eating episodes with the Pharisees—the Gospels relate that Jesus is turning the tables, quite literally, on proper hospitality at God's feast. The kingdom of God—essentially the revival of the national covenant—would come by purging the nation of all that defiles. For Jesus, the Pharisees defile more than anyone else. They not only plot his death but are keeping sinners from coming to him for mercy. It is legalistic purity, not forgiveness and justification, that they believe will provoke God to descend and inaugurate his kingdom on earth. Second Temple Judaism was their context, and there was no room for a crucified Messiah in their eschatology.

That was because they did not really acknowledge that their greatest problem was the need for forgiveness, justification before God, which the tax collector recognized in his simple prayer. "I tell you," Jesus said, "this man went down to his house justified, rather than the other" (Luke 18:14). Like Abraham, he was justified then and there, when he trusted in God's promise (Gen 15:6).

Third, the Pharisee is not a Pelagian. Whether feigned piety or genuine conviction, the Pharisee thanks God that he is not like the tax collector. He professes evidence of God's grace in his life: fasting, tithing, and so forth. But he is the one rejected, while the tax collector "beat his breast, saying, 'God, be merciful to me, a sinner.'" This harks back to Luke 7:32, where the ministry of John the Baptist is too austere and the ministry of Jesus is too libertine for the Pharisees. Failing to understand the seriousness of the coming wrath, they imagine that they can escape it by their own righteousness, which keeps them from dancing when the Bridegroom comes.

Luke places this parable in chapter 18 before the encounter with the rich young ruler, which is itself significant. The aspiring rabbi asks, "What must I do to inherit eternal life?" (Luke 18:18). It matters little whether it is a sincere question or a trap. Jesus told him that the answer was obvious: obedience to the whole law, love of God and neighbor. "All these I have kept from my youth" (v. 21). *Really?* That response was enough to provoke Jesus to tell him that if he really loved his neighbors (and God), he would sell off his enormous wealth and give it all to the poor. Leaving sad, the ruler shows that he was not who he said he was. Disillusioned by the law, he did not wait around for the gospel. Immediately afterward, Jesus foretells his death to the disciples. "But they understood none of these things" (v. 34).

The sermons in Acts are demonstrations of Christ's insistence that the Scriptures are about him and that salvation—for gentiles as well as Jews—is found in his name alone (*solus Christus*), acknowledged at the Jerusalem Council (Acts 15). For his part, Peter declared:

> And God, who knows the heart, bore witness to them, by giving them the Holy Spirit just as he did to us, and he made no distinction between us and them, having cleansed their hearts by faith. Now, therefore, why are you putting God to the test

by placing a yoke on the neck of the disciples that neither our fathers nor we have been able to bear? But we believe that we will be saved through the grace of the Lord Jesus, just as they will. (Acts 15:8–11)

Christ is sufficient, apart from the works of the law—for Jews as well as gentiles. The answer was a decisive victory for Paul's argument in the letter to the Galatians. Christ *plus nothing* is the conclusion. There must be decorum and respect for distinctive cultural practices, but no requirement of circumcision and dietary laws as entrance requirements. This is not the only thing that the debate was about, but it was a flashpoint for the question: "Is Jesus alone sufficient for our salvation?" Again and again in the book of Acts, people believed and were immediately transferred from being a sinner to being justified, from being an outcast to being forgiven, in the worldwide family of God. Christ is the seed in whom the families of all nations would be blessed.

Once more, the Reformation view is less reductionistic than alternatives. For example, it does not deny that by "works of the law" Paul includes boundary markers that separate gentiles from Jews, but it insists that this phrase includes any and every work of human obedience, even to the moral law, offered to God as a meritorious reward. In Romans 4, for example, Paul's contrast is not between some works and others but between faith and all works, comparing the latter to "wages":

> For what does the Scripture say? "Abraham believed God, and it was counted to him as righteousness." Now to the one who works, his wages are not counted as a gift but as his due. And to the one who *does not work* but *believes in him who justifies the ungodly*, his faith is counted as righteousness, just as David also speaks of the blessing of the one to whom God *counts righteousness apart from works* . . . (Rom 4:3–6, emphases added).

So, what about the alleged discrepancy between James and Paul? We must recall, first of all, that it was James who made the decisive speech at the Jerusalem Council that probably he would not have made before the controversy initiated by Paul. Second, James's concern was that people were abusing Paul's message to say—contrary to the apostle's teaching—that obedience to the *moral* law was no longer necessary. If we read James's epistle in that context, it makes perfect sense—just as Paul himself said that, although it is not circumcision, "faith working through love" is the ethic of the Christian family (Gal 5:6). Yet the deeper structure of Paul's argument is that "the law is not of faith" (Gal 3:12). The law creates slaves, not sons and daughters. Paradoxically, it is only through faith in Christ that we have not only justification but the fruit of faith working by love. The legal tests that some in Galatia were imposing had generated a sect of backbiting, jealousy, self-righteous exclusion, and division (much like the Pharisee in Jesus's parable above), while the gospel creates a communion around Christ alone. There are two different covenants—the Abrahamic, based on God's promise, and the Sinaitic, based on Israel's oath, "all this we will do" (Gal 4:24; cf. Exod 19:8). To reduce the difference to circumcision and keeping kosher is to miss a great deal not only in Paul's interpretation of Israel's history but in the Old Testament narratives themselves.

Elsewhere in Paul's corpus it is evident that "works of the law" include all efforts to merit God's favor by obedience and that the "righteousness *of* God" condemns while the "righteousness *from* God" justifies. The Roman Catholic teaching is that justification is a process of becoming holy. A similar rejection of the judicial character of the *dik-* word group characterizes most contemporary critiques of the Reformation position. A dubious trajectory since Hermann Cremer treats the "righteousness of God" in the Old as well as the New Testament as a relational rather than a legal concept.[9] However, for Paul *dikaiōsis* ("justification") is the antithesis of *katakrima* ("condemnation"), not of moral sickness or a broken relationship. Once again, these latter symptoms are comprehended within a Reformation account, but are resolved only on the basis of Christ's imputed righteousness.

Romans is of course a principal source for the Reformation perspective. The epistle is not a systematic theology, but it is a systematic

---

9. Lee Irons offers a masterful treatment of the history of this development in biblical studies and, more importantly, a detailed rebuttal in *The Righteousness of God: A Lexical Examination of the "Covenant-Faithfulness" Interpretation*, WUNT 2/386 (Tübingen: Mohr Siebeck, 2015); cf. Horton, *Justification*, 2:151–94; Joseph Fitzmyer, "Justification by Faith in Pauline Thought: A Catholic Perspective," in *Re-Reading Paul Together: Protestant and Catholic Perspectives on Justification*, ed. David E. Aune (Grand Rapids: Baker Academic, 2006), 77–94.

argument—in the line of rabbinical teaching—that one thing follows from another. All people are condemned, not only lawless gentiles (who still have some sense of civic morality), but also the Jews, who have failed to keep the law in which they boast. The upshot of the argument is disclosed in verses 19–20 of chapter 3: "Now we know that whatever the law says it speaks to those who are under the law, so that every mouth may be stopped, and the whole world may be held accountable to God. For by works of the law no human being will be justified in his sight, since through the law comes knowledge of sin."

This cannot be reduced to circumcision and the dietary laws. After all, Paul himself refers to "you shall not covet" as the command that killed him (Rom 7:7–10). There is the righteousness *of* God, revealed in the law, which condemns:

> But now the righteousness of God has been manifested apart from the law [as a covenant], although the Law and the Prophets [as Scripture] bear witness to it—the righteousness of God through faith in Jesus Christ for all who believe. For there is no distinction: for all have sinned and fall short of the glory of God, and are justified by his grace as a gift, through the redemption that is in Christ Jesus, whom God put forward as a propitiation by his blood, to be received by faith. This was to show God's righteousness, because in his divine forbearance he had passed over former sins. It was to show his righteousness at the present time, so that he might be just and the justifier of the one who has faith in Jesus.
>
> Then what becomes of our boasting? It is excluded. By what kind of law? By a law of works? No, but by the law of faith. For we hold that one is justified by faith apart from works of the law. (Rom 3:21–28)

The rest of the epistle is an outworking of that thesis. The distinction between the Abrahamic promise of God and the Sinaitic oath of the people runs throughout the epistle. No one has ever been justified by obedience to the law; the theocratic economy constituted by the Sinaitic covenant pertained strictly to long life in the land, not to everlasting salvation. To miss this is to misunderstand not only Galatians, but Romans and Ephesians. For Paul, it was the heart of the debate with his critics.

Response and Benefits

I will treat the response and benefits together with living worthily of the gospel. As I have mentioned, we are not saved by appropriating the gospel. Rather, we are saved *by the gospel*: actually, by the work of Christ himself in his incarnation, obedient life, death, resurrection, ascension, and return. The gospel itself does not include anything that we do in response. It is pure gift, an announcement of what God in Christ has accomplished for sinners.

At the same time, we are justified *through* faith. I will not digress into the Barthian quarter of Pauline scholarship at this point, represented well by Douglas Campbell.[10] I will only register what seems to me to be as obvious as anything in the New Testament: that only those who trust in Christ are united to Christ. Paul rarely speaks of justification without the clause "through faith" (*ek pisteōs*). We are not justified because we believe, as if faith were the basis of acquittal. The law must be fulfilled in order for one to be justified; faith cannot substitute for obedience. Yet through faith in Christ, we receive all that he is and has accomplished for us as our covenant head. Since the Reformation, Lutheran and Reformed traditions have used the phrase: *propter Christum per fide*—"on account of Christ, through faith." Expressed in Aristotelian categories, Lutheran and Reformed traditions teach that God's grace is the efficient cause, Christ's merit is the material cause, and faith is the instrumental cause. When Scripture refers to being justified by faith, it is shorthand for being justified by Christ's righteousness through faith.

Being united to Christ by faith, we receive *all* that Christ is and has accomplished for us. This means that we are elect in him, redeemed by him, adopted coheirs of his estate, beneficiaries of his toppling of the dominion of sin and death, and objects of his Spirit's indwelling and sanctifying work and the resurrection-glorification that awaits us (Rom 8:30). It is all of grace, all in Christ, received through the gift of faith, all to the glory of God alone.

---

10. See, e.g., Douglas A. Campbell, *The Deliverance of God: An Apocalyptic Rereading of Justification in Paul* (Grand Rapids: Eerdmans, 2013).

Defenders of the traditional Reformation view are often charged with having no place for sanctification. However, history has proved otherwise. Luther and Melanchthon minced no words against antinomianism. Bucer, Vermigli, Calvin, and Knox can hardly be regarded as treating the Christian life as an irrelevant matter. The spiritual literature that often goes by the name "Puritan" represents a profound interest in justification and sanctification. A fair reading of Lutheran and Reformed confessions and catechisms, liturgies, songs, and aids for family and personal devotions reveal a deep piety. It is a piety that grows out of a confidence in God's grace as both favor *and* gift: Christ with all of his benefits, including the gift of the Holy Spirit. It is a piety that emerges first of all not within the individual but through the external action of the Father, in the Son, by the Spirit through the tangible means of hearing the Word, baptism, and the Supper.

I suppose what people mean when they level this charge is that the doctrine *shouldn't* support such piety. All I can say to this is that it reflects a misunderstanding of the position. The Reformation confessions do not reduce the whole Christian faith to a central dogma, including justification, but reflect the breadth and richness of catholic and evangelical conviction. We take the doctrine of justification so seriously not because we consider it the sum of Christianity but because it assures the legal basis for God to adopt, to sanctify, and to glorify all who are united to Christ.

In my view, it is actually rival positions that are reductionistic. In quite different outlines, Eastern Orthodox, Roman Catholic, and Arminian systems endorse a synergism that does not allow for a completely unilateral and gratuitous gift of new birth. Neither sanctification nor glorification (deification) is possible apart from justification. Reformation theology rejoices in all of these benefits, but Orthodox and Roman Catholic traditions deny the one benefit that secures the others. Reformation theology affirms genuine human participation in the growth from sanctification to glorification. No longer "dead" in trespasses and sins (Eph 2:1–5), the regenerate are willing agents, bearing the fruit of the Spirit. We do not press a choice between justification, sanctification, or glorification. Yet only if one is legally wedded to Christ, adopted and justified, is there any basis for growing into this relationship. It is of no use to pit relational against legal categories here.

As in marriage, adoption, and definitely in the politics of the ancient Near East that form the background of the biblical world, the relationship arises out of the legal constitution.

Faith comes from the gospel, and joyful and grateful obedience comes from faith. After relating our election, calling, justification and glorification, Paul exclaims, "What, then, shall we say then in response to these things? If God is for us, who can be against us?" (Rom 8:31 NIV). The gospel is now not only a riveting drama or a set of propositional doctrines but provokes us to move out of our seats and onto the stage. No longer spectators, we are cast by the Spirit as supporting actors in Christ's story. From the overflowing doxology of our hearts springs a life of discipleship.

It is important that Paul instructs, "Only let your manner of life be worthy of the gospel of Christ, so that whether I come and see you or am absent, I may hear of you that you are standing firm in one spirit, with one mind striving side by side for the faith of the gospel" (Phil 1:27). There is a qualitative distinction between the *gospel* (Christ's work) and a "manner of life" that is "worthy of the gospel" and striving together "for the faith of the gospel." How should we live in the world—as those who are still dead in "trespasses and sins" (Eph 2:1), or as those who have been saved by grace to live a new life (vv. 8–10)? And to be united to Christ is also to be united to the members of his ecclesial body, granting access not only to the Father but to the communion of saints. We relate to them not as competitors for divine favor but as equally unworthy and yet also equal beneficiaries of mercy: "faith working through love." Paul always grounds the imperatives to holy living in the indicatives of the gospel. It is as experientially liberating as it is theologically decisive that justification is the origin, not the goal, of the Christian life.

As the Reformers emphasized, we cannot separate one of the gifts of our union with Christ from the others. Anyone who is chosen, redeemed, called, and justified in Christ is also a beneficiary of his Spirit-wrought sanctification and will certainly be glorified. We do not hold ourselves up as the "righteous" who can plead our case before God, in contrast to the wicked. Rather, every day, we take our place with the tax collector, crying out, "God, be merciful to me, a sinner" (Luke 18:13). It is in our confession of sin as much as our godly comportment that we testify to the world that we are on the receiving end of God's rescue operation.

Like those upbraided by the prophets, as well as hypocrites chastised by Paul for making a mockery of God before the watching world, many who profess to believe and spread the gospel today are preaching themselves rather than Christ (2 Cor 4:5).

It is only when we come humbly to the cross and seek the forgiveness and justification found only in Christ that we are able to live a life that is worthy of the gospel. The gospel is not a means to an end, though. It is not a first step to getting us back on the path of securing our own righteousness. The gospel is an end in itself. The fruit of it, including a life worthy of the gospel, is dependent at every moment on whether we actually embrace the gospel—and the triune God of the gospel—as the goal of our existence.

Conclusion

"Therefore, since we have been justified through faith, we have peace with God" (Rom 5:1). The justification of the ungodly cannot be the only piece of good news. To be united to Christ is to be a recipient of all of his gifts. Yet it is because of forensic justification that the other gifts can be granted. At its heart, the message to which the Reformers testified is simply, "Christ alone!" (*solus Christus*)—for everything, not only for justification but for election, regeneration, adoption, sanctification, and glorification. Union with Christ is the whole gospel horizon. We do not look for our justification in Christ and our sanctification in ourselves. Nor do we hope that we will be worthy of glorification; on the contrary, we know that "those whom he predestined he also called, and those whom he called he also justified, and those whom he justified he also glorified" (Rom 8:30). The pieces of the puzzle fit together, so it is very tough to say, "Here is the 'kicker.'" The whole message testifies to this gospel, from Genesis 3:15 to the Bible's last verse, "The grace of the Lord Jesus be with all. Amen" (Rev 22:21).

RESPONSE TO MICHAEL HORTON

SCOT MCKNIGHT

I teach New Testament. My discipline, beginning especially in my doctoral work, is the Gospels, in particular the Gospel of Matthew and the Synoptic Gospels. My professor was James D. G. Dunn, and I began my work in the heady days of the arrival of what Dunn called the "New Perspective on Paul," which was built upon the groundbreaking work of E. P. Sanders's reframing of covenantal nomism as the core of Judaism. So, from the get-go my quest was to comprehend Jesus and the Gospel of Matthew in the context of Judaism. Michael Horton's essay on the Reformation Gospel, which is about as clear an example of the Reformation gospel as one will find in short compass, is more of a theological approach that methodologically creates tension for me. This methodological tension is not a criticism of Horton or the Reformation gospel as he sketches it, but it is fair to say that Horton and I think in different categories. In reading his essay, I came to understand his view much better. Like David deSilva's essay on the Wesleyan gospel, Horton's essay frames the gospel as a soteriological system, and his soteriology is deep and wide. His covenant-formed soteriology, or a two-covenants theology, has always been a lore to me.

The Reformation gospel, as historians of theology have often observed, is based in the book of Romans, and the Bible's narrative is read with much influence from Paul's amazing set of contrasts in Romans 5:12–21. Horton says, "Romans is of course a principal source for the Reformation perspective" (p. 81). The frame for Horton's use of Romans 5:12–21 is law versus gospel. Horton writes on page 80:

There are two different covenants—the Abrahamic, based on God's promise, and the Sinaitic, based on Israel's oath, "all this we will do" (Gal 4:24; cf. Exod 19:8).

The primary context, then, is the history of the covenant of grace, with distinct lines of law and promise.

This contrast of law and gospel does not divide Old from New Testaments, however. The covenant of grace established in Genesis 3:15 and with Abraham and his "Seed" (Christ) is the larger narrative, with the national covenant as a typological drama, something like Hamlet's play-within-a-play. (pp. 72–73)

The Reformed covenant of grace can be connected profitably with the magnificent work of John M. G. Barclay (*Paul and the Gift*), who has shown not only what grace meant in Judaism but has dipped into the larger framework of gift-giving with its essential power of social bonding.[1] Barclay's theology of grace, expressed now in a number of publications, challenges (and confirms) in important ways the framing of grace in Horton's essay:

The contrast between law and gospel is exhibited in the New Testament. John the Baptist's ministry is contrasted with that of Jesus's in such terms. Jesus compares John's urgent call to repentance in light of the coming judgment to a dirge and his own ministry to a joyful feast. (p. 73)

The lodestar for the law-gospel contrast is Galatians, where the Sinai covenant is distinguished clearly from the Abrahamic. (p. 74)

His framework for the Reformation gospel is thickened with a universal (all humans) story versus a particular (Israel) story. This bifocal nature of the Bible's story would work even better if it examined the

---

[1] John M. G. Barclay, *Paul and the Gift* (Grand Rapids: Eerdmans, 2015).

kingdom narrative of Jesus. In fact, though "law and gospel" can raise plenty of red flags, it can work with a variety of narratives present in the New Testament. Many Bible scholars today would want to put into play a variety of narratives at work in the Bible, and they would challenge any single metanarrative of the Bible's storyline. Here are important lines from Horton for how he frames the Bible's narrative:

> Like Hamlet's play-within-a-play, the history of Israel is the subplot of universal sin and redemption. Human sin and fallenness are the universal context, with Israel finding itself "in Adam," having "broken the covenant" (Hos 6:7). (p. 69)

> Some of the tensions in defining the gospel no doubt turn on whether one privileges the former (e.g., the story of Israel) or the latter (e.g., the "plan of salvation"). However, these should be seen as integrally related. The drama is the source of the doctrine, which leads to doxology and discipleship. From the drama we learn, for example, that Christ was crucified, buried, and raised on the third day in accordance with the Scriptures (1 Cor 15:3–4). Yet it is the doctrine that announces its significance for us: "who was delivered up *for our trespasses* and raised *for our justification*" (Rom 4:25). I suppose that if I had to summarize the gospel in a tweet, I could not find a better one. (p. 67)

Horton's essay has numerous instances of some clever shadow boxing with his opponents. For instance, he says "In the first place, they believed they were recovering the apostolic gospel, not coining a new one" (pp. 63–64). And then "secondly, anyone familiar with the writings of Luther, Bucer, Melanchthon, Calvin, Vermigli, and other Reformers as well as those of Lutheran and Reformed orthodoxy is aware that the 'Reformation Gospel' is not reduced to justification. Especially in the Reformed tradition ever since Calvin, the work of Christ has been treated under the integrative rubric of prophet, priest, and king" (p. 64). It would have helped had he named names here. I've heard "the gospel is justification" quite often in the last two decades, so I'm not sure Horton's simple denial can turn the tide. And, he says, "The Reformers did not reduce the gospel to the crucifixion" (p. 64). He's right about the Reformers, of that there is no doubt. But the power of the resurrection, with which Horton's Reformation clearly agrees in his treatment of Romans 4:25, is ignored in many presentations of the gospel today that one hears in sermons and reads in tracts. I agree with Horton here (about the Reformers) and I, too, think we would agree about those presentations of the gospel that do ignore the resurrection.

Horton has a robust Christology when it comes to soteriology, and his lengthy quote from Calvin inspired me and led me to worship. He frames it this way, "We see that our whole salvation and all its parts are comprehended in Christ. We should therefore take care not to derive the least portion of it from anywhere else" (p. 64). Polemics arrive when Horton writes, "By contrast, alternatives to the so-called Reformation Gospel are reductionistic in their view of the plight and solution" (p. 65). He's now brushing up against at least Sanders if not Wright and Dunn. Reformers had a robust soteriology, and simple binaries between various branches of the church won't do, but his binaries turn on the same dime: "Unlike Roman Catholic and Eastern Orthodox theology, the Reformers affirmed justification as the basis for sanctification and deification" (p. 65). So, any simplification of the gospel to just justification won't be compatible with the robust soteriology of the Reformation gospel. He says it this way, "Consequently, the gospel cannot be reduced to justification. Yet apart from this fact—our guilt imputed to Christ and his righteousness imputed to us—there is no good news" (p. 68). Perhaps we can ask, How central is justification? Or, is justification an adequate framing category for the gospel?

Horton presses against the arrival of very serious and endless contextual studies, not least the development since the discoveries of the Dead Sea scrolls, that provide fresh perspectives on what was formerly (mis)understood (or accused of misunderstanding). Here my opening paragraph and the following quotation from Horton's essay raise the old eyebrow of methodology: "It is first-century Judea where the promise is fulfilled—and misunderstood by the religious leaders and even by the disciples until Pentecost. Second Temple Judaism is therefore a *context*, but not a *norm* for what we should expect the gospel to be (contra Sanders, Dunn, and Wright)" (pp. 68–69). Sanders, Dunn, and Wright do not say Judaism is the norm, or at least Horton doesn't document his claim. All three see an explosion of newness in Jesus, who spoke out of and into and against a context. So the questions arise: What does "norm" mean here, and where does he see it in the scholars who baptize Jesus all over again into his first-century Jewishness?

The gospel is first and foremost a Christology and only then a soteriology. Those who flip that script, if I may say so, turn Jesus into an Agent and miss the centrality of the Person. Thus, the gospel is actually defined in the New Testament in 1 Corinthians 15:1–8. Horton comments: "From the drama we learn, for example, that Christ was crucified, buried, and raised on the third day in accordance with the Scriptures (1 Cor 15:3–4)" (p. 67). To which is quickly added Romans 4:25, a text that magnificently sketches the soteriological benefits of the gospel. The sermons in the Book of Acts are records of early Christian gospeling. Horton writes: "The sermons in Acts are demonstrations of Christ's insistence that the Scriptures are about him and that salvation—for gentiles as well as Jews—is found in his name alone (*solus Christus*), acknowledged at the Jerusalem Council (Acts 15)" (p. 78). I like that "about him," but I asked myself, Why not just spell out the centrality of Jesus as a person? Why not let the New Testament itself define the gospel, as in 2 Timothy 2:8, which tells us facts about the story of Jesus? Jesus's own framing of the gospel was with the term *kingdom*. Horton writes: "The kingdom of God—essentially the revival of the national covenant—would come by purging the nation of all that defiles" (p. 77). A question: Can the message of Jesus about kingdom be reduced to the "revival of the national covenant"?

The gospel is defined in the New Testament in 1 Corinthians 15, in the sermons in Acts, in 2 Timothy 2:8, and in the Gospels—and they are the gospel. That gospel is the story of Jesus—his life (which implies all his life as stated in the Gospels), his death, his burial, his resurrection, his ascension, his return—and that story brings redemption, with all its gloriously dancing terms—justification, reconciliation, redemption, liberation. But the gospel, again, is the story *about* Jesus first and foremost, and only second does it talk about the benefits of the gospel. To tell the story of Jesus, in biographical form as Richard Burridge has said over and over, is to tell the gospel.[2] The gospel is the story about Jesus.

---

2. Richard Burridge, *What Are the Gospels?: A Comparison with Graeco-Roman Biography*, 3rd ed. (Waco, TX: Baylor University Press, 2020).

For Horton's (only clear) exposition of the gospel according to Jesus, which could be buttressed with a clear exposition of Jesus's own term, the *kingdom*, he turns to Luke 18:9–14, the parable of the Pharisee and tax collector. I return to the methodological tension I stated to open this response. His study illustrates the problem that recent studies of Judaism and of the Pharisees have pointed out. He expresses—and this was helpful for me to see so clearly stated—the problem of the Pharisees by appealing to the covenant story of the Reformation gospel:

> However, the Pharisees had confused the Sinai covenant (their oath to keep the law and thus live long in the land with God as their king) with the Abrahamic covenant (God's unilateral promise of grace in Christ). Moreover, they were not actually righteous but preferred their own rules to God's law. They were hypocrites, as Jesus charges repeatedly. (p. 77)

Every claim in the paragraph has been seriously challenged in recent scholarship, and I recommend Joseph Sievers and Amy-Jill Levine's *The Pharisees* as the place to start.[3] Horton continues:

> It is legalistic purity, not forgiveness and justification, that they believe will provoke God to descend and inaugurate his kingdom on earth. Second Temple Judaism was their context, and there was no room for a crucified Messiah in their eschatology. That was because they did not really acknowledge that their greatest problem was the need for forgiveness, justification before God, which the tax collector recognized in his simple prayer. "I tell you," Jesus said, "this sinner, not the Pharisee, returned home justified before God" (Luke 18:14). Like Abraham, he was justified then and there, when he trusted in God's promise (Gen 15:6). (pp. 77–78)

Horton's understanding of the Pharisees comes from an old Lutheran-based scholarship that made them the proponents of a

---

3. Joseph Sievers and Amy-Jill Levine, eds., *The Pharisees* (Grand Rapids: Eerdmans, 2021).

graceless religion, and proponents of a legalism based on merit-seeking with God. I must say this, however strong it is: one cannot say these things unless one misunderstands Judaism, law, grace, and covenant. To his brief study of Luke 18 he adds the rich young ruler who was "disillusioned by the law" and "did not wait around for the gospel" (p. 78).

On the response to the gospel, Horton has nothing less than a brilliant statement of a Reformed soteriological approach:

> Expressed in Aristotelian categories, Lutheran and Reformed traditions teach that God's grace is the efficient cause, Christ's merit is the material cause, and faith is the instrumental cause. When Scripture refers to being justified by faith, it is shorthand for being justified by Christ's righteousness through faith. (p. 82)

In the words of Jesus this is what his paragraph looks like: "The kingdom of God has come near. Repent and believe the good news!" (Mark 1:15), which is then followed up with, "Come, follow me" (v. 17).

RESPONSE TO MICHAEL HORTON

DAVID A. DESILVA

In his sermon on "Catholic Spirit," Wesley—who was no stranger to offering strong criticism—urged that we who hold to differing opinions on several points concerning the scriptural witness to God's saving acts and agenda should nevertheless continue to embrace one another as sisters and brothers in Christ and as partners in ministry to the world. It seems particularly important to affirm this where a person approaching the gospel from an "Arminian" perspective addresses remarks to a person approaching the gospel from a Reformed, or Calvinist, perspective, for these perspectives—and all too often those holding these different perspectives—are typically regarded as inimical one to the other.

I would agree that "the good news is as encompassing as the bad news," and the "bad news" is larger than my guilt and impending condemnation (p. 66). I fail, in the first place, to give God the honor and obedience that is God's due as my Creator. Justification is, as Horton says well at one point, the *entrance* into the gospel mansion, and there is far more to the good news. We are not yet rescued from the plight in which we find ourselves by acquittal or by the imputation of a righteousness that does not also characterize us in reality. Rather, we are rescued from our larger plight as God brings us, through his Holy Spirit's operation, closer and closer to that point where we are living no longer for ourselves but "for him who died . . . and was raised" on our behalf (2 Cor 5:15). Our full salvation is to become and to do what God loves and to cease to be and to do what provokes God's wrath.

Michael Horton invokes Philippians 3:8–11 as a scriptural testimony against the value of *anything* that might be considered "a righteousness of my own." The only qualifier that *dis*qualifies this righteousness for Paul, however, is that it is based on the law, because the law does not ultimately set people in alignment with what God has done for *all* people in the Christ, who brought the term of the Torah to an end and secured for us the greater gift of the Holy Spirit, the law written on our hearts, to guide us into and empower us for genuine righteousness. Giving fair weight to Philippians 3:10–11 alongside 3:8–9, it becomes clear that living in ever-greater conformity to Christ in his death—what Paul earlier described as living with the mind that was in Christ (Phil 2:1–11)—leads to the righteousness that Paul seeks, the righteousness that he believes will lead ultimately to his resurrection from the dead after the pattern of the Lord to whose pattern the Spirit had conformed him. Such righteousness is never "our own" in the sense that we manufacture it; it is the gift of God through the Spirit. It is, however, "our own" in the sense that it really *characterizes* what we have become in Christ; it is not merely *imputed* to us in a moment of divine make-believe.

Horton objects: "What good news could it be to me that the Spirit gradually conforms me to Christ's image when I know that this good work begun in me will not be perfect in this life?"[1] First, I would ask: How do you *know* this? What makes you so sure of the Spirit's inadequacy, in the face of your flesh, to complete his work in you? Didn't Paul promise precisely the opposite? "Walk by the Spirit and you will certainly not consummate the flesh's desires!" (Gal 5:16, my trans.). Paul expects "the righteous requirement of the law" to "be fully met in us, who do not live according to the flesh but according to the Spirit" (Rom 8:4). Is "anthropological pessimism" more appropriate in the face of such promises than "pneumatological optimism"?[2] Horton is correct when he writes that "the law must be fulfilled in order for one to be justified; faith cannot substitute for obedience" (p. 82). But he is mistaken not to look, with Paul, to the Holy Spirit sent from God to accomplish this very thing within us. The faith that saves us is not merely trust in Jesus and his redemptive death; it also involves trust in the Holy Spirit that Jesus died to secure for us (Gal 3:13–14). Horton ironically quotes Hebrews

---

1. One also bumps up against the assumption here, which I've encountered frequently enough to call "typical" for Reformed thinkers, that our God is an all-or-nothing God. If perfection is not attained, all is lost; therefore not only perfection, but even *progress* in Christlikeness, cannot be part of the answer to the question, "What must I do to be saved?"

2. Michael Bird, *The Saving Righteousness of God: Studies on Paul, Justification and the New Perspective* (Milton Keynes: Paternoster, 2007), 173.

12:14 in the context of arguing that only the forensic declaration that we are "righteous" allows confidence before God's throne of judgment, for the point of Hebrews 12:14 is to impel its hearers to *keep pursuing* "the holiness without which no one will see the Lord" (NRSV). Yielding ourselves to the sanctifying work of God's Holy Spirit is prerequisite to enjoying God's unveiled presence forever.

I would be reluctant, therefore, to affirm that the takeaway from Paul's letter to the Galatians is "Christ *plus nothing*" as the means by which God's promise of life is granted to believers. Paul spends so much of Galatians focused on the Holy Spirit that this formula no longer seems adequate. "Jesus alone is sufficient for our salvation" only *if* we make room for the Holy Spirit, whom Paul certainly believed to be the "plus" that Jesus died to secure for us (Gal 3:2–5, 13–14), so that, "through the Spirit," we might indeed arrive at the "hoped-for righteousness by faith" (Gal 5:5). Christ coming alive in us, the life of the new person taking shape within us, the "new creation" that is all that counts (Gal 6:15)—this is all God's gift to us in the Spirit, and it is an essential part of every account of that great salvation, that new "life," into which God has invited us. It would be a truer summary of Galatians to say: Christ plus the Torah equals nothing; Christ plus the Spirit equals everything (cf. Gal 5:6; 6:15).

I was surprised by Horton's claim that "the least likely candidate for a 'context' [for the Reformation gospel] is the Reformation" (p. 70). It seems quite disingenuous to set aside the contextual role that Luther's break from the Roman Catholic Church of the early sixteenth century played in the formulation of "the Reformation gospel"—and not a little ideological to claim *this* gospel to be purely a recovery of the "apostolic gospel." While Horton is correct that the problem of guilt before a holy God did not originate in Luther's conscience but rather reaches back far into the experience of ancient Israel, the radicalization of the apostolic gospel in the "five *solas*,"[3] for example, and the radical aversion to the

---

3. It is telling that Paul himself never found it necessary to couple the word "alone" with either "faith," "grace," "Christ," or "Scripture." Indeed, the only appearance of "faith alone" in the New Testament appears in the context of James's negation of the sufficiency of "faith alone" to save a person apart from works (Jas 2:24). (We naturally find "God" and "alone" linked quite a bit, generally in the context of claims concerning the uniqueness of Israel's God and his qualities and authority.) The "five *solas*" are evidence that the Reformation gospel is not merely a recovery of the apostolic gospel but has taken on a certain edge that arose from the historical and theological contexts of the sixteenth century and later.

Catholic (or is it *apostolic*?) emphasis on God's work of actually making us righteous in Christ, are clearly consequences of the particular contextual struggles of the sixteenth, not the first, century. The failure to acknowledge and grapple seriously with the historical context out of which the Reformation gospel emerged represents a significant weakness in this essay.

It is admittedly tangential to Horton's principal thrust, but I am concerned about the manner in which he continues to represent Jesus's and Paul's contemporaries. Horton speaks of the dispute, reflected in Paul's letters, between "Paul and the legalists" (p. 69). There are *some* things we can learn from the New Perspective on Paul—and the fact that the rival teachers in Galatia (for example) were driven by more than mere "legalism" is certainly one of them. Referring to the parable of the Pharisee and the tax collector, Horton claims that "here, Jesus especially contrasts his message with the piety of Second Temple Judaism" (p. 76). But Jesus is closely following the cautions that Ben Sira (a scribe in Jerusalem whose teachings became very popular among Essenes and latter rabbis—and thus, one might surmise, also among nonsectarian Jews) uttered two centuries prior against presuming upon God's grace and forgiveness because of their piety or gifts (Sir 7:5, 8–9). One could also turn to the hymn that ends the Rule of the Community at Qumran as well as the Thanksgiving Hymns produced within that community, the Prayer of Azariah, or the Prayer of Manasseh to find examples of a piety in the Second Temple period that would agree that the most proper stance to take before God is to beat one's breast and say, "Lord, have mercy on me, the sinner." We really must stop holding up a parable's caricature of a Pharisee as a mirror of "the piety of Second Temple Judaism"—and thinking that Jesus's piety has no home in Second Temple Judaism.

In closing, I would suggest a different reading of Jesus's encounter with the rich young man than one that concludes: "Disillusioned by the law"—that is, by Jesus's practical unpacking of the command to love one's neighbor as oneself, he "did not wait around for the gospel" (p. 78). No, Jesus's instructions to him *were* gospel. Unwilling to obey Jesus, the young man chose not to follow him and walk into the kingdom life that made such demands upon him, failing to recognize that those demands would lead him—and his poorer neighbors!—to a place of good news, of deeper connection with one another and with their Lord! Such obedience was an essential part of answering Jesus's invitation to come with Jesus as his disciple. The expectation that we will fully live out the command to love our neighbor never goes away (see Rom 13:8–10; Gal 5:13–15). Horton's treatment of this episode raises for me the question: Does our "gospel" serve, in the end, to insulate us from *Jesus's* gospel invitation and from the demand to bear actual kingdom fruit—and thus give us a false assurance concerning our place in that kingdom?

RESPONSE TO MICHAEL HORTON

JULIE MA

Pentecostals like myself are Protestant in the historical sense, so we are concerned with salvation by grace through faith. We can even say that the Holy Spirit was a force of renewal in the Protestant Reformation. The main point of differences is that we don't think the Spirit abandoned us after Martin Luther nailed his ninety-five theses on the door of Wittenberg Castle Church (1517) or even after the Westminster Confession was written (1646). I wonder then if the Reformation Gospel needs to be further reformed to be more robustly spiritual and holistic in its contents and concerns. There is then much in Michael Horton's Reformed gospel view that I can affirm and question.

Horton notes and affirms the connection between the cross, resurrection, and incarnation quite brilliantly. He is correct that the salvific significance of the Word's assumption of our nature cannot be adequately explained by a theology that is just cross centered, and the incarnation by itself does not remove the barrier to communion with God. In addition to demonstrating Jesus's deity, the resurrection is another instance of his redemptive work. Furthermore, Christ's ascension is not only a culmination of his resurrection but a new step in the process of his atonement. All of these incidents in Christ's life result in the forgiveness, justification, sanctification, and glorification of those who are linked to him. In the end, as Horton observes, Christ is the victor over the evil powers, to be sure, but the ground of his triumph was canceling the legal record of debt by nailing it to the cross (Col 2:14–15). Horton gives a lot of attention to the Holy Spirit, which is both wise as it is sensible for a theologian to do. Horton, too, is open to the possibility that the gospel is good news for oppressed and marginalized groups in society.

Horton provides his viewpoint on covenants in the Old Testament. Only three of the five covenants—the Adamic, Mosaic, and a small amount of the Abrahamic covenant—were effectively covered by him. He merely mentions the rest of the covenants. To give the full picture of covenants in the Old Testament, I will go into further detail about other covenants. Adamic, Noahic, Abrahamic, Mosaic, and Davidic covenants are the five covenants, which were made at various points throughout history.

Horton omitted a crucial element of the Abrahamic covenant in the study. God chose Abram for this covenant in order to make a covenant with him to become "a father of many nations" (Gen 17:5). "Scripture foresaw that God would justify the Gentiles by faith, and announced the gospel in advance to Abraham: 'All nations will be blessed through you,'" writes Paul. He names this promise the gospel (Gal 3:8). Since the beginning of time, God's redemptive mission has been to save mankind via trust in Jesus the Messiah (Eph 1:3–10). God only has one gospel to share with the human race. It can only be obtained by faith in Christ Jesus. Whoever seeks God by faith in Christ Jesus will find God and become "children of God" and "Abraham's seed, and heirs according to the promise," regardless of whether they are a Jew or a gentile (Gal 3:26–29).

In 2 Samuel 7:18–19, the Davidic covenant is constrained. David received a consoling word from God (v. 11). In addition, the "Seed" in whom David put his hope and his faith for salvation would now emerge from David's own flesh (v. 12). God would also bestow upon him an eternal throne and kingdom (v. 16). There are five instances of "Adonai Yahweh" or "Lord Yahweh," in verses 18–19, 22, 28, and 29 (NIV: "Sovereign Lord"). In Genesis 15:2, 8, God had previously used this special compound word to promise Abraham a seed. The term "instruction for mankind" in 2 Samuel 7:19 deserves our attention (ESV). What was this Torah—this rule or "instruction" or charter that applied to the entire human race? This was a point David did not miss. He understood that the everlasting dynasty, dominion, and kingdom he had just received were all connected to the continual promise that God had been making repeatedly. The destiny of the entire human race would be at stake. That unquestionably represents missions at its best. That this is "instruction for mankind" or the charter for humanity relates to the revelation David had just received regarding the "seed," which carries another significant implication.

What Horton observes in addressing the relationships between the old (Abrahamic and Davidic) and the new covenant is unclear. He needs to present the continuity and discontinuity between the two. Another related question is which prophets foretold the new covenant with what new features. Also, Horton's following phrase would require qualifications: "eschatological continuity of one covenant of grace alongside covenantal discontinuity" (p. 71). I tend to disagree with this, as I view it as continuity. The Christian life should be eschatological until the consummation of the return of Jesus Christ.

Horton mentions the grace of Christ quite frequently. This common biblical term is so significant when we experience it in real life. The phrase "God's life, power, and righteousness are given to us by unmerited favor" could be used to define grace. God powerfully changes our hearts and lives through grace. Grace offers us a new life that is not under God's condemnation. In applying God's grace in my Christian life, I gladly forgive my fellow believer who hurts me deeply, by his grace, as Jesus forgave Peter who denied his Master three times. Colossians 3:13 says, "forgive as the Lord forgave you."

Horton highlights being humble before the cross and asking the forgiveness and justification discovered only in Jesus Christ. Living a humble life, being forgiven and forgiving others, will bring us to a new dimension that will make our lives worthy of the gospel. Horton profoundly states that the gospel is not the primary stage to bringing us toward establishing our righteousness. The word of God is an end in itself. To live our lives worthy of the gospel is to make the word alive, as applied in our daily life.

RESPONSE TO MICHAEL HORTON

SHIVELY T. J. SMITH

Michael Horton's essay on the Reformation Gospel engaged in a helpful corrective, which responded to a series of oversimplistic alternatives. Pulling the curtain back on reductionist understandings of "the plight and solution" at work in the Reformers' gospel readings reset my understanding about the dynamic and constructive interaction between Reformed theology and biblical interpretation easily misconstrued in the excesses of the (mis)information age. The essay was written with a clear understanding that the Reformation and the gospel might too quickly be reduced to matters of crucifixion, justification, and sanctification. Indeed, Horton opens by taking on that oversimplistic connection with a historical lesson on the Reformers' understanding about their mission—namely, to recover "the apostolic gospel," rather than "coining a new one." This opening point shaped my expectation about the essay's agenda and awakened me to some connections I had not considered, and Horton does not disappoint as he takes readers on a guided tour that adjusts how the Bible is understood to be at work in the Reformed view.

One thread running through Horton's essay that resists oversimplification is the way he describes the "integrative" synthesis at work between Reformation thought and biblical interpretation. He opens by saying, "The work of Christ has been treated under the integrative rubric of prophet, priest, and king" (p. 64). The mixture contributes to a more robust theological tapestry undergirding matters of crucifixion and resurrection than one might anticipate. As Horton's interpretive approach demonstrates, this integrative rubric involves thick cross-testament readings, in which the Old Testament speaks forward to the New and the New Testament speaks back to the Old. The essay is rich with intertextual considerations and showcases the constructive nature of gospel interpretation in the Reformed view.

In the section on the plight and solution to which the Reformation Gospel responds, Horton deploys two terms—intensive and extensive—which prove helpful in understanding what Reformed readings of the gospel see at work in Scripture. He says, "Reformed theology has always been eager to affirm that the nature created by God remains good yet corrupted; depravity is total in its *extensiveness* (heart, intellect, will, and body), not in *intensiveness* (as if the image of God could be eradicated)" (p. 66). Such a juxtaposition was instructive to understanding what is at stake in Horton's treatment of the Reformation Gospel. Matters of heart, intellect, will, and body are up to redemption, justification, and sanctification, while the image of God remains eternally intact. My concern with this thought is that I question what happens when particular hearts, intellects, wills, and bodies are deemed unjustifiable, at least fully in this life. How has this juxtaposition impacted certain people, based on their cultural and social locations, differently? What happens when the human condition of the heart, intellect, will, and body is imposed? One has to wonder how the Reformation Gospel responds to the depravity of those who force and create those conditions for others while claiming justification and righteousness for themselves? It is unclear to me how Horton's Reformation Gospel reading addresses those different "Christian" experiences and acknowledges their existence in the first place. Merely suggesting "decorum and respect" in the face of "distinctive cultural practices" (p. 79) and histories can distort the gospel message and render its application in morally uneven ways.

I found several points of agreement and nuanced distinction between the Reformed and Liberation Gospel views. First, the centrality of Jesus to the gospel message is uncontested. Jesus, as Horton suggests, is "the incarnate gospel" and unifying feature of gospel-focused reading of Holy Scripture (p. 66). But what happens when biblical literacy, specifically, and literacy in general, is denied to people? What is the Reformation view about the non-textual experience of Jesus that privileges experience as opposed to doctrine because that is all some of those subscribing to the Reformed view permitted? I am thinking specifically about a South Carolinian African-American freedwoman who explained her knowledge about Jesus to a white missionary around the 1860s: "Oh! I don't know nothing! I can't read a word. But oh! I read Jesus in my heart, just as you read him in the book. . . . I read and read him here in my heart just as you read him in the Bible. O, . . . my God! I got him! I hold him here all the time. He stay[s] with me!"[1] From my reading, this view does not address an accounting of knowledge about Jesus Christ and matters of justification, sanctification, and righteousness that are not mediated or shaped by textual gospel engagement. How does Horton's Reformation Gospel account for traditions of gospel faith from the discarded and disposed underside of society not included in gospel-faith communities with the privileges to determine cultural and social norms for all?

Both the Reformed and Liberation Gospel readings, as well as those of our other colleagues, are unified on the centrality of Jesus to gospel understanding. What is slightly different, however, is the degree to which the other topics and actors interacting in the Incarnate One's activities is secondary to the thrust of the gospel message of salvation and liberation. Horton accurately notes the Protestant Reformers' confessional commitment to determine the scope of Scripture as "Christ as he is clothed in his gospel" (p. 66), but he does not stop there. He qualifies this focus, saying, "There are of course other topics, genres, supporting actors, and subplots, but all are subservient to this single message that grows clearer as the story unfolds" (p. 66). Whereas Horton places supporting actors and subplots as secondary to the chief point of gospel proclamation as Christ among us, the Liberation view treats those supporting roles and secondary storylines as the very point for why Jesus's inaugural announcement in Luke 4:18–19 was necessary.

One curious moment in Horton's overview of the Reformation Gospel was his selection of the Lukan parable on the Pharisee and the publican (Luke 18:9–14). To be sure, Horton's interpretive use of this parable is masterful. He demonstrates the correlation between righteousness and justification discourse in the Reformation Gospel, locating that conversation within the gospel narrative. Unpacking the contrast between the Pharisee and the tax collector in the parable, he captures well the difference in religious observance and orientation between the two figures, which the Gospel sets up by saying, "The

---

1. Quoted in Allen Callahan, *The Talking Book: African Americans and the Bible* (New Haven: Yale University Press, 2006), 186.

Pharisee, standing by himself.... But the tax collector, standing far off..." (Luke 18:11, 13 NRSV), Horton nuances distinction between the Pharisee and tax collector in several ways. First, the distance highlights a confusion about the difference between living into the Sinai covenant or the Abrahamic covenant. Horton says, "The Pharisees had confused the Sinai covenant (their oath to keep the law and thus live long in the land with God as their king) with the Abrahamic covenant (God's unilateral promise of grace in Christ). Moreover, they were not actually righteous, but preferred their own rules to God's law. They were hypocrites, as Jesus charges repeatedly" (p. 77). What is telling from Horton's distillation is how the promise of grace in the Abrahamic covenant links directly to Christ, conflating the distance between the ancient Near Eastern historical moment of the covenant's enactment and the ancient Roman imperial context in which the Gospel writers and Jesus existed. The Israelite covenants are understood through a christological reading, and this Lukan parable from Horton's reading is an example of that interpretive strategy. He characterizes the Reformation Gospel view as involved in seeing signposts of Christ across the Old and New Testaments. Horton describes it best when he says, "Expounded in narrative, poetry, apocalyptic, wisdom, and didactic literature ... the varied biblical texts evidence a coherent historical plot" (p. 66). Although talking about the New Testament in particular, this statement holds true for his understanding about the Reformation gospel's treatment of both canons. He summarizes it well at the end of the essay, "At its heart, the message to which the Reformers testified is simply, 'Christ alone!'" (p. 85).

Another interesting feature in Horton's interpretation of the parable as a resource for understanding the Reformation Gospel view is how it helps him to outline the relationship between matters of purity, forgiveness, and justification. The parable demonstrates the difference between a legalistic religious adherence to laws and regulations compared to the position of one observant of those traditions (the tax collector) who yet violates those observances in his professional decisions. As Horton says, "For Jesus, the Pharisees defile more than anyone else.... It is legalistic purity, not forgiveness and justification, that they [Pharisees] believe will provoke God to descend and inaugurate his kingdom on earth.... That was because they did not really acknowledge that their greatest problem was the need for forgiveness, justification before God, which the tax collector recognized in his simple prayer" (pp. 77–78).

Out of all the parables from which to select, why choose one so singular? Luke, by far, includes more parables than any other Gospel, but this parable constitutes one of the nineteen unique Lukan parables not shared with the others. Given the matters of justification, forgiveness, and purity are so crucial to the Reformation Gospel view, particularly in a form that is nonreductionist as Horton asserts, why not choose one of the parables shared across the Synoptic Gospels to demonstrate how important these concepts are for much of the gospel narrative? For example, the short parable about the wedding guests and fasting (Matt 9:15; Mark 2:19–20; Luke 5:34–35) explicitly names the law-observant practice observed by the Pharisees and the disciples of John in contrast to the practices of Jesus and his disciples eating and drinking. The same matter of legalistic observance versus Christ as justification runs as a thread in this parable, and it appears as a fixture in the gospel tradition.

Moreover, when one considers that Jesus spoke of fasting while not evidencing any fasting practices in the gospel narrative, it appears Jesus saw himself as the messianic fulfillment of Sabbath joy in the parable (Exod 16:22–30). According to Jewish law, it is forbidden to fast on the Sabbath because it is set aside as a time of joyful communion with God and the family of God (Isa 58:3–10; Jub. 50.11–12). The absence of a practice of fasting in Jesus's ministry indicates he understands himself to be the fulfillment of the Sabbath's joy and communion. Additionally, Sabbath fulfillment involves the work of social acknowledgment and a reckoning for social inequities. For example, in the prophecy of Isaiah 58, God responds to Israel's claim of fasting observance by stating they have missed the very purpose of the religious practice: "Is not this the fast that I choose: to loose the bonds of injustice, to undo the thongs of the yoke, to let the oppressed go free, and to break every yoke? Is it not to share your bread with the hungry, and bring the homeless poor into your house; when you see the naked, to cover them, and not to hide yourself from your own kin?" (Isa 58:6–7 NRSV). As Horton says, Jesus is the Incarnate One, which highlights what Jesus casts fasting, prayer, and repentance to be chiefly about—namely, unity with God. "Christ alone," in this way, embodies God's response to Israel's failed fasting aims, and it carries a sense of social response that is missing from Horton's articulation.

In summarizing Paul's thoughts on the gospel of Christ, Horton states, "Paul always grounds the imperatives to holy living in the indicatives of the gospel. It is as experientially liberating as it is theologically decisive that justification is the origin, not the goal, of the Christian life" (p. 84). What a poetic articulation of the Christian life in origin and aims. Yet, one wonders what origination means in the believer's living response. The question is not answered with Horton's turn to the epistle of James. He interprets James as a response to Paul, keeping them in a genealogical and theological conversation instead of parallel canonical discussions. What is the Reformation Gospel's sense of social responsibility and care for the believing community? That matter seems to continually evade the conversation, leaving this liberationist gospel interpreter yet wondering, What is our Christian responsibility to care for the dignity of each other's justification in the current moment and beyond?

CHAPTER THREE: THE WESLEYAN GOSPEL

DAVID A. DESILVA

By God's grace from start to finish, those who trust in Jesus Christ are saved from the guilt and penalty of their former sins, renewed in God's image, and empowered by the Holy Spirit to love and serve God and neighbor in true holiness all the remaining days of their lives.[1]

The Wesleyan Gospel: An Overview

John Wesley shares with the tradition of all historic Christian denominations the conviction that the gospel is "the power of God for salvation to everyone who has faith" (Rom 1:16 NRSV). This gospel, however, announces God's appointed means for deliverance from the *twin* problems that have beset human beings—their alienation from the life of God through disobedience and the deformation of their very nature as a consequence of that alienation. Thus the salvation that God's power works to accomplish is also twofold, incorporating both justification and sanctification: "by justification we are saved from the guilt of sin, and restored to the favour of God; by sanctification we are saved from the power and root of sin, and restored to the image of God."[2] It was Wesley's particular genius to join these two elements of Christian theology as inseparable and equally indispensable facets of the saving work of God. Wesley was adamant that his ministers should "preach the whole

---

1. Adapted from John Wesley, Sermon 6.I.10 (*WJW* I.208).
2. Wesley, Sermon 85.II.1 (*WJW* III.204).

gospel, even justification and sanctification, preparatory to glory," not rending asunder what God had joined, but giving equal attention to "Christ dying for us, and Christ living in us."[3]

This dual focus on God delivering us not only from the *guilt* and *penalty* of sin but also from the *power* of sin is the core conviction at the heart of the Wesleyan gospel.[4] Salvation is not merely about "going to heaven," though salvation is *consummated* in an eternity in the presence of God and the company of all the redeemed. This is that final salvation that is "nearer to us now than when we became believers" (Rom 13:11 NRSVue). Salvation, however, encompasses the whole, ongoing work of God—not merely what occurred "the hour I first believed." It reaches across the whole span of a person's life, beginning with the divine empowerment to perceive and respond to the truth of the gospel (what Wesley called "prevenient grace") and continuing until "mortal life shall cease," when believers are at last ushered into what we "shall possess within the veil"[5] of God's eternal kingdom. Salvation involves the work both of the Son and Holy Spirit, the Son in "giving himself to be 'a propitiation for the sins of the world,'" the Holy Spirit in "renewing men in that image of God wherein they were created,"[6] working in us "both to will and to work for his good pleasure" (Phil 2:13 NRSVue). The Wesleyan gospel thus proclaims not merely our change in status "from guilty to forgiven" but also our "gracious and gradual restoration . . . to God-likeness,"[7] particularly as the image of God is revealed in Jesus Christ. God's full work is only fully achieved when the believer is fully transformed—when he or she is no longer a person that contributes to the ongoing degradation of self and others, but has rather become a person *in* whom God has renewed a right spirit and *through* whom

---

3. John Wesley, "Thoughts Concerning Gospel-Ministers," in *The Works of John Wesley*, 14 vols. (London: Wesleyan Conference Office, 1872; repr., Grand Rapids: Zondervan, 1958), X.456 (henceforth *WJW*).

4. See, e.g., Wesley, Sermon 5.III.3 (*WJW* I.191): "he saves from the guilt of sin (and at the same time from the power) sinners of every kind"; idem, Sermon 6.proem.3 (*WJW* I.204): "'believe and thou shalt be saved'; now saved both from the guilt and power of sin, and of consequence from the wages of it."

5. Quotations taken from verses 2 and 5 of the hymn "Amazing Grace" by John Newton, published in John Newton and William Cowper, *Olney Hymns: In Three Books* (Glasgow: William Collins, 1829), 101–2.

6. Wesley, Sermon 85.proem.2, *WJW* III.200.

7. Randy Maddox, *Responsible Grace: John Wesley's Practical Theology* (Nashville: Abingdon, 1994), 67.

God works to elevate the dignity and experience of all those whom the restored believer touches.

What Context?

John Wesley's spiritual biography constitutes one important context for the emergence of his understanding of the gospel.[8] He was profoundly dissatisfied with the lack of impact that the Scriptures and church life were having on his contemporaries and profoundly aware of the gap between the scriptural vision for how Christ was to transform Christ-followers and the actual condition of his fellow clergy, the people in their parishes, and *himself*, despite the relative seriousness of his intentions in this regard.[9] This became the seedbed for his rediscovery of the full scope of the good news in Jesus Christ—namely, God's empowerment of the believer for the full transformation of heart and life that the gospel proclaims. This was, of course, an empowerment that he had first to discover in his own experience before he could affirm that he himself had been transformed from an "almost Christian" into an "altogether Christian."[10]

The theological context for the Wesleyan Gospel is the creation of humankind in the image of God and the consequences of our willful disobedience of, and alienation from, our Creator, as typified in the sin of Adam. God had created human beings in his image (Gen 1:26–27), which Wesley understood to indicate humanity's reflection of God's nature. This meant that humanity shared, at first, God's immortality; God's freedom, which was prerequisite to the exercise of genuine

---

8. A foundational treatment of this subject can be found in Richard P. Heitzenrater, *Wesley and the People Called Methodists* (Nashville: Abingdon, 1995).

9. An early sermon preached in Oxford, "The Almost Christian," and all the more the draft sermon that he had written first for that occasion but prudently abandoned—"Hypocrisy in Oxford" (Sermon 150, *WJW* IV.392–407), the text for which was "how the faithful city has become a harlot" (Isa 1:21)!—provide windows into this dissatisfaction. On the complexities of understanding the relationship of the emergence of the Methodist movement to the spiritual health or slackness of the Anglican Church, see Jeremy Gregory, "The Long Eighteenth Century," in *The Cambridge Companion to John Wesley*, ed. Randy L. Maddox and Jason E. Vickers (Cambridge: Cambridge University Press, 2010), 13–39. The reading that Wesley undertook for his ordination in the Anglican Church, which included such works as Thomas à Kempis's *The Imitation of Christ*, Jeremy Taylor's *Rule and Exercises of Holy Living*, and William Law's *Christian Perfection* significantly nurtured his vision for the transformation of heart and life.

10. Wesley, Sermon 2.II.6, *WJW* I.139.

virtue;[11] and God's moral character, which is "true righteousness and holiness" (Eph 4:24) and "love" (1 John 4:8).[12]

In choosing not to be ruled by God—that is, to disobey God's sole command—human beings "lost the life of God: he was separated from Him, in union with whom his spiritual life consisted."[13] As Randy Maddox observes, "The essence of the first sin was the severing of this relationship, the desire to be independent of God."[14] Alienated from life-giving communion with God, human beings no longer possessed the natural or moral faculties of the divine image. People would henceforth be born in the likeness of Adam (Gen 5:3; cf. Rom 5:12–21) rather than that of God: "the natural consequence of this is, that everyone descended from him comes into the world spiritually dead, dead to God, wholly dead in sin; entirely void of the life of God; void of the image of God, of all that righteousness and holiness wherein Adam was created."[15] The result was the multiplication of wickedness, misery, sickness, pain, and death.[16] Having failed to honor God as the source and goal of their being, human beings have degraded themselves, and no longer seeing the image of God in others, degrade one another through exploitation, oppression, and violence (cf. Rom 1:18–32).

As hostile ingrates abusing the very gift of life and abusing one another, human beings could expect only to meet with the wrath of the Creator whom they affronted so egregiously—a wrath revealed and experienced already in their degradation (Rom 1:18) but also awaiting its full manifestation when all would stand before God at God's visitation to judge the earth (Rom 2:5, 8). But precisely at this point the announcement of what this God has done on behalf of alienated humanity in the life, death, and resurrection of Jesus and in the gift of the Holy Spirit breaks into the human situation as "gospel"—as "good tidings, good news for guilty, helpless sinners."[17] God has not visited human beings

---

11. Wesley, Sermon 17.proem.1, *WJW* II.401.
12. Wesley, Sermon 45.I.1, *WJW* II.188; see also Sermon 141 ("The Image of God") I.1–4, *WJW* IV.293–295.
13. Sermon 45.I.2, *WJW* II.189.
14. Maddox, *Responsible Grace*, 81.
15. Sermon 45.I.4, *WJW* II.190.
16. These consequences are developed in Sermon 44 ("Original Sin"), launching from Gen 6:5, and Sermon 57 ("On the Fall of Man"), concerning the deleterious consequences of the fall and the death that "in Adam all died."
17. John Wesley, Sermon 7.II.8 (*WJW* I:229).

in wrath but, contrary to all expectation and deserving, with further grace. Indeed, the very awareness that "this isn't how it should be for human beings" and, all the more, "I'm not who *I* should be as a human being," is already a gift from God. It is the voice of God calling us out from perpetuating (or at least colluding with) the forces that destroy human life toward becoming something new—people whose ambitions and energies will have decidedly different effects upon human experience as far as our impact can reach. Wesley would name this a facet of God's "prevenient grace," God's intervention in the lives of those who do what is destructive of human flourishing, who have lost all sense of that moral compass that would tell them to change direction so as to swim up toward the air rather than farther down toward drowning utterly.[18]

John Wesley understood the good news that came to the world in Jesus Christ as the promise of assured deliverance ("salvation") from this condition in every respect. Given the context of the human predicament, for a gospel truly to bring "good news" it would need to solve not merely one, but two fundamental problems: first, the reconciliation of rebellious and alienated creatures to their Creator; second, the restoration of the image of God that these creatures had lost. Wesley thus combined both the Western Christian "*juridical* emphasis on guilt and absolution" and the Eastern Orthodox "*therapeutic* concern for healing our sin-diseased nature" in one unified view of God's saving work.[19]

What Texts?

It is challenging, in Wesley's case, to select just a few key texts as representative pillars of his particular understanding of the gospel. He demonstrates an encyclopedic facility in the Scriptures and tends to develop his theological understanding more after the manner of a mosaic, drawing many texts together over the course of a sermon or tract to fashion a biblical theology that sought to take in the whole counsel of God. Nevertheless, we may consider a few particular texts that are closely associated with fundamental pillars of the gospel.

---

18. Here one must simply acknowledge that, throughout the history of the past two millennia, many who identified themselves as Christians have not only failed to advance God's goals of setting things right in human experience but, in fact, have so frequently done the opposite that the name of God has fallen into disrepute because of them.

19. Maddox, *Responsible Grace*, 23 (see also pp. 142–43).

1. Saved by the Atoning Death of Jesus: Justification

Paul's reflections on the significance of Jesus's life and death for renewing the relationship between alienated human beings and their Creator are, of course, of central importance for the Wesleyan Gospel as they are for the gospel in any reckoning. Jesus Christ, the incarnation of God the Son, lived a life of perfect righteousness. He was both fully human and fully committed to (and successful in regard to) falling into no inward or outward sin, to doing all that the Father wished, and ultimately to suffering all that the Father had ordained in dying on behalf of alienated humanity. This offering of a righteous life became the basis upon which all whose hearts were drawn to the Son in faith and in love would be pardoned for their past sins:

> Since all have sinned and fall short of the glory of God; they are now justified by his grace as a gift, through the redemption that is in Christ Jesus, whom God put forward as a sacrifice of atonement by his blood, effective through faith. (Rom 3:23–25 NRSVue)

Wesley defines justification and the "reckoning of righteousness" in precisely the terms that Paul does in Romans 4:6–8: it means "pardon, the forgiveness of sins."[20] And with the pardon of the guilt—and dismissal thereby of the consequences—comes deliverance from "all servile fear" of God, which is replaced by confidence that God in his favor will bring to completion the work that God has begun.[21]

Wesley was adamant that justification does not involve God pretending that believers are righteous when they are not. God could not give way to such pretense in the judgment, for "the judgment of the all-wise God is always according to truth."[22] Rather, God has set in

---

20. Sermon 5.II.5 (*WJW* I.189); see most especially Rom 4:7–8.
21. Sermon 1.II.2–4 (*WJW* I.121–23); 8.II.1–2 (*WJW* I.237–238). "A filial fear of offending" God, such as loved children bear toward loving parents, would still have a place in Christian life.
22. Sermon 5.II.4 (*WJW* I.188). Wesley would affirm "imputed righteousness" insofar as "all believers are forgiven and accepted, not for the sake of anything in them, or of anything that ever was, that is, or ever can be done by them, but wholly and solely for the sake of what Christ hath done and suffered for them" (Sermon 20.II.5; *WJW* I.455), but adamantly opposed the notion that God judges me righteous "because another [that is, Christ] is so."

motion those divine forces that will make us righteous *if* we diligently give ourselves ever over to them. Thus, as Wesley stresses repeatedly, God has delivered those who trust in Jesus not only from the guilt of sin, but also its power. The former is justification, the latter is sanctification. The former is what God "*does for us* through his Son," the latter is what God "*works in us* by his Spirit" so that we become "actually just and righteous."[23] He affirms, with Paul, that "just as by the one man's [Adam's] disobedience the many were made sinners, so by the one man's [Jesus's] obedience the many will be made righteous" (Rom 5:19 NRSV), but with a distinctive accent: Jesus's obedient death and rising again on our behalf has secured for us also the new birth that inaugurates a life of righteousness.

2. Saved by Being Transformed into a New Person: The New Birth

The third chapter of John's Gospel gives us the phrase that, more than any other, has come to be associated with evangelical preaching and revivals: "no one can see the kingdom of God unless they are born again" (John 3:3 NIV). We must be born again because, though humanity was created in God's image and was meant to continue to bear that image through all its generations, we no longer bear that image by virtue of our natural birth alone.[24] The dialogue between Jesus and Nicodemus in John 3:3–8 was of great importance to Wesley's formulation of the gospel, leading him to identify the "new birth" alongside justification as an indispensable work of grace. While justification represents "what God does *for us*, in forgiving our sins," the new birth is "what God does *in us*, in renewing our fallen nature."[25]

Wesley draws an illumining parallel between natural birth and spiritual rebirth. Just as the unborn child has no perception of light, the faintest perception of sound, and almost no sensation from the outside world—there being a wall of flesh that separates the child from the world beyond the womb—so the natural person goes about not perceiving the light of God, hearing the voice of God as faint murmurings at best, and feeling almost nothing of the promptings of the Spirit. But when he or she is "brought to the birth"—*delivered* in multiple senses

---

23. Sermon 5.II.1 (*WJW* I.187).
24. Sermon 45.I.4 (*WJW* II.190).
25. Sermon 45.proem.1 (*WJW* II.187). See also Sermon 19.proem.2 (*WJW* I.431–32).

of the word—he or she enters upon a much larger existence, seeing "the light of the knowledge of the glory of God in the face of Christ" (2 Cor 4:6 NRSVue), hearing the voice of God with the ears of the spirit, feeling the love of Christ and the empowering guidance of the Holy Spirit, "and all his spiritual senses are then exercised to discern spiritual good and evil."[26]

This "new birth" is the gateway to sanctification, that process by which we "grow up in every way into him who is the head, into Christ" (Eph 4:15 NRSVue). But this new life must be sustained, even as natural life must be sustained. Wesley speaks therefore of a kind of spiritual "respiration" that sustains the life of the new person. God now continually breathes God's Spirit into the soul—the work of "sanctifying grace"—and, "as it is continually received by faith, so it is continually rendered back by love, by prayer, and praise, and thanksgiving. And by this new kind of spiritual respiration, spiritual life is not only sustained but increased day by day, together with spiritual strength and motion and sensation; all the senses of the soul being now awake, and capable of 'discerning' spiritual 'good and evil.'"[27]

This Godward orientation is essential to the life of the "new person" that begins with the "new birth." The believer who preserves an ongoing awareness of God's grace and reception of God's Spirit, and who "returns the grace he receives in unceasing love, and praise, and prayer," is thereby kept—and keeps himself or herself—from sin. Here 1 John plays a central role in Wesley's understanding of the good news.

> No one who abides in him sins; no one who sins has either seen him or known him. . . . Those who have been born of God do not sin, because God's seed abides in them; they cannot sin, because they have been born of God. (1 John 3:6, 9 NRSV)

The believers who keep the love of God in Christ ever in view, who maintain constant communion with God in inward conversation, "cannot voluntarily transgress any command of God, either by speaking or acting what he knows God hath forbidden." The divine "seed," which

---

26. Sermon 45.II.4 (*WJW* II.192–93); see also Sermon 19.I.4–10 (*WJW* I.433–35).
27. Sermon 19.I.8 (*WJW* I.434–35); see also Sermon 45.II.4 (*WJW* II.193).

Wesley identifies as "that loving, praying, thankful faith," will not permit them to do what would offend the Father they love and whose love they have known.[28] Where sin happens, it is a consequence of not "keeping" ourselves in the knowledge and experience of God's love and presence, not remaining in constant communion with God in our thoughts and intentions: "so long as 'he that is born of God keepeth himself' (which he is able to do, by the grace of God) 'the wicked one toucheth him not.'"[29]

It is in this same passage that the author of 1 John declares that "everyone who commits sin is a child of the devil; for the devil has been sinning from the beginning. The Son of God was revealed for this purpose, to destroy the works of the devil" (1 John 3:8 NRSV). Wesley understood the devil's work in particular as perpetuating the reign of sin in the lives of human beings. The Son of God did not take on mortal flesh and suffer death on the cross only for the purpose of reconciling alienated humanity to God. Rather, the incarnation, death, and resurrection of Jesus also had in view the undoing of the devil's work as here understood. Thus "we see in the clearest, strongest light, what is real religion: A restoration of man by Him that bruises the serpent's head [Gen 3:15], to all that the old serpent deprived him of; a restoration not only to the favour but likewise to the image of God, implying not barely deliverance from sin, but the being filled with the fullness of God. It is plain, if we attend to the preceding considerations, that nothing short of this is Christian religion."[30]

3. Saved by Dying with Christ and Rising to New Life

Wesley brings Johannine and Pauline streams of thought together as he considers the "new birth" and the new life that it begins. Here Romans 6:1–23, a passage that appears frequently throughout Wesley's

---

28. Sermon 19.II.1–2 (*WJW* I.435–36).
29. Sermon 19.II.7 (*WJW* I.437–38), quoting 1 John 5:18. There is an important discrepancy in the textual tradition of this verse—namely, the direct object of the clause "the one begotten of God keeps." In Codex Sinaiticus and the text known to Origen, the object is the reflexive "himself" (as in the KJV and CEB); in Codices Vaticanus and Alexandrinus, the object is "him" (rendered more inclusively as "them" in the NRSV, NIV, and NLT), so that the subject of the clause is now read as Christ (who can also be described as "the one begotten of God"). Wesley's Bible followed the former textual tradition.
30. Sermon 62.III.5 (*WJW* II.482).

preaching, plays an important role. A new *birth* is necessary because a *death* is also necessary—the death of "our old self" that lived enslaved to self-centered passions and thus to sin (Rom 6:5–6). This death is prerequisite to the flourishing of the new life (v. 4) into which the new birth initiates us. Christ's death and resurrection *for us* thus becomes something in which we are invited to participate. It becomes a means by which to leave behind one way of life—what Paul will elsewhere describe as the "old self, corrupt and deluded by its lusts" (Eph 4:22 NRSV)— and to step fully into another—what Paul elsewhere describes as "the new self, created according to the likeness of God in true righteousness and holiness" (Eph 4:24 NRSV). Here again we see the seriousness with which Wesley took Paul's vision for the life of those whom God had redeemed. There was no room for continuing "in sin" (Rom 6:1) and splitting one's devotion between God and self (or "sin"; vv. 15–16). The proper response to God's grace was to use one's redeemed life fully in service to God, in righteousness and holiness.

Sanctification, living into this "new life" and "new person," has two aspects. Negatively, it means that the believer abstains from committing sins: "Do not let sin exercise dominion in your mortal bodies, to make you obey their passions. No longer present your [bodily] members to sin as instruments of wickedness. . . . For sin will have no dominion over you" (Rom 6:12–14, my trans.). This includes both inward sin (indulging opinions, emotions, desires, or intentions contrary to God's will for God's creatures), such as Jesus had identified as already culpable in God's sight (see Matt 5:22, 28), and outward sin (acting upon such opinions, emotions, desires, or intentions).[31] Thus, while in justification believers are delivered from the condemnation of former sins, for they have been forgiven, it is through sanctification that believers are delivered from the condemnation of present and future sins, for they no longer *commit* them, since they no longer "walk after the flesh, but after the Spirit."[32]

Positively, it means that the believer gives his or her life in the body over to doing what pleases God rather than continuing to use the same to serve himself or herself. As Paul wrote, "Present yourselves to God

---

31. Sermon 40.II.4 (*WJW* II.106); 40.II.21–24 (*WJW* II.117–18).
32. Rom 8:4, quoted in Sermon 8.II.4 (*WJW* I.238).

as those who have been brought from death to life, and present your members to God as instruments of righteousness" (Rom 6:13 NRSV). This includes manifesting the fruit of the Holy Spirit in all its variety: "love, joy, peace, patience, kindness, generosity, faithfulness, gentleness, and self-control" (Gal 5:22–23 NRSV), with love, both of God and of one's neighbors for God's sake, being chief. It means living consistently from the "mind" that "was in Christ Jesus," promoting the interests of others before one's own (Phil 2:3–5 NRSV), and thus the full reversal—the complete redemption—of what human beings have become.[33] "Thus doth Jesus 'save his people from their sins.'"[34]

Wesley regarded sanctification as essential to salvation. It was the means by which people would be fitted with that "holiness without which no one will see the Lord" (Heb 12:14 NRSV).[35] But sanctification is not an onerous obligation laid upon the believer to bring about by his or her own power.[36] Rather, it is a path to deliverance generously provided for the believer and sustained in the believer by the same God who graciously pardoned his or her past sins—and Wesley was far more optimistic about the power of the Holy Spirit than he was pessimistic about the frailties of the disciple. It is not a prize that comes without cost, however, for it requires no less of believers than to die to the person that they were apart from the Holy Spirit (and would otherwise continue to be), so that the new person, re-created in the likeness of God, might indeed come alive and take shape fully within them.

Romans 6:23 has long been isolated as one of the paving stones on the "Romans Road," that familiar, if severely truncated, tool for evangelism:

---

33. Sermon 7.II.12 (*WJW* I.231).
34. Sermon 40.II.27 (*WJW* II.119), quoting Matt 1:21.
35. Sermon 45.III.2 (*WJW* II.195).
36. Wesley is consistently clear that, while it is the Christian's joy ever to be "loving God and keeping his commandments," we do not keep "them as if we were thereby to fulfil the terms of the *covenant of works*; as if by any works or righteousness of ours we were to procure pardon and acceptance with God. Not so: we are already pardoned and accepted through the mercy of God in Christ Jesus. Not as if we were by our own obedience to procure life, life from the death of sin. This also we have already through the grace of God. 'Us hath he quickened, who were dead in sin.' And now we are 'alive to God, through Jesus Christ our Lord'. But we rejoice in walking according to the *covenant of grace*, in holy love and happy obedience. We rejoice in knowing that 'being justified through his grace,' we have 'not received that grace of God in vain'; that God having freely (not for the sake of our willing or running, but through the blood of the Lamb) reconciled us to himself, we run in the strength which he hath given us the way of his commandments" (Sermon 12.20 [*WJW* I.312–13]).

"for the wages of sin is death, but the gift of God is eternal life in Christ Jesus our Lord" (NIV). Wesley deserves credit for holding this verse to its immediate context: "but now that you have been set free from sin and have become slaves of God, the benefit you reap leads to holiness, and the result is eternal life" (Rom 6:22 NIV). The gift of God is a new life that God empowers, a life for which God has liberated sin's captives—a life of holiness that leads to eternal life. The genuine "Romans Road" brooks no detours around sanctification.

Response and Benefits

The subheads set for the essays in this volume prove somewhat problematic for representing Wesley's gospel on his own terms, for he understood the gospel itself to speak of God's initiatives in empowering us both to respond and to live lives worthy of God's call. The gospel itself proclaims God's work "in us" to renew his image in our minds and hearts, with direct consequences for our living. This empowerment to "live a life worthy of the gospel" is also a principal "benefit" announced as part and parcel of the gospel. Moreover, Wesley understands the salvation that the gospel proclaims to encompass this whole process—both justification and sanctification, and these inseparably—unto final glorification. Our "response" to God's gracious initiatives likewise *indispensably* involves "living a life worthy of the gospel." Nevertheless, we will here speak of "faith" (in its fullest, Wesleyan sense) as the essence of our response to the gospel and the indwelling Holy Spirit as the principal benefit that makes the whole journey from justification through sanctification to glorification possible in the lives of those who possess, and act from, a genuine faith.[37]

A Living Faith

The benefits of pardon for what is past (justification) and holiness for the time that remains in the body (sanctification) are given to those who *trust* God's promise to provide the same in Jesus Christ. That is

---

37. Where justification signals our deliverance from "the *penalty* of sin" and sanctification our deliverance from "the *plague* [or disease] of sin," glorification means "our deliverance from the very *presence* of sin . . . in the eschatological recreation of all things" (Maddox, *Responsible Grace*, 144, 190).

to say, "faith" is the only thing required of human beings. There is no precondition for faith: we can never be sufficiently religious, good, or contrite "to merit acceptance."[38] We can only believe, accept the gift of pardon and restoration to God's favor, and live thenceforward "no longer for" ourselves "but for him who died and was raised" on our behalf (2 Cor 5:15 NRSV). But this faith must be more than "a bare assent to this proposition, 'Jesus is the Christ;' . . . indeed to all the propositions contained in our creed, or in the Old and New Testament."[39] Even demons have faith of this kind.[40] It must also involve "a sure trust in the mercy of God through Christ Jesus" and a trust of a very personal kind: not merely that "'God was in Christ, reconciling the world to himself, not imputing to them their former trespasses'" but also, in particular, that the Son of God "'loved *me* and given himself for *me*,'" with the result that "I, even I, am now reconciled to God by the blood of the cross."[41] Such faith, moreover, "cannot fail to show evidently the power of him that inspires it, by delivering his children from the yoke of sin, and 'purging their consciences from dead works'; by strengthening them so that they are no longer constrained to 'obey sin in the desires thereof'; but instead of 'yielding their members unto' it, 'as instruments of unrighteousness,' they now 'yield' themselves entirely 'unto God, as those that are alive from the dead.'"[42] In short, the faith by which the believer is "saved" (Eph 2:8) is "faith expressing itself through love" (Gal 5:6 NRSV). "Whosoever has this faith, thus 'working by love,' is not almost only, but altogether a Christian."[43]

The Work of the Holy Spirit

It is not only the human being who responds, however, for God's Holy Spirit plays an essential part in the process of turning this "good news" into lived experience. The Holy Spirit, the great gift secured by Jesus for those who put their trust in him (cf. Gal 3:2–5, 13–14), brings the

---

38. Sermon 6.3.1–4 (*WJW* I.214–15).
39. Sermon 18.I.2–3 (*WJW* I.418–19); see also Sermon 7.II.10 (*WJW* I.230).
40. Sermon 2.II.4 (*WJW* I.138); Sermon 1.I.2 (*WJW* I.119–20); see Jas 2:19.
41. Sermon 7.II.10 (*WJW* I.230), quoting 2 Cor 5:19 and Gal 2:20 (as also in Sermon 43.II.2 [*WJW* 2.161]). Emphases original.
42. Sermon 17.I.8 (*WJW* I.406), quoting Heb 9:14 and Rom 6:12–13.
43. Sermon 2.II.6 (*WJW* I.139).

good news of God's pardon, love, and adoption home to the person who will respond with genuine faith. It is the Spirit that "directly 'witnesses to my spirit that I am a child of God'; that Jesus Christ hath loved me, and given himself for me; that all my sins are blotted out, and I, even I, am reconciled to God."[44] This inward communication of God's pardoning love for the believer arouses love for God in response and, as a consequence of this, love for all those whom God loves.[45] It is also the basis for the believers' assurance of having been accepted by God into God's family and of standing before a God who is ever ready to help them live into the fullness of the salvation *from* sin and salvation *for* holiness that God has set before them.[46] This assurance frees believers from any servile fear of God, but also manifests itself in honoring God's kindness by responding to it with a glad heart and full energy rather than despising the riches of God's goodness (Rom 2:4).

The Holy Spirit continues to empower and guide believers toward this end as the agent of their sanctification. The Spirit nurtures the "mind" that was "in Christ Jesus" in and among believers (Phil 2:5), for the Holy Spirit is none other than "the Spirit of Christ" (Rom 8:9). Wesley considered this mind of Christ to be synonymous with the cultivation of "those holy 'fruits of the Spirit' which whosoever hath not 'is none of his'" (cf. Rom 8:9; Gal 5:22–23). The Spirit enables believers to put to death "the flesh with its passions and desires" (Gal 5:24) and, "in consequence of that *inward change*, to fulfil all *outward* righteousness, 'to walk as Christ also walked,' in the 'work of faith, the patience of hope, the labour of love'" (cf. 1 Thess 1:3; 1 John 2:6).[47] Wesley believed Paul when he wrote: "keep walking in the Spirit, and you will surely not carry out the cravings of the flesh" (Gal 5:16, my translation). The first clause issues a command; the second assures the doer of the certain results of obeying the command.[48] The Spirit makes a life of holiness

---

44. Sermon 10.I.7 (*WJW* I.274), quoting Rom 8:16 and recontextualizing Gal 2:20. See also Sermon 1.II.3 (*WJW* I.122); 7.II.11 (*WJW* I.231).
45. Sermon 10.I.8–9 (*WJW* I.274–75), where Wesley draws on 1 John 4:13–21.
46. Sermon 17.I.9 (*WJW* I.406).
47. Sermon 4.proem.4–5 (*WJW* I.160–61).
48. Paul uses a grammatical construction that grammarians label a "future emphatic negation." The NRSV (1989), incidentally, mistakes the form for a second imperative and thus misses Paul's point—an error not corrected in the NRSVue (2021).

genuinely practicable: "those who continue to sow to their own flesh will harvest only decomposition from the flesh; those who continue to sow to the Spirit will harvest eternal life from the Spirit" (Gal 6:7–8, my translation). A long obedience under the direction of the Spirit was precisely the path to final salvation.

So important was this work of the Spirit in the heart and life of the believer that Wesley identified the Holy Spirit himself as "this great salvation from sin,"[49] the divine gift that would enable each believer and the community of believers together to realize what is truly meant in the word "Christianity" beyond its pale shadows evident everywhere in Wesley's England.[50] Once again, it was not Wesley's optimism about what is possible for human beings to achieve that drove his understanding of the full scope of the good news in Jesus Christ. Rather, it was his confidence (indeed, his *faith*) in the working of the Holy Spirit to empower believers "to love God and their neighbour with a love which is as 'a well of water, springing up into everlasting life,'" to lead them "onto every holy desire, into every divine and heavenly temper, till every thought which arises in their heart is holiness unto the Lord."[51] The good news is also thus not something to be merely believed but to be experienced and lived as it transformed the believer and, through him or her, also transformed the conditions of those who would be impacted by the believer's Spirit-directed and other-centered life.

The transformation that the Holy Spirit brings about in the believer's life becomes itself a second source of assurance for believers. Their obedience to God's commandments (which Wesley summarizes as "the doing good to all men, the doing no evil to any, and the walking in the light" such as supported "a good conscience toward God"), the transformation of their character in the direction of the "mind" that was "in Christ Jesus," and the manifestation of the "fruit of the Spirit" would all provide evidence that the Holy Spirit was genuinely at work in them and thus that they had indeed been accepted as children of God, their heavenly Parent whose image they were growing increasingly to resemble.[52]

---

49. Sermon 40.II.12 (*WJW* II.111).
50. Sermon 4.proem.5 (*WJW* I.161).
51. Sermon 8.I.4 (*WJW* I.236), paraphrasing John 7:38–39.
52. Sermon 10.II.7, 12 (*WJW* I.280, 283), where Wesley draws on John 14:21 and 1 John 5:3.

Renewal of the Image of God

A principal benefit of the gospel as Wesley understood it is the recovery of the divine image that humankind lost through sin and alienation from God:

> The great end of religion is to renew our hearts in the image of God, to repair that total loss of righteousness and true holiness which we sustained by the sin of our first parent.... All that stops short of this, the renewal of our soul in the image of God, after the likeness of Him that created it, is no other than a poor farce.[53]

This renewal is linked consistently to the new birth. As our natural parents impressed upon us their own image (and thereby the image of fallen humanity) in our natural birth, so God renews his own image upon us when we are born from above:

> Know your disease! Know your cure! Ye were born in sin: Therefore, "ye must be born again," born of God. By nature ye are wholly corrupted. By grace ye shall be wholly renewed. In Adam ye all died: In the second Adam, in Christ, ye all are made alive.... Now, "go on from faith to faith," until your whole sickness be healed; and all that "mind be in you which was also in Christ Jesus!"[54]

With such language Wesley emphasizes that salvation involves a process of transformation—indeed, a process of *healing*—alongside and consequent upon salvation as a change of status before God. He also affirms that this transformation, whether expressed as recovering the image of God or having the mind that was in Christ Jesus or Christ living in the believer, is an indispensable benefit offered in the good news of Jesus Christ.

---

53. Sermon 44.III.5 (*WJW* II.185).
54. Sermon 44.III.5 (*WJW* II.185). Or, in the words of a typically omitted verse of "Hark! The Herald Angels Sing": "Adam's likeness now efface, / Stamp Thine image in its place: / Second Adam from above, / Reinstate us in Thy love."

A Faith That Works: Does Wesley Promote Synergism?

The accent in many presentations of "the gospel" falls on *receiving* God's grace. The Wesleyan gospel has a double accent that falls both on receiving *and responding* to God's grace. Wesley affirmed that, on the one hand, all that God would accomplish for and in us reflects God's gracious initiatives; he also affirmed that, on the other hand, God's grace must find us responsive and intent on giving due attention to the Giver and his sustaining help. Some have criticized Wesley for promoting a "synergistic" model of salvation, where "synergism" is a bad word because it suggests that human beings contribute something to their own salvation. It would be more accurate to say that Wesley had recovered a proper, contextual understanding of the inseparability of grace and grateful response that shaped *all* New Testament reflection on how God's grace became effective for the transformation of its recipients.[55] God's grace attains its full effect in the person who remains fully mindful of God's grace, who maintains his or her awareness of the "unceasing presence of ... the loving, pardoning God," who is fully responsive to grace, making an "unceasing return of love, praise, and prayer, offering up all the thoughts of our hearts, all the words of our tongues, all the works of our hands, all our body, soul, and spirit, to be an holy sacrifice, acceptable unto God in Christ Jesus."[56]

Philippians 2:12–13 is another key text for Wesley in this regard. It proclaims: "First, that grand truth, which ought never to be out of our remembrance, 'It is God that worketh in us, both to will and to do of his own good pleasure'; Secondly, the improvement we ought to make of it: 'Work out your own salvation with fear and trembling'; Thirdly, the connection between them: 'It is God that worketh in you'; therefore

---

55. On this point, see D. A. deSilva, *Honor, Patronage, Kinship and Purity: Unlocking New Testament Culture* (Downers Grove, IL: InterVarsity Press, 2000), 95–156; more briefly, idem, *The Letter to the Galatians*, NICNT (Grand Rapids: Eerdmans, 2018), 254–62. See also J. M. G. Barclay, *Paul and the Power of Grace* (Grand Rapids: Eerdmans, 2020). Randy Maddox (*Responsible Grace*, 151) intuited the relationship between Wesley's soteriology and the ethos of grace (reciprocity) in the New Testament world when he wrote: "A good image ... to capture salvation's co-operant nature is that of a *dance* in which God always takes the first step but we must participate responsively, lest the dance stumble or end. Besides highlighting the Divine prevenience in salvation, this image conveys that such responsive interaction takes place over time."

56. Sermon 19.III.2 (*WJW* I.442).

'work out your own salvation.'"⁵⁷ All depends upon God working in the believer "to will" and "to do," corresponding to inward and outward holiness. This conviction leads, however, to the necessary corollaries for Wesley: "God works; therefore you *can* work.... God works; therefore you *must* work."⁵⁸ Similarly, after giving full weight to the proclamation of salvation by grace through faith in Ephesians 2:8-9, Wesley insists that the divine purpose for that salvation become the business of all believers:

> It is incumbent on all that are justified to be zealous of good works. And these are so necessary that if a man willingly neglect them, he cannot reasonably expect that he shall ever be sanctified. He cannot "grow in grace," in the image of God, the mind which was in Christ Jesus; nay, he cannot retain the grace he has received, he cannot continue in faith, or in the favour of God.⁵⁹

Wesley was not particularly concerned where he fell in terms of the categories of monergism (whereby God, and God alone, is responsible for our salvation) and synergism. He was concerned, however, to proclaim and to live the full scriptural vision for the redeemed life. Randy Maddox rightly observes, however, that definitions of synergism vary and, with them, their applicability to Wesley's gospel. If the term indicates some *initiative* on the part of human beings, some unassisted contribution to their own deliverance, then the term would not apply to Wesley. If, however, the term merely indicates "the preservation of a role for grace-empowered human co-operation in salvation," then it applies to Wesley's gospel—but just as much to Paul's own!⁶⁰

Living a Life Worthy of the Gospel: Christian Perfection

So great was Wesley's confidence in the power of the Holy Spirit that he fully believed that God could make the Scriptures' vision for Christian life a reality in the experience of all believers who fully gave themselves over to the Spirit's work. The goal came to be known as *Christian*

---

57. Sermon 85.proem.4. (*WJW* III.202).
58. Sermon 85.III.1 (*WJW* III.206).
59. Sermon 43.III.5 (*WJW* II.164); cf. also Titus 2:14.
60. Maddox, *Responsible Grace*, 91.

perfection, reflecting the seriousness with which Wesley took Jesus's own charge to his disciples: "Be perfect, therefore, as your heavenly Father is perfect" (Matt 5:48 NIV). While the name led to grave misunderstandings both on the part of those who embraced and those who opposed this ideal, Wesley himself was quite clear concerning what "Christian perfection" was and was not. It did not promise perfection of knowledge, whether of God or the Scriptures, on the one hand, or of people and their circumstances and motivations on the other, for believers would always be subject to error and misperception—and "from wrong judgments wrong words and actions will often necessarily flow."[61] It did not promise freedom from the weaknesses imposed by our physical nature, from temptation, or even from the need to continue ever to "grow in grace."[62]

Christian perfection involved nothing more and nothing less than the full realization in experience of what Wesley read in the New Testament texts, believing as he did that "a promise is implied in every commandment of God"—that is, that God had commanded nothing that God would not also empower.[63] Wesley grounds this expectation also in explicit promises from God, notably drawing on texts from the Old Testament that he read as early announcements of God's plan to restore the divine image in human beings.

> The Lord your God will circumcise your heart and the heart of your descendants, so that you will love the Lord your God with all your heart and with all your soul, in order that you may live. (Deut 30:6 NRSV)

> I will sprinkle clean water upon you, and you shall be clean from all your uncleannesses, and from all your idols I will cleanse you. A new heart I will give you, and a new spirit I will put within you; and I will remove from your body the heart of stone

---

61. Sermon 76.I.3 (*WJW* III.73). Wesley understood the promise of the author of 1 John that "you have an anointing from the Holy One, and all of you know the truth" (1 John 2:20) to pertain only to matters necessary for salvation and not to matters of theological speculation (Sermon 40.I.1–2 [*WJW* II.100–101]).

62. Sermon 40.I.7–9 (*WJW* II.103–5).

63. Sermon 76.II.11 (*WJW* III.80). This might perhaps have arisen as an inference of the future indicative tense with which many commandments (e.g., the greatest two) are expressed, as opposed to the bare imperative.

and give you a heart of flesh. I will put my spirit within you, and make you follow my statutes and be careful to observe my ordinances. (Ezek 36:25–27 NRSV)[64]

"Christian perfection" is thus itself also ultimately sought and received on the basis of faith, for the one who would attain it must first believe that God promised it, that "what God hath promised he is able to perform," and, finally, that "He is able and willing to do it now."[65]

Wesley described Christian perfection as arriving at a place where one truly and consistently lived out the twin commandments that Jesus elevated as the weightiest: "you shall love the Lord your God with all your heart, and with all your soul, and with all your might" (Deut 6:5 NRSV); "you shall love your neighbor as yourself" (Lev 19:18 NRSV; see also Matt 22:37–40; Mark 12:29–31; Gal 5:14).[66] This twinned love becomes the driving impulse of the believer's life, indeed to the exclusion of every contrary impulse: "It is love excluding sin; love filling the heart, taking up the whole capacity of the soul. It is love rejoicing evermore, praying without ceasing, in everything giving thanks."[67]

"Christian perfection" could also be conceived of as living consistently from the "mind" that was also "in Christ Jesus," applied not only to the humility of our Lord but also to his self-giving, other-centered love, with the result that the believer now "walk[s] in love, as Christ loved us and gave himself up for us" (Eph 5:2 ESV).[68] Paul had arrived at the place where he could exclaim, "It is no longer I who live, but it is Christ who lives in me. And the life I now live in the flesh I live by faith in the Son of God, who loved me and gave himself for me" (Gal 2:20 NRSV); Paul longed and labored to see Christ "formed" similarly in his own converts (4:19). The good news was that the Spirit could and would indeed bring this to pass in all who believe, such that the believer's affections, intentions, and actions consistently manifested Christ, "the

---

64. These appear at the climax of the sermon "On Christian Perfection" (40.II.29 [*WJW* II.120–21]). See also the references to Deut 30:6 and Jer 31:31–34 as promises on which to build such a hope in Sermon 76.II.1–2 (*WJW* III.76–77).
65. Sermon 43.III.15–16 (*WJW* II.167–68).
66. Sermon 76.I.4 (*WJW* III.74).
67. Sermon 43.I.9 (*WJW* II.160).
68. Sermon 76.I.5 (*WJW* III.74).

righteous one," living in and through him or her—and thus restoring the believer to righteousness as well! This would mark the decisive putting aside of "your former way of life . . . your old self," and the putting on of "the new self, created to be like God in true righteousness and holiness" (Eph 4:22–24),[69] with the expectation of continuing in this new state "blameless" unto "the coming of our Lord Jesus Christ" (1 Thess 5:23).[70]

Wesleyan scholar William Abraham acknowledged that "the attainment of perfection involves a radical spiritual reorientation beyond conversion."[71] But the authors of the New Testament call for precisely such a "radical reorientation" as an indispensable facet of deliverance (of "salvation"). One might think of Paul's statement concerning Christ's purpose in his death: "he died for all in order that those who continued living might live no longer for themselves, but for him who died and was raised on their behalf" (2 Cor 5:15, my trans.). Christ's self-giving death here has not only the forgiveness of sins in view but also the "radical reorientation" of the remainder of one's life such as would restore the God-centered orientation that ought always to have characterized the creature. This is what it means that God should "save to the uttermost them that come unto God through him,"[72] that is, through Jesus: to be saved not merely from the penalty of sin, nor even from its power, but ultimately from its very presence in the lives of those Christ has redeemed and the Spirit has filled with the very life of Christ. It is this larger view of salvation that allowed Charles Wesley to speak of arriving at "Christian perfection" *as* salvation:

---

69. See Sermon 76.I.7 (*WJW* III.75). William Abraham claims with no little justification that "Wesley's aggressive optimism of grace fits much more aptly with the witness of Scripture and the wider canonical heritage of the church than does the systematic pessimism of Luther or Calvin or the sombre moderation of Anglicanism" ("Christian Perfection," in *The Oxford Handbook of Methodist Studies*, ed. James E. Kirby and William J. Abraham [Oxford: Oxford University Press, 2011], 598). On "entire sanctification," see further also Kevin M. Watson, *Perfect Love: Recovering Entire Sanctification, the Lost Power of the Methodist Movement* (Franklin, TN: Seedbed, 2021).

70. Sermon 76.I.9 (*WJW* III.75). It is worth noting that, in his final months, Wesley reflected on this particular teaching as "the grand depositum which God has lodged with the people called Methodists; and for the sake of propagating this chiefly He appeared to have raised us up" (John Wesley, "Letter to Robert Carr Brackenbury," September 15, 1790, in *The Letters of John Wesley*, ed. John Telford, 8 vols. [London: Epworth, 1931], 8:238).

71. Abraham, "Christian Perfection," 588.

72. Sermon 76.III.12 (*WJW* III.87), quoting Heb 7:25.

> *Finish, then, thy new creation,*
> *Pure and spotless let us be;*
> *Let us see thy great salvation*
> *Perfectly restored in thee;*
> *Changed from glory into glory....* [73]

Salvation begins with justification and the new birth. It attains its mark when we are "perfectly restored" to God's image and character (reflected, for example, in the fruit of the Spirit) as a result of being "in" Christ. It is consummated when

> "in heaven we take our place,
> [and] cast our crowns before Thee,
> lost in wonder, love, and praise."[74]

It thus carries with it the hope, indeed the assurance, of the verdict of being recognized as "righteous" on that day (that is, at the last judgment), since God will recognize Christ, "the righteous One," in all those whom the Spirit has thus transformed.[75]

As with the whole process of sanctification, it would be entirely wrong to regard "Christian perfection" as an obligation laid upon believers' shoulders to attain by their own efforts, though it would certainly call for diligence in attending to the means of grace and be worthy of

---

73. Charles Wesley, "Love Divine, All Loves Excelling" (*WJW* VII.546–47).
74. Wesley, "Love Divine, All Loves Excelling."
75. See Sermon 15.V.5 (*WJW* I.375): "Why should one of you be found on the left hand at his appearing? He 'willeth not that any should perish, but that all should come to repentance'; by repentance to faith in a bleeding Lord; by faith to spotless love, to the full image of God renewed in the heart, and producing all holiness of conversation" (i.e., "of conduct"). The context of Matt 25:31–46 (a vision of judgment) supports Wesley's implicit claim here that the journey toward a fullness of love, not only for God but also for neighbor, is an indispensable facet of the fuller journey from conversion to approval when "we must all appear before the judgment seat of Christ" (2 Cor 5:10, the text on which the sermon is based). See also Maddox, *Responsible Grace*, 172: "Wesley's understanding of the relation of justification and sanctification expressed structurally his fundamental conviction about the inherent relation of *grace* and *responsibility*: our very capacity for growth in Christ-likeness (New Birth) is contingent upon God's gracious pardoning prevenience (initial justification), while the continuance of God's acceptance (final justification) becomes contingent upon our responsive growth in Christ-likeness (sanctification). Justification is not a stage that we leave behind to enter sanctification, it is a facet of God's saving grace permeating the entire Way of Salvation."

the label "spiritual *disciplines*."[76] It remains, rather, the gracious promise of the work that God greatly desires to accomplish in believers by the power of God's Holy Spirit. It marks at last the restoration of the once-lost image of God in human beings, the full formation of the "mind" that was "in Jesus Christ," who is the image of the invisible God (Phil 2:5; Col 1:15), manifested in all that these human beings think, desire, and do in God's world. Human beings become at last what they were always meant to be, and the experience of *all* human beings is elevated as a result.

Conclusion

The good news that has come to the world in Jesus Christ is that human beings, once alienated from God and cut off from the life of righteousness, are reconciled to God through Jesus's obedient death. They are delivered "from the guilt and penalty for their former sins, renewed in God's image, and empowered by the Holy Spirit to love and serve God and neighbor in true holiness all the remaining days of their lives."[77]

Wesley was so intent that those whom God had redeemed should "conduct [them]selves in a manner worthy of the gospel of Christ" (Phil 1:27) that it can fairly be said that there is no genuine *reception* of the gospel apart from the wholesale reorientation of the life of the one who embraces it. The gospel calls us into a life of intentional discipleship. It bands us together to help one another to recognize and die fully to the life of the "old self," deformed by sin and the structures within which it took shape, and to learn to walk consistently in "newness of life" (Rom 6:4, 6), using all the spiritual disciplines and means of grace bequeathed to us by the rich heritage of the Christian tradition.[78] It calls for rigorous

---

76. The "means of grace" is the subject of the important sermons "The Circumcision of the Heart" (Sermon 17 [*WJW* I.401–14]) and "Self-Denial" (Sermon 48 [*WJW* II.238–50]), but it also undergirded the whole of the Methodist program of society, class, and band meetings, frequent participation in the Lord's Supper, daily study of the word, prayer, and self-examination, and commitment to devote oneself to works of mercy (tending both to one's neighbors' physical and spiritual needs). For other catalogs of what Wesley delineated as "means of grace," see Sermon 85 ("On Working Out Our Own Salvation") II.4 (*WJW* III.205), and the full discussion in Sermon 16 ("On the Means of Grace") (*WJW* I.378–97).

77. Adapted from John Wesley, Sermon 6.I.10 (*WJW* I.208).

78. On Wesley's band and class meetings and their formative effect, see Kevin M. Watson and Scott T. Kisker, *The Band Meeting* (Franklin, TN: Seedbed, 2017) and Kevin M. Watson, *The Class Meeting* (Franklin, TN: Seedbed, 2014).

commitment to discover the full dimensions of the life of the new person opened up through the power of the Holy Spirit, and it calls us to "let perseverance" in this commitment "attain its full effect, in order that [we] may be mature and complete, lacking in no respect" (Jas 1:4, my translation). It calls us not merely to "accept Christ" but to have the "mind" that was "in Christ"—to live a life devoted to serving the interests of others (Phil 2:3–5), both *divesting* ourselves of the practices that perpetuate harm and *investing* ourselves in doing "good to all people, especially to those who belong to the family of believers" (Gal 6:10), to the fullest extent of our capacity and imagination. For God's purpose is not only to "redeem us from all iniquity" but also to "purify for himself a people of his own who are zealous for good deeds" (Titus 2:14 NRSV; see also Eph 2:10).

Wesley himself pleads with us on precisely this point:

> "O do not take anything less than this for the religion of Jesus Christ! Do not take part of it for the whole! What God hath joined together"—justification and sanctification under the single banner of salvation!—"put not asunder! Take no less for his religion, than the 'faith that worketh by love' all inward and outward holiness. Be not content with any religion which does not imply the destruction of 'all the works of the devil'; that is, of all sin. . . . He is able, he is willing, to destroy it now, in all that believe in him."[79]

---

79. Sermon 62.III.6 (*WJW* II.483). Wesley refers here to Gal 5:6; 1 John 3:8.

RESPONSE TO DAVID A. DESILVA

SCOT MCKNIGHT

It brings me honor to respond to David deSilva's essay on the Wesleyan Gospel, in part because I have been reading his work for years and in part because it was his invitation to me to speak at Ashland Theological Seminary where I laid out my approach to the gospel that became the book *The King Jesus Gospel*. Kind host that he was, we did not engage in any serious disagreements. His essay in this volume is an example of extraordinary analytics of texts, ideas, and soteriology. His style presses the English language into elegant formulas and more than a dozen quotable turns of phrase. Take this as an example of many I could have chosen:

> Wesley thus combined both the Western Christian "*juridical* emphasis on guilt and absolution" and the Eastern Orthodox "*therapeutic* concern for healing our sin-diseased nature" in one unified view of God's saving work. (p. 111)

Or this one:

> This dual focus on God delivering us not only from the *guilt* and *penalty* of sin but also from the *power* of sin is the core conviction at the heart of the Wesleyan gospel. (p. 108)

Wesleyan soteriology becomes remarkably concise under deSilva's careful study, and I have learned much about Wesley in reading it. It could become a standard essay to be read in seminaries where students are taught the variety of post-Reformation theologies. The entire holiness tradition can benefit from deSilva's "The Wesleyan Gospel."

To expose the *method* of the Wesleyan gospel, deSilva mines the writings of John Wesley. He provides nearly eighty footnotes, and nearly all of them are from Wesley's own writings. Over the years I have profited from reading Wesley's sermons and a few of his writings. This essay not only confirmed what I had learned about Wesley's approach, but it deepened everything I (thought I) knew. Because Wesley was who he was, or how he was who he was, not only does deSilva support his observations by citing Wesley but he cites over and over the New Testament Scriptures so vital for Wesley's understanding of the gospel. Which is to say, Romans, with clear resonances of, and overlaps with, the contributions of the Reformation's emphasis on justification and sanctification. It may sound like someone running fingernails over a chalkboard if I say this, but there are considerable overlaps between John Murray's *Redemption Accomplished and Applied* and the substance of deSilva's definitions of terms in this chapter.[1]

Wesley, not unlike George Whitefield, Charles Finney, and D. L. Moody, had both a context and an agenda for their gospeling missions. Their concerns were not as simple as "getting people saved." Instead, their aim in preaching and teaching was repentance, regeneration, revival, and transformation, but not just of an individual but also of the whole of a city and nation. They all believed the problem of culture could only be resolved by a spiritual awakening. David deSilva is nothing if not a true heir of this holistic transformation in the Wesleyan tradition.

Thus, deSilva's essay shows that the gospel's aim in Wesley is holistic salvation, one that combines justification and sanctification. His conclusion says it this way:

> The good news that has come to the world in Jesus Christ is that human beings, once alienated from God and cut off from the life of righteousness, are reconciled to God through Jesus's obedient death. (p. 129)

Wesley saw the solution to the problems to be the separation of justification (as personal forgiveness for many) from sanctification, and

---

1. John Murray, *Redemption Accomplished and Applied* (repr., Grand Rapids: Eerdmans, 2015).

Wesley's gospel, through the importance of the Holy Spirit, laid claim to the essential importance of sanctification for salvation. Thus, "the gift of God is a new life that God empowers, a life for which God has liberated sin's captives—a life of holiness that leads to eternal life. The genuine 'Romans Road' brooks no detours around sanctification" (p. 118). Here is deSilva's full-orbed statement:

> The Wesleyan gospel thus proclaims not merely our change in status "from guilty to forgiven" but also our "gracious and gradual restoration . . . to God-likeness," particularly as the image of God is revealed in Jesus Christ. God's full work is only fully achieved when the believer is fully transformed—when he or she is no longer a person that contributes to the ongoing degradation of self and others, but has rather become a person *in* whom God has renewed a right spirit and *through* whom God works to elevate the dignity and experience of all those whom the restored believer touches. (pp. 108–9)

As such, deSilva's sketch of the Wesleyan Gospel makes the gospel about the benefits of redemption: regeneration, justification, and sanctification. It is vital for deSilva to demonstrate that Wesley was not a synergist and that humans are called to respond in trust and to deepen one's spiritual life by discipline, but the redemptive work is everywhere and always God's. One will have a hard time discovering a finer way of putting the importance of the work of God than observing how Wesley emphasized the Holy Spirit, something neglected (if I may) in some Reformed and Bible traditions. Thus, the Holy Spirit's work is an inward communication arousing love for God and all whom God loves.

Once again, it was not Wesley's optimism about what is possible for human beings to achieve that drove his understanding of the full scope of the good news in Jesus Christ. Rather, it was his confidence (indeed, his *faith*) in the working of the Holy Spirit to empower believers "to love God and their neighbour with a love which is as 'a well of water, springing up into everlasting life,'" to lead them "onto every holy desire, into every divine and heavenly temper, till every thought which arises in their heart is holiness unto the Lord" (p. 121).

No Wesleyan will leave the human wondering what must be done. DeSilva again:

> Wesley affirmed that, on the one hand, all that God would accomplish for and in us reflects God's gracious initiatives; he also affirmed that, on the other hand, God's grace must find us responsive and intent on giving due attention to the Giver and his sustaining help. (p. 123)

> It would be more accurate to say that Wesley had recovered a proper, contextual understanding of the inseparability of grace and grateful response that shaped *all* New Testament reflection on how God's grace became effective for the transformation of its recipients. (p. 123)

Such an approach to a soteriological-based gospel, with serious implication for human response, has always raised the importance of one's assurance of redemption, and deSilva anchors this in the Wesleyan approach to the gospel in the work of the Holy Spirit. One could hardly disagree.

I like, too, that deSilva broadens his scope so often to bring in other angles on this soteriological gospel. Hence, he discusses it all in terms I first learned in college, in the creation, fall, and restoration of humans as made in God's image. My reading at the time was about the fourfold state of humans in the work of, if I recall aright, Thomas Boston. What happens to the human over time in the work of redemption features as a prominent theme in deSilva's sketch of the Wesleyan Gospel.

Yet, I have never had inclinations for the Wesleyan concern with perfection. It was never the easy criticism that "no one is sinless" that attracted me, but the term itself just doesn't fit how the New Testament depicts the life of the followers of Jesus. The disciples of Jesus flop and fail often enough, and Paul's own writings, even when he thinks he's saying and doing the right thing, have their negatives—say, his confrontation of Peter in Galatians 2:11–14 or his carping in 2 Corinthians 10–13. If perfection be not found with them, then with whom?, would be my question. Yes, deSilva's nuances give perfection a fresh sense, but even then the term sticks in my throat. I leave his nuances for you to read:

> So great was Wesley's confidence in the power of the Holy Spirit that he fully believed that God could make the Scriptures' vision for Christian life a reality in the experience of all believers who fully gave themselves over to the Spirit's work. (p. 124)

> Wesley described Christian perfection as arriving at a place where one truly and consistently lived out the twin commandments that Jesus elevated as the weightiest: "you shall love the Lord your God with all your heart, and with all your soul, and with all your might" (Deut 6:5); "you shall love your neighbor as yourself" (Lev 19:18; see also Matt 22:37–40; Mark 12:29–31; Gal 5:14). (p. 126)

Yes, but saying it like this doesn't make it a reality in the life of enough people to give me much sanguinity about Wesleyan perfectionism.

I don't, however, agree with the Wesleyan framing of the gospel. Which is not to say I disagree with deSilva's own framing of the gospel but with the Wesleyan gospel itself. Here are my concerns.

First, there is for me a profound absence of Jesus-centeredness in the Wesleyan gospel. The first four books of the New Testament are about Jesus—every pericope tells us about Jesus, the human being. What he said, what he did, what happened in his life. That he lived, died, was buried, and was raised. There is not enough Jesus in the Wesleyan gospel. The Wesleyan gospel is too much soteriology, not enough Christology. Notice how it is framed, and again I quote deSilva's summary:

> John Wesley shares with the tradition of all historic Christian denominations the conviction that the gospel is "the power of God for salvation to everyone who has faith" (Rom 1:16 NRSV). This gospel, however, announces God's appointed means for deliverance from the *twin* problems that have beset human beings—their alienation from the life of God through disobedience and the deformation of their very nature as a consequence of that alienation. Thus the salvation that God's power works to accomplish is also twofold, incorporating both justification and sanctification: "by justification we are saved from the guilt of sin, and restored to the favour of God; by sanctification we are

saved from the power and root of sin, and restored to the image of God." (p. 107)

This set of lines tells us about the *benefits* of the gospel not, I would argue, the gospel itself. The gospel, according to 1 Corinthians 15:1–28, 2 Timothy 2:8, the gospel summaries in the book of Acts's sermons, is the story of Jesus, not the articulation of the soteriological facets of justification and sanctification. These are the benefits Jesus brings, but a method that focuses on the explicit statements of the gospel leads us to press forward a first step in Christology and not in soteriology. A true Christology leads to a soteriology, but a soteriological centering will lead, as this Wesleyan gospel reveals, to a gospel that does not need the stories in the Gospels to know what the gospel is.

Second, the Wesleyan gospel, when framed in the soteriological themes of justification and sanctification, lacks emphasis on the story of Israel, it lacks a substantive ecclesiology, and because of its focus on a soteriology framed by Romans, with a little John 3 tossed in to get the new birth, doesn't find room for the kingdom of God as taught by Jesus as the framing vision for his life and mission. Again, I'm not saying this of deSilva's own view of the gospel but of the Wesleyan gospel as framed in this essay.

Third, I am not persuaded of the strong separations one finds in much Reformation and post-Reformation thinking between justification and sanctification.[2] These terms overlap in attempting to describe the regenerative, redemptive, and transformative work of God in both the individual and the church/collective. What God has joined together let not our theologies split asunder. The act of God that redeems is an act that not only justifies but also sanctifies because the very act of redemption is not only a right-making but a holy-making—at the same time. We do not move down a path from justification to sanctification. We participate in both at the same time and all the time.

In offering these criticisms of the Wesleyan gospel I am not disagreeing with the soteriology or the many nuances characteristic of deSilva's careful study. I am rather contending the whole needs to be fronted with the story of Jesus—that is, with the gospel about Jesus before it gets to the gospel's benefits from Jesus.

---

2. Peter Toon, *Justification and Sanctification* (Westchester, IL: Crossway, 1984).

RESPONSE TO DAVID A. DESILVA

MICHAEL HORTON

William Willimon told me he has his students at Duke Divinity School ask themselves one question after they finish writing a sermon: "Would Jesus have had to have died on a cross for this sermon to be true?" Not only is Christ central in John Wesley's sermons, but our Savior's death in our place to reconcile us to God is a marked emphasis in which, especially through Charles Wesley's hymns, all of us rejoice. Doing a bit of genealogical work, I've discovered that about the very moment my ancestors touched American soil they became Methodists. I even have the worn Bible my great grandfather carried around as a circuit-riding preacher, attesting to the tradition's evangelistic zeal. Tucked in the Bible is his obituary written by his wife with the line, "Our people die well."

David deSilva emphasizes the inseparable bond between justification and sanctification, as salvation not only from guilt to acceptance but from bondage to restoration of God's image. "It was Wesley's particular genius," he says, "to join these two elements of Christian theology as inseparable and equally indispensable facets of the saving work of God" (p. 107). Happily, though, Lutheran and Reformed confessions join him in celebrating the "double cure."[1] All who are united to Christ are not only chosen, redeemed, and justified but are being sanctified and will be glorified (Rom 8:29–30). To imagine justification without sanctification is to "sever Christ," says Calvin, "to rend him in pieces."[2] Union with

---

[1]. By the way, I include here the Anglican tradition among the Reformed. The Thirty-Nine Articles as well as Cranmer's Homilies and the Book of Common Prayer are among the jewels of the English Reformed tradition.

[2]. John Calvin, *Institutes of the Christian Religion*, ed. John T. McNeill, trans. Ford Lewis Battles, 2 vols., The Library of Christian Classics (Louisville: Westminster John Knox, 2011), 3.1.1.

Christ is the overarching motif. "Blessed be the God and Father of our Lord Jesus Christ, who has blessed us in Christ" not just with some blessings but "with every spiritual blessing in the heavenly places" (Eph 1:3), which the apostle then enumerates. We do not make Jesus our personal Savior and then, if we seek a higher blessing, make him Lord of our lives. In fact, we don't *make* him anything: he *is* Savior and Lord. He rules to save and saves to rule, breaking both the guilt and dominion of sin.

DeSilva helpfully distinguishes the context of Wesley's spiritual biography (the "emergence of his understanding of the gospel") and the "theological context" of creation, fall, and salvation. I was surprised to learn that according to Wesleyan theology "human beings no longer possessed the natural or moral faculties of the divine image. People would henceforth be born in the likeness of Adam (Gen 5:3; cf. Rom 5:12–21) rather than that of God . . . 'void of the image of God'" (quoting Randy Maddox) (p. 110). And later: "we no longer bear that image by virtue of our natural birth alone" (p. 113).

This is a rather important point of difference, of which I had not been aware until now. It would suggest, ironically, that Wesley had a more radical view of total depravity than Calvinists! Reformed churches not only affirm but emphasize that it is the excellence rather than the image itself that has been lost. In agreement with patristic and medieval writers, Reformed theology maintains that *nothing* that is natural to humanity has been *eradicated*, yet *everything* has been *corrupted*. This is what is meant by "total depravity." Depravity is not the destruction but the pollution of something good. Human beings are totally good, as created good by a God who can only make good things. As Calvin stipulates, "For the depravity and wickedness, whether of man or of the devil, and the sins thence resulting, [are] not from nature, but from the corruption of nature."[3]

After the fall, no aspect of this good nature is left uncontaminated and unbound by original and actual sin. Yet even one who is spiritually dead is a person. After offering a litany of contributions to the arts, sciences, and human welfare by non-Christians, Calvin concludes, "Let us, accordingly, learn by their example how many gifts the Lord left

---

3. Calvin, *Institutes* 1.14.3.

to human nature even after it was despoiled of its true good."[4] In fact, Calvin again and again returns to this point to ground the call to justice: "Our neighbors, bear the image of God. To use him, abuse him, or misuse him is to do violence to the person of God who images himself in every human soul, the Fall notwithstanding.... Not only do I despise my flesh when I wish to oppress someone, but I violate the image of God which is in me."[5] This high office is not only a measure of our dignity but of our disgrace.

Much depends on how one defines the image of God. The ultimate goodness of which human nature has been "despoiled" is that true righteousness and holiness that would lead to everlasting life. Perhaps it is this perfection of the image that Wesley and his heirs have in mind. If so, we would agree that this has been lost, but not the image itself.

DeSilva's discussion of Wesley's view of justification reveals both similarities and differences with Lutheran and Reformed confessions. "Wesley defines justification and the 'reckoning of righteousness' in precisely the terms that Paul does in Romans 4:6–8: it means 'pardon, the forgiveness of sins'" (p. 112). While affirming that this is an essential part of justification, we add that the imputation of righteousness is included. The ungodly must not only be forgiven but judged as righteous in order to be accepted by God. Thus, the active obedience of Christ—his fulfillment of the law as the last Adam—is as essential as his atoning death for our justification.

It seems from deSilva's summary that for Wesley justification involves only the nonimputation of guilt (i.e., forgiveness) based only on the atonement. Indeed, Wesley "adamantly opposed the notion that God judges me righteous 'because another [that is, Christ] is so'" (p. 112). But this is the heart of the doctrine, from a Reformation perspective. It seems that Wesley would disagree, for example, with the Heidelberg Catechism's answer to the question, "How are you righteous before God?" (Q. 60):

---

4. Calvin, *Institutes*, 2.2.15.
5. Calvin, *Corpus Reformatorum* (*CR*) 50:251, quoted in John H. Leith, *John Calvin's Doctrine of the Christian Life* (Louisville: Westminster John Knox, 1989; repr., Eugene, OR: Wipf & Stock, 2010), 187. Leith provides several relevant quotes from *CR* 26:226–27, 304–5, 325, 351; 27:204; 33:660; 51:18; 55:402; 52:78.

Only by true faith in Jesus Christ. Although my conscience accuses me that I have grievously sinned against all God's commandments, have never kept any of them, and am still inclined to all evil, yet God, without any merit of my own, out of mere grace, imputes to me the perfect satisfaction, righteousness, and holiness of Christ. He grants these to me as if I had never had nor committed any sin, *and as if I myself had accomplished all the obedience which Christ has rendered for me,* if only I accept this gift with a believing heart.

DeSilva adds, "Wesley was adamant that justification does not involve God pretending that believers are righteous when they are not.... Rather, God has set in motion those divine forces that will make us righteous *if* we diligently give ourselves ever over to them" (emphasis original, pp. 112–13). "Pretending" is precisely what the Reformers' critics charged them with teaching. However, it is not a legal fiction when Christ's status before the law is *credited* (imputed) to believers. Moreover, seeing justification as setting in motion a process conditioned on our diligent cooperation is precisely what the Reformers rejected. A quotation from Maddox in a footnote adds, "Our very capacity for growth in Christ-likeness (New Birth) is contingent upon God's gracious pardoning prevenience (initial justification), while the continuance of God's acceptance (final justification) becomes contingent upon our responsive growth in Christ-likeness (sanctification)" (p. 128). I cannot see how this formulation differs from that of the Council of Trent.

The Reformers interpreted Scripture as teaching that justification is the future verdict of the final judgment rendered in the present: "There is therefore now no condemnation for those who are in Christ Jesus" (Rom 8:1 ESV). If a different verdict can be rendered in the future based on our "responsive growth" (i.e., good works), justification is relevant only for past sins. This is precisely Wesley's view, deSilva tells us. The good news is that believers are saved "from the guilt and penalty of *their former sins*" (emphasis added, p. 107). Unless one is "zealous of good works ... he cannot retain the grace he has received, he cannot continue in faith, or in the favour of God" (p. 124). "Thus, while in justification believers are delivered from the condemnation of former sins, for they have been forgiven," deSilva explains, "it is through sanctification that

"If we say we have no sin, we deceive ourselves, and the truth is not in us. If we confess our sins, he is faithful and just to forgive us our sins and to cleanse us from all unrighteousness" (1 John 1:8–9 ESV). It seems that the sort of Christian perfection commended by Wesley for "all believers who fully gave themselves over to the Spirit's work" (p. 124) must define *transgression* to mean involuntary shortcomings. DeSilva mentions "weaknesses imposed by our physical nature," "error and misperception—and 'from wrong judgments wrong words and actions will often necessarily flow'" (p. 125).

However, it is *sins* that we confess daily, and it is difficult to imagine how these failures to love God and our neighbor could be considered anything but voluntary. "Wesley described Christian perfection as arriving at a place where one truly and consistently lived out the twin commandments that Jesus elevated as the weightiest . . . 'It is love excluding sin'" (p. 126). This strikes me as a misreading of 1 John 4:18, which reads, "There is no fear in love, but perfect love casts out fear. For fear has to do with punishment, and whoever fears has not been perfected in love" (ESV). First, it is not "love excluding sin" in general, but "love casting out fear." Second, it is "fear of *punishment*" (*kolasis*), says John. To the extent that we fear God's punishment, our response is cowering resentment rather than love. Third, the phrase "drives out" (*exō ballei*), used for Jesus casting out demons, expresses this incompatibility. Love and fear of punishment are no more compatible *within* us than justification and condemnation are *toward* us. Yet they often do dwell together, which is why the promises of the gospel must always be driving out the threats of the law in our conscience. In short, John's point seems to be not only different than Wesley's but to engender the opposite response.

When asked, "But can those who are converted to God perfectly keep these commandments?" I can only answer honestly along with the Heidelberg Catechism, "No, but even the holiest of people, while in this life, have only a small beginning of this obedience; yet so, that with a sincere resolution they begin to live, not only according to some, but all the commandments of God" (Q. 114).

A Reformed understanding of the Christian life affirms both the "small beginning" and the "sincere resolution." Only the believer can experience this tension. Those who are not regenerate feel regret, believers are delivered from the condemnation of present and future sins, for they no longer *commit* them, since they no longer 'walk after the flesh, but after the Spirit'" (emphasis original, p. 116). Perhaps I am misunderstanding the position, but the argument seems to go like this: present and future justification depend on sanctification. Further, this sanctification that determines the final justification is not merely a sincere beginning and continuance in modest obedience (as in the Roman Catholic view) but is Christian perfection. We would agree that nothing short of complete, perfect, and perpetual obedience is the ground of our justification, but that this righteousness is found in Christ rather than in us. Our sanctification remains incomplete, while our justification remains perfect and secure. To suggest that a believer is accepted as righteous currently because he or she does not commit sins is to make the believer's obedience the ground of justification. Is it no longer necessary to pray daily, "Forgive us our debts . . ."? And if we do sin, are we justified again each time we confess?

The note of conditionality continues in deSilva's treatment of Wesley's doctrine of the new birth: "The believer who preserves an ongoing awareness of God's grace and reception of God's Spirit, and who 'returns the grace he receives in unceasing love, and praise, and prayer,' is thereby kept—and keeps himself or herself—from sin" (p. 114). The idea of returning grace *to God* is foreign to our tradition. God is the only giver of grace; what we return is gratitude. This renders love, praise, and prayer a means of thanksgiving rather than a means of grace. "The believers who keep the love of God in Christ ever in view, who maintain constant communion with God in inward conversation," Wesley teaches, "'cannot voluntarily transgress any command of God, either by speaking or acting what he knows God hath forbidden'" (p. 114).

This is quite different from confessing, with the Heidelberg Catechism above, that "I am still inclined to all evil." According to both Lutheran and Reformed churches, the believer is *simul iustus et peccator*, just and sinner at the same time. This paradox is evident in the paradox of Romans 6 and 7. Assuming that Paul is speaking autobiographically of the normal Christian experience, we confess that every believer is always completely worthy of everlasting life in Christ and worthy condemnation in ourselves; fully alive in Christ and yet volunta transgressing the very commands that we know are true and remorse, and even guilt, but they do not acknowledge, "Against you, you only, have I sinned and done what is evil in your sight, so that you may be justified in your words and blameless in your judgment. Behold, I was brought forth in iniquity, and in sin did my mother conceive me" (Ps 51:4–5 ESV). Paul could say, "How I love your law" even when he was breaking it (Rom 7:12, 22). That is why only the believer experiences himself or herself as the "wretched man" of verse 24.

As deSilva's summary makes clear, Wesley eschewed any form of Pelagianism. It is because God works that we work. Even our cooperation is dependent on God's grace. Pelagius held that God would never command something that one did not have the moral ability to fulfill, while Wesley taught that God would never command something that he did not have the grace to empower. What we need is a new birth, not a new leaf. I also understand Wesley's reaction against nominal church membership and antinomian tendencies in hyper-Calvinism. The Spirit's empowerment for a life of love and holiness is a crucial emphasis of Scripture. We share the Wesleyan opposition to antinomianism, expressed in the attitude, "God likes to forgive; I like to sin—what a perfect relationship!" But sometimes we assume, "I'm just a sinner saved by grace—what did you expect?" We should expect more—because God gives more.

Yet I worry about a weakening of the law that is required to accommodate the doctrine of Christian perfection and a weakening of the gospel by "ifs, ands, or buts." I appreciate the affirmation of our need always for God's grace, but those who are "dead" in "trespasses and sins" need not only *prevenient* grace that makes faith possible but *effective* grace that grants us faith. We need to hear that "even when we were dead in our trespasses, [he] made us alive together with Christ—by grace you have been saved" (Eph 2:5 ESV). This is not the result of cooperation, but also not of coercion. "Meanwhile," notes Calvin, "we deny not the truth of Augustine's doctrine, that the will is not destroyed, but rather repaired, by grace—the two things being perfectly consistent."[6] Once we are regenerated by God's effectual grace, we do begin to yield obedience to God's commands. Yet the imperative always rests

---

6. Calvin, *Institutes* 2.5.15.

on the indicative: "Since we live by the Spirit, let us keep in step with the Spirit" (Gal 5:25).

Wesley's view strikes me as offering gospel at the beginning but a new law for the rest of the journey. DeSilva quotes William Abraham: "The attainment of perfection involves a radical spiritual reorientation beyond conversion" (p. 127). At best, it seems to divide believers into merely converted and perfect. However, if present and future justification depend on perfection (no longer committing sin), then are those who are *merely* converted even justified? Forgiveness is a marvelous gift. But apart from the "breastplate of righteousness"—being clothed in Christ's perfect righteousness by imputation—I cannot repel Satan's accusations for a moment. When it comes to finding rest for the conscience, the law gives no quarter, only accuses, and makes only conditional promises with threats for transgression. As John Murray said, "The law can do no more in sanctification than in justification." It can only tell me what I must do; the gospel tells me that it's done. And only on the basis of that triumphant indicative can I even begin to hold up my head in praise and prayer, looking up to Christ in faith and out to my neighbor in love.

RESPONSE TO DAVID A. DESILVA

JULIE MA

It was a pleasure to read David deSilva's essay, as his Wesleyan tradition is not too far from my own Pentecostal tradition, which will be clear even as there are things I would nuance differently or unpack in other ways. Several thoughts crossed my mind as I read deSilva's essay.

First, the study of the Wesleyan Gospel is well presented by deSilva. He accurately reflects the gospel from the great tradition of the church that "it is the power of God for salvation to everyone who has faith" (Rom 1:16 NRSV). His study further contends that the gospel proclaims God's preferred approach for delivering people from two issues that have plagued them: their separation from God's purposes via disobedience and the resultant marring of their fundamental nature. Therefore, deSilva rightly points out how justification and sanctification are both included in the twofold salvation that God seeks to bring about; by justification, we are saved from the guilt of sin and restored to God's favor; by sanctification, we are saved from the power and root of sin and restored to the image of God.

Unique to deSilva is his resourcing Wesley's specific brilliance in combining these two tenets of Christian theology as integral and equally crucial components of God's redemptive activity. Wesley insisted that his fellow preachers proclaimed the whole gospel, justification and sanctification, anterior to glory, not tearing asunder what God had united but giving equal attention to Christ dying for us and Christ living in us. DeSilva further goes on to note that the fundamental belief at the center of the Wesleyan Gospel is that God will free us from sins and guilt and its consequences. Both the Son and the Holy Spirit are involved in salvation; the Son gives himself up as a propitiation for the sins of the world, the Holy Spirit renews mankind in that image of God wherein they were formed, and together they operate in us both to will and to work for his good pleasure (Phil 2:13). As a Pentecostal, this emphasis on the Holy Spirit meets with my warm approval.

Second, deSilva notes the consequences of our intentional disobedience of and alienation from our Creator, as symbolized in the sin of Adam, and the fact that humankind was created in the image of God provides the theological backdrop for the Wesleyan Gospel. I concur because Genesis 1:26–27 states that God made humans in his image, which Wesley interpreted to mean that humans are reflections of God. This meant that God's moral nature, which is "true righteousness and holiness" (Eph 4:24) and "love," was initially shared by humanity. God's freedom was also shared by humanity at first (1 John 4:8). Rightly then, deSilva argues that people, alienated from a life-giving connection with God, no longer possessed the natural or moral capabilities of the divine image. He further presents the theological viewpoints of Randy Maddox, arguing that the core of the first sin was the breaking of this relationship, the desire to be independent of God. The result of this is that everyone descended from Adam enters the world spiritually dead to God, fully dead in sin, completely devoid of God's life, devoid of the image of God, and devoid of all the righteousness and holiness in which Adam was created (Gen 5:3; cf. Rom 5:12–21). I concur because deSilva accepts the realities of sin, death, and spiritual death, something Pentecostals take very seriously.

Third, deSilva's section on "Saved by Being Transformed into a New Person: The New Birth" is highly interesting. As things proceed, deSilva makes useful points about the necessity of being born again, as based on John 3:3, "no one can see the kingdom of God unless they are born again." He argues, "We must be born again because, though humanity was created in God's image and was meant to continue to bear that image through all its generations, we no longer bear that image by our natural birth alone" (p. 113). In the conversation between Jesus and Nicodemus in John 3:3–8, Jesus leads off the conversation with an attempt to identify the "new birth." My question is how could Nicodemus be born again, and further, how are Christians born again? Does the Bible tell us about it? If so, deSilva should provide biblical references for a clear understanding. And the next question that arises is: What are a person's duties as a newborn believer?

There is much to agree with here because in my Pentecostal tradition "new birth" is the gateway to sanctification, a process by which we "grow up in every way into him who is the head, into Christ" (Eph 4:15 NRSV). But this new spiritual life must be sustained, even as natural life must be sustained by nourishment. So it is right to agree with deSilva agreeing with Wesley that sanctification is "essential to salvation" (p. 117). That is valid, but one important thing that should be borne in mind is this: we have to acknowledge that sanctification is a lifelong process, not a one-time occurrence, not a passing attainment of perfection that then ebbs away. Although we come to the sphere of salvation and become a child of God, transformation and sanctification will not happen immediately but must be nurtured and nourished. Many times, Christians fail due to human weaknesses, and we must seek God's power, strength, and help. Through such a process, we can experience transformation and further sanctification. So part of my disagreement with deSilva is on the lifelong struggle to sustain our sanctification. It is a battle, a duty, a command, and a power that we aspire to live in.

Fourth, I would like to comment on deSilva's account of holiness as part of sanctification. I suspect something is missing. He notes that we must pursue the "holiness without which no one will see the Lord" (Heb 12:14 NRSV). True enough! But it would be great if deSilva reflected more on Wesley's perspective on holiness as a correlation with God's character and ultimately derived from the holy constitution of the Holy Trinity. Wesley's view of sanctification is closely tied to his robust Trinitarian theology. God's distinctiveness is manifested in its deepest respect in the person of Jesus Christ, who is the exalted Lord and whose dynamic presence is manifested in the world via the work of the Holy Spirit. Jesus brings us into the holiness of the Father by giving us the Holy Spirit for our holiness and hope. This Trinitarian aspect of Wesley's sanctification and holiness also necessitates reflecting on the practical side of a sanctified and holy life for the believer. For example, in showing God's love in our relationship with others, Henri Nouwen rightly stated that if our need for solitude and prayer is not motivated by a desire to better the lives of those around us, we will quickly grow disinterested in our own spiritual lives. Finding fellowship in the outside world, in warm and intimate relationships that are growing and expanding, is the best insurance for a safe voyage within. Other than by showing them our love, we have no other method to influence them to be receptive to relationships with God and their fellow humans. Otherwise, people would continue to be fortresses that can be overpowered and brought under control but are closed to new connections. Therefore, our Christian spirituality is lived out and manifested through love and relationships. I'm of the mind that deSilva's notion of holiness needs to be combined with Wesley's Trinitarian theology and even an ecclesiology based on friendship.

Fifth, deSilva rightly observed that faith needs to be active. He notes that those who put their faith in God's promise centered on Jesus Christ are granted the benefits of forgiveness for the past (justification) and holiness for the present (sanctification). DeSilva notes that the only thing needed from people is "faith." But deSilva seems to major on the passive part of faith, as something believed, truths accepted, benefits conferred. I'm more of the mind that for this faith to be effective, it must go beyond a simple acceptance to this claim, Jesus is the Christ, to every claim made in our creed or the Old and New Testament. As a Pentecostal, I want to emphasize more on faith as living and lived, not belief and boundaries, but a trust that results in obedience, love, holiness, action, activity, and community.

Sixth, deSilva argues that a Godward orientation is essential to the life of the "new person" that begins with the "new birth." I concur because the believer receives God's Spirit and rests in God's grace, which if cultivated and curated, keeps one from sin. I think deSilva wonderfully captures how the spiritual life is not only sustained but increased day by day, together with spiritual strength and motion and sensation; all the senses of the soul are now awake and capable of discerning spiritual good and evil. God's continual breathing of his Spirit into the soul is called the work of "sanctifying grace," and as it is continually received by faith, it is constantly rendered back by love, prayer, praise, and thanksgiving.

Seventh, deSilva writes, "Wesley was far more optimistic about the power of the Holy Spirit than he was pessimistic about the frailties of the disciple" (p. 117). Very true! The Holy Spirit empowers Christians. It looks like this empowerment has to do with internal cultivation, sowing holiness into our hearts, nurturing the fruit of the Spirit, and tending to our virtues in faith and love. These are all marvelous. However, what needs to be stressed is our need for divine empowerment. As Acts 1:8

says, "But you will receive power when the Holy Spirit comes on you; and you will be my witnesses in Jerusalem, and in all Judea and Samaria, and to the ends of the earth." Through experiencing empowerment, the church needs to implement the task of being the witness of Christ and bringing in the souls who are in the darkness. Isaiah 49:6 notes that the task of being "a light for the Gentiles" is given to his Servant, Israel. Such a witness should not be carried out in Israel's power but rather through the Holy Spirit who would come like rain on the dry and thirsty land. So Israel must be a witness on behalf of the Lord. In Acts 13:47, Paul applies this promise to himself and Barnabas: "I have made you a light for the Gentiles, that you may bring salvation to the ends of the earth." Both the New Testament and Old Testament indicate the role of the Spirit's empowerment, which is being a witness to the gentiles, to bring them to hope and holiness, love and life, redemption and renewal. I wished deSilva had more on the Spirit as God's power for mission and witness.

Finally, I must offer some passing comments on the Wesleyan notion of perfectionism. Wesley took very seriously Jesus's admonition to his disciples, "Be perfect, therefore, as your heavenly Father is perfect" (Matt 5:48 NIV). This verse, and Wesley's exposition of it, became the basis of the idea that Christians really can in this life attain perfection. DeSilva explains what Wesley's view was and wasn't. The topic has caused much confusion and been liable to misunderstanding. Because believers would always be prone to error and misperception, and because "from wrong judgments wrong words and actions will often necessarily flow" (p. 125), it did not guarantee the perfection of knowledge, whether of God or the Scriptures on the one hand, or people and their circumstances and motivations on the other. It did not guarantee escape from temptation, from the limitations imposed by our bodily nature, or even from the need to constantly "grow in grace."

I am grateful to deSilva's exposition of a Wesleyan gospel that supports much of my own Pentecostal perspective and buttresses my own attempt to resource the Wesleyan tradition as a Pentecostal believer.

RESPONSE TO DAVID A. DESILVA

SHIVELY T. J. SMITH

The "sound" of David deSilva's essay on the Wesleyan aim of "living a life worthy of the gospel" resonates with me as a member of the African Methodist Episcopal (AME) Church.[1] Much in deSilva's treatment reminds me of the prophetic message reverberating through many of the Wesleyan communities I engage as member, teacher, preacher, and scholar. My gratitude for deSilva's contribution cannot be overstated. From his use of John Wesley's autobiography, to how he highlights the metaphors and images populating Wesley's sermonic expositions, to the thick descriptions about the meaning of terms like justification and sanctification—deSilva curates a rich immersion in Wesleyan biblical thought and perspective.

In his essay, multiple images and biblical passages collide in Wesleyan parlance on matters of justification (e.g., Rom 3:23–25), sanctification (e.g., Rom 6:12–14), and the life and death of Jesus. While the commitments and teachings of John Wesley shape deSilva's description of the content and significance of the gospel, he paints rich imagery funding the Wesleyan Gospel as generative and refreshing. DeSilva, in turn, recasts the Wesleyan Gospel in a form that can awaken the imaginations of Bible readers and biblical theologians. I found myself pondering the metaphors, which shape my thinking about the gospel literature and tradition. Water. Wind. Breath. Light. Fire. Birth. The biblical register

---

1. The notion of "sound" recalls one of Howard Thurman's famous phrases, "the sound of the genuine." In one of his essays, he describes it this way: "one man's response to the sound of the genuine in another man is to ascribe to the other man the same sense of infinite worth that one holds for oneself." There is much in deSilva's essay I am grateful for as I reflect on my own Methodist gospel roots. See Howard Thurman, "Excerpt from *The Luminous Darkness* (1965)," in *A Strange Freedom* (Boston: Beacon, 1998), 248.

of images for reading, hearing, believing, and acting out the gospel message is infinite, and deSilva's essay is a refreshing reminder of this fact.

Represented as a rich repository of gospel imagery, deSilva's description of the Wesleyan Gospel shifts when considering Africana Methodist gospel-reading spaces.[2] It offers an important critical edge to understanding sanctification, for instance. With accuracy, deSilva defines Wesley's understanding of sanctification as including both "inward sin (indulging opinions, emotions, desires, or intentions contrary to God's will for God's creatures)" and "outward sin (acting upon such opinions, emotions, desires, or intentions)" (p. 116). Yet, deSilva's view on the twofold aspect of Wesleyan understandings about sanctification misses the prophetic insight characteristic of Africana Wesleyan gospel interpretations.

Africana Wesleyan communities historically question, in demonstrative ways, a Wesleyan Gospel that touts itself as living out the process of justification, sanctification, and ultimately glorification without challenging the matter of separation and segregation it imposes and upholds among its Christian siblinghood. For example, the movement toward founding the AME Church began with African American Christians departing from St. George's Methodist Church in Philadelphia in 1787. Founding figures like Richard Allen and Absalom Jones were emboldened by their Wesleyan faith to leave their "assigned" pews and practice their Christian freedom by praying at the front of the church as equal members in their racially mixed Christian community. In response, their Wesleyan Christian siblings violently ripped them from praying at the altar because they were "out of place" in the congregation.

As deSilva describes, Wesley understood a "principal benefit of the gospel" to be "the recovery of the divine image that humankind lost through sin and alienation from God" (p. 122). But the gospel, as Africana Wesleyan communities understand it, also requires redress and repair of the sin and alienation human beings forge among themselves.

---

2. *Africana* will be used in correlation with African American to recognize how Wesleyan gospel traditions permeate the African diaspora. Indeed, the African Methodist Episcopal church is a worldwide Wesleyan tradition with diverse Africana histories and communities interacting as a Christian kinship and connectional body. *Africana* signals that diversity. *African American* will be used alone when speaking about a specific historical moment located within an African American Wesleyan body.

From this perspective, the Wesleyan gospel inherently carries social critique that turns the mirror on the gospel carriers who proclaim salvation while mandating exclusion, difference, and oppression. An Africana Wesleyan perspective looks for the explicit commitment of a gospel of a grace to full inclusion of all human beings.

In an 1839 address demanding the end of slavery titled "Slavery Brutalizes Man," Daniel A. Payne, former bishop of the AME Church (elected in 1852), depicted the African American Wesleyan gaze as one defined by observation and interpretation.

> The slaves are sensible of the oppression exercised by their masters; and they see these masters on the Lord's Day worshiping in his holy Sanctuary. They hear their masters professing Christianity; they see their masters preaching the Gospel; they hear these masters praying in their families, and they know that oppression and slavery are inconsistent with the Christian religion. . . . I have heard the mistress ring the bell for family prayer, and I have seen the servants immediately begin to sneer and laugh; and have heard them declare they would not go in to prayers, adding, if I go in she will only just read, "Servants obey your masters"; but she will not read, "Break every yoke, and let the oppressed go free."[3]

According to Payne's description, gospel believers notice and interpret the actions of Christian powerholders. As Payne explains, they question where in the Bible readers go to assert God's mandates and what they avoid. Driving their interrogation of gospel reading practices is the question, "To what end do they read the Bible this way?" Africana gospel readers record the patterns of Christian proclamation used to enslave and dehumanize, as well as those patterns that liberate, humanize, and care for all God's creation.

DeSilva records Wesley's correlation between sin and disease. Wesley says, "Know your disease! Know your cure! Ye were born in sin:

---

3. Daniel A. Payne, "Slavery Brutalizes Man," in *Lift Every Voice: African American Oratory, 1787–1900*, ed. Philip Sheldon Foner and Robert J. Branham (Tuscaloosa: University of Alabama Press, 1998), 176–77.

Therefore, 'ye must be born again,' born of God" (p. 122). For Africana gospel readers, Wesley's metaphor of sin as disease does not merely address internal moral corruption. The disease of sin is external and social, manifesting in the interrelationships and caste systems Christian stakeholders install and support. Gospel proclamations that uphold forms of separation and segregation, suppression of voting rights, inequitable educational opportunities, and limited healthcare for those without the financial resources to afford it themselves are potential sites for critique.

And yet, when one returns to John Wesley's gospel interpretations, as deSilva's essay so masterfully achieves, one discovers the seeds of authentic Christian community and care. It aligns well with Africana gospel-reading imperatives shaped by our stories of faith, resilience, and life. The Wesleyan gospel couples the theological context of biblical themes like human creation (Gen 1:26–27), new birth (John 3:3), and grace (Eph 2:8–9) with moral imperatives like justice (Eph 4:24; or "righteousness," as *dikaiosynē* is often translated) and love (1 John 4:8). In a collection of his prayers, Wesley resources his own religious experience and revelatory moment as an authoritative source for describing the responsibility of Christian communities to each other: "I continue to dream and pray about a revival of holiness in our day that moves forth in mission and creates authentic community in which each person can be unleashed through the empowerment of the Spirit to fulfill God's creational intentions."[4]

When other contexts beyond John Wesley articulate the implications of his gospel perspectives from their social and spiritual realities, however, Wesley's "Godward orientation" recalibrates. Some matters are not quickly glossed over. Matters of whole human experience uncolored by social constructions of race, class, gender, and identity (to name a few) become enormously important. Africana Methodist perspectives question gospel messages that do not speak directly to the inequities that are possible not just in the world but within *gospel*-proclaiming communities across the world. By so doing, the tenor of many potent

---

4. *How to Pray: The Best of John Wesley on Prayer* (Uhrichsville, OH: Barbour, 2007), 70. It should be noted that there is some debate as to whether the prayer actually originated with Wesley.

images of gospel experience that Wesley deploys deepens. The image of new birth, for example, casts the gospel as a message that is *in motion*. The gospel unfolds as an active and dynamic movement in believers' lives. In addition to Wesley speaking "of a kind of spiritual 'respiration' that sustains the life of the new person" (p. 114), deSilva notes the gospel is a way of being godlike that compels believers forward. The initial moment, which demands the process of maturation and expansion, is birth. DeSilva says, "Wesley draws an illumining parallel between natural birth and spiritual rebirth. . . . When he or she is 'brought to the birth'—*delivered* in multiple senses of the word—he or she enters upon a much larger existence, seeing 'the light of the knowledge of the glory of God in the face of Jesus Christ' (2 Cor 4:6 NRSVue)" (pp. 113–14, emphasis his). Resourcing the human experiences of birth and growth, the Wesleyan view extracts gospel meaning from both gospel literature and the way those who read the gospel live with it—be it faithfully or unfaithfully. In speaking about the simple theory of incarnation threaded through the spirituals, Howard Thurman cites one song as a reference to how God and Jesus are used interchangeably while talking about the faithful soul:

> *Did you ever see such a man as God?*
> *A little more faith in Jesus,*
> *A preaching the Gospel to the poor,*
> *A little more faith in Jesus.*[5]

In considering the faithful gospel message located in Wesleyan gospel readings, I cannot help but reflect on my tradition as an itinerant elder in the AME Church, the oldest Methodist tradition specifically of African American origin. I serve at Metropolitan AME Church as a resident scholar, which sits on the oldest plot of land owned by African Americans in the capital city of the United States, Washington, DC. It is a church of Frederick Douglass, Paul Laurence Dunbar, and others. It is the church that was attacked and vandalized by the Proud Boys in December 2020 while many people quarantined at home during the

---

5. Howard Thurman, *Deep River and The Negro Spiritual Speaks of Life and Death* (Richmond, IN: Friends United Press, 1990), 38.

COVID-19 pandemic.[6] Even before that public spectacle, however, our Africana/African American church space, which is a member of the Wesleyan gospel tradition, required security at the door because we had received threats of attacks in the past. The events of the massacre of the Emanuel Nine in Charleston, South Carolina on June 17, 2015, at Emanuel AME Church, is an eerie echo back to some of the worst acts of Christian hatred in twentieth-century America—such as the 1963 bombing of a Baptist Birmingham Church by Christian-proclaiming hate groups. These are not relics from the past for my Wesleyan gospel-proclaiming congregation. We face an ever-present danger as we faithfully congregate in Christian faith and gospel hope. Such a position calibrates the Wesleyan sound deSilva plays and emboldens its message of salvation, justification, and faith. Coupling deSilva's essay on the Wesleyan Gospel with the histories of African Methodism, I am reminded that at the heart of our gospel is a belief that hope carries grace, love, and care for one another. I am grateful for how deSilva's essay cultivates a rediscovery of the power of the gospel message to transgress human boundaries of difference and separation and embrace a faith that seeks Christian kinship and our souls' salvation in tandem.

---

6. Lawyers' Committee for Civil Rights under the Law, "Proud Boys Ordered to Pay More Than $1 Million for Racially-Motivated Attack on Historically Black Church," Press release, July 1, 2023. https://www.lawyerscommittee.org/proud-boys-ordered-to-pay-more-than-1-million-for-racially-motivated-attack-on-historically-black-church.

CHAPTER FOUR: THE PENTECOSTAL GOSPEL

JULIE MA

Introduction

My understanding of the gospel is the good news of Jesus Christ to nonbelievers who are in darkness. I begin with my personal experience of the salvation of Christ, which will help me explain the gospel in a more tangible way. I heard the good news of salvation when I was a high school student. Speaking of my background, I was born and raised in a southern port town in Korea and grew up in a family where several religions were practiced: Buddhism, shamanism, and Confucianism. The most religious person in my family was my grandmother who was a well-known shaman or medium, especially popular among her clients for her ability to call up the spirits of the deceased. My exposure to Christianity was quite radical, as my high school teacher played a recording of a conversation with "angels" and with Jesus, which she had while in a trance-like state. As a teenager, this had such a strong influence on me that I later found myself in an empty local church in prayer. Even though I did not directly hear the gospel of salvation nor about the cross, death, and resurrection of Jesus, this event impacted me so profoundly that I started attending a church. In the fall of that year (1971), I attended a revival meeting where I experienced the baptism of the Holy Spirit. That was obviously my salvation experience. I was practically disowned by my family because of my new belief, and I decided to begin my theological education away from home. After much prayer for the salvation of my family, many years later the entire family heard the good news of Christ and experienced his salvation.

Pentecostals sharing the gospel for saving souls is accomplished through evangelistic mission. The mission is assumed in its most direct way as "facilitating" God's power for witness "to the ends of the earth" (Acts 1:8). "The Pentecostal movement shares this soteriological driven mission as the evangelization of the lost."[1] Through repentance, people believe that their sins are washed by the blood of Jesus, and they become the children of God. The Pentecostal gospel of salvation, along with hope and optimism, is particularly well accepted by people in destitute, socially marginalized situations, and the sick. This chapter will discuss the Pentecostal gospel, the Pentecostal evangelistic mission along with its holistic mission, biblical texts that mention the baptism of the Spirit for witness, Jesus's ministry by the anointing of the Spirit, the gift of the Spirit, Spirit-empowered mission, and further transformation of life after conversion.

What Is the Pentecostal Gospel?

"Pentecostals believe that all people have sinned, sin being defined as breaking God's law and also as offending or displeasing God."[2] Sin affected human beings' rapport with God. It also affects people's relations with one another, and further it affects the entire creation as well. The Son of God came in human flesh to become an atoning sacrifice for the sins of the world. Jesus Christ was a sacrifice to pay that penalty, hence the relationship between God and humanity was reestablished through his blood.[3]

In the beginning, humankind was made in the image of God, and life through God's breath (*ruakh*) was given. God and the first human beings, Adam and Eve, had an exceptional and faultless relationship together in the garden of Eden. Adam and Eve were "created pure and

---

1. Wonsuk Ma and Julie C. Ma, "Missiology: Evangelization, Holistic Ministry, and Social Justice," in *The Routledge Handbook of Pentecostal Theology*, ed. by Wolfgang Vondey (Abingdon: Routledge, 2020), 282.

2. Keith Warrington, *Pentecostal Theology: A Theology of Encounter* (London: T&T Clark, 2008), 35.

3. Grace Milton, "Salvation: Participating in the Story Where Earth and Heaven Meet," in Vondey, *Routledge Handbook of Pentecostal Theology*, 228.

upright"⁴ and with free will, but through "voluntary transgression"⁵ yielded to the lure of sin, "rending man subject to God's wrath and condemnation."⁶ Pentecostal soteriology is rooted in this fundamental account and understanding of the fall, and it is from this narrative that Pentecostals comprehend the "origins of sin" in humanity.⁷ The defeating of sin is not something that human beings can achieve by themselves, but rather God must enter into history and the individual believers' lives to provide "atonement and to restore the broken relationships."⁸

Critically, due to their exclusive position in creation and the extraordinary relationship with God before the fall, Adam and Eve were given the responsibility to be in charge of God's creation, and thus their sin affected not only humanity but the entire creation. The sin is realized primarily as disobedience to God and as generating a discontinuity in the relationship between God and human beings, making their removal from paradise necessary. This broken relationship and inclination to sin affected the condition of the entire human person and is the fundamental issue of "theological concerns regarding salvation."⁹

The overcoming of sin is not something that humans can accomplish on their own, but rather God needed to step into history and into the lives of individual believers, in order to provide atonement and restore the broken relationship.¹⁰ Therefore, Pentecostals believe that the Son of God came in the flesh and eventually gave his life as an atoning sacrifice for the sins of the world. The predominant atonement model for Pentecostals is that of penal substitutionary atonement, whereby God required a penalty to be paid for sin, and Jesus Christ, God's pure and sinless Son, acted as a sacrifice to pay that penalty, thus restoring humanity to a right relationship with God through his blood.¹¹

---

4. Assemblies of God (Great Britain), "What We Believe," 2018.
5. Assemblies of God (Great Britain), "What We Believe," 2018.
6. Elim Foursquare Gospel Alliance, "Statement of Beliefs," 2018.
7. Milton "Salvation," 228.
8. Edmund Rybarczyk, "Towards a Pentecostal Perspective on Salvation," in *Pentecostals in the 21st Century: Identity, Beliefs, Praxis*, ed. by Corneliu Constantineanu and Christopher Scobie (Eugene, OR: Cascade, 2018), 80–82.
9. Milton, "Salvation," 228.
10. Edmund Rybarczyk, *Beyond Salvation: Eastern Orthodox and Classical Pentecostalism on Becoming Like Christ* (Cumbria: Paternoster, 2018), 80–82.
11. Church of God in Christ, Statement of Faith, 2018.

The entire human being is purified through repentance and faith in the costly blood of Jesus Christ to rebuild a true relationship with God and to advance that person to sanctity and "restored purpose."[12] Repentance is measured to be personal rather than public. It is frequently regarded to be "where the conversion experience is thought to end." Acknowledgment of sin and repentance is the human response to the effort already established by God.[13]

Pentecostals tend to expand the account of salvation beyond the cross so that the "soteriological narrative" prongs to the "resurrection and ascension of Christ" that made it possible to pour out the Holy Spirit on all flesh (Acts 2:38). Frank Macchia claims that "the vocation of the human race was to bear the Spirit of God, and the entire mission of Jesus was to provide how this can occur. Justification and sanctification consequently belong to the same work of salvation,"[14] and humankind's response to the atoning work of Christ is found as unswervingly corresponding to the response of the early Christians to the outburst of the Spirit: "Pentecostal soteriology is Christocentric only insofar as the work of Christ is interpreted through and extended by the work of the Holy Spirit."[15]

As understood in general, Pentecostal evangelism is indoctrinated in the theological stress on the Spirit's empowerment that activates every Christian to be a witness to the gospel to the "ends of the earth" (Acts 1:8), to save an individual soul to Christ. Healing is a chief and noticeable distinctive of Pentecostal evangelists, helping to bring in huge gatherings. "The experiential manifestation of God's supernatural power has turned many animistic communities to Christ."[16] Countless people in diverse Asian countries such as China, Cambodia, Korea, Sri Lanka, Myanmar, Nepal, and Malaysia who primarily practice animism came to the salvation of Christ through divine healing experiences. Huge and small open-air healing "crusades" turn out to be the trademark of Pentecostal evangelism.[17]

---

12. Matthew Thomson, "Eschatology a Soteriology: The Cosmic Full Gospel," in *Perspectives in Pentecostal Eschatologies*, ed. by Peter Althouse and Robbie Waddell (Eugene, OR: Pickwick, 2010), 189–204.

13. Milton, "Salvation," 228.

14. Frank Macchia, *Justified in the Spirit: Creation, Redemption, and the Triune God* (Grand Rapids: Eerdmans, 2010), 186.

15. Milton, "Salvation," 228–29.

16. Ma and Ma, "Missiology," 281.

17. Ma and Ma, "Missiology," 281.

Needless to say, salvation is for all humanity, all of whom are sinners. Hence, Pentecostals bring the good news of salvation to the sinful world as a mission mandate. As they share the message of salvation, they encounter human suffering as a consequence of sin. Thus, from the early days of the Pentecostal mission, serving those who suffer has been the other side of the "mission" coin. Sin engenders human struggles, and greed compounds the plight of billions of people. The truth is that bringing souls to Christ for eternal life must be complemented by serving the saved to be faithful disciples of Christ for witnessing. Thus, the Pentecostal mission is holistic.

As an example of holistic ministry, let me attempt to elaborate the connection between sin and social issues, for instance HIV/AIDS. Sin and HIV/AIDS are mostly linked, and this connection is clear when viewed from the perspective of commissioned neighborly love. Humans were made to live in loving connections with God, other people, and the environment. Sin is the negative force that obliterates the divine image in people and ruptures the aforementioned essential human connections. Such shattered partnerships are a blatant sign of a crisis in love. Sin can be viewed as the absence of love, which may be viewed as the main cause of HIV/AIDS in society.[18] For the Pentecostal gospel, responding to such issues is an essential expression of the good news.

People in the Context: The Poor and the Marginalized

Along with the stress on Spirit-empowered evangelism and healing, Pentecostals utilize a holistic mission in which the gospel is the remedy for social issues such as the plight of orphans and widows, the HIV/AIDS epidemic, and the like. "Responding to human suffering has significantly broadened the purview of Pentecostal mission from a focus on saving the lost to a mission to the poor and destitute."[19] With such a notion, nearly from its inception, Pentecostal beliefs and practices have shown a specific appeal to the deprived and socially marginalized.

The assurance of good health and blessing reconstituted the understanding of Christian redemption to individuals, families, communities, and the here and now. This message is ready to tackle life's unrelenting

---

18. Frederick N. Kakwata, "Strategies for Dealing with Sin in Relation to Poverty," *Stellenbosch Theological Journal* 2.2 (2016): 273–94.
19. Ma and Ma, "Missiology," 282.

problems, such as sickness, shortage, job loss, loneliness, and disaster. As the faith closely interacts with the given context, it tends to be elastic, quick to reinterpret and expand the existing belief to counter a new challenge. This makes the Pentecostal faith extremely agile, relevant, and dynamic in any given sociocultural context. In various east and southeast Asian countries, Pentecostal believers form an alternative social movement, addressing society's common challenges.[20] As a result, Pentecostal Christianity has recorded significant growth over many decades throughout the world.

As expected, the Pentecostal notion of mission is integral and holistic, with the evangelistic mission as the ultimate outcome, nonetheless. A few Pentecostal missionary practices, such as Teen Challenge, reveal theological rationality in dealing with the impoverished—in this case, drug addicts in urban centers. There was a simple theological logic: "as the current state of human transgression started from rebellion against God, its undoing will have to begin with the spiritual realm of human existence."[21] In Latin America, the Pentecostal faith has produced social upward mobility among its followers, and this has attracted many to its faith.[22]

I will present a couple of examples to illustrate the potential and practice of Pentecostal holistic mission.

1. The Orphanage Mission in Ethiopia

Lillian Trasher, an American Pentecostal missionary in Egypt (1910–1961), served Egyptian children after breaking her engagement to answer God's call. Trasher had had a strong desire to begin an orphanage, even though there was neither support nor committed supporters. In 1915, her orphanage began with several children, which grew to fifty children by 1916. With this rapid growth, the adequate resources to support them and to secure a large house was critical. To solve this acute challenge, she came up with a creative idea: to make bricks utilizing the

---

20. Donald E. Miller and Tetsunao Yamamori, *Global Pentecostalism: The New Face of Christian Social Engagement* (Berkeley, CA: University of California Press, 2007), showcases such Pentecostal communities in the Global South.

21. Wonsuk Ma, "'When the Poor Are Fired Up': The Role of Pneumatology in Pentecostal-Charismatic Mission," *Transformation* 24.1 (2007): 28–34.

22. David Martin, *Tongues of Fire: The Explosion of Protestantism in Latin America* (Oxford: Basil Blackwell, 1990), 90–92.

labor force of the children.²³ Soon, feeding programs were added, and by 1941 she served 2,700 meals every day. In the 1960s, her orphanage housed 1,500 children and she served 4,500 meals each day on a campus that contained more than eleven buildings.²⁴

In addition, Trasher provided housing for widows who had no place to live after the death of their husbands. She dedicated most of her adult life, fifty years to be exact, to take care of children and women in Egypt. Besides providing physical necessities, she also cared for the spiritual growth of a person. Of the children and widows who came to Trasher for care, some were believers, but others were not. Hence, she constantly looked over their spiritual growth, and for those who were uncertain of their salvation in Christ, she made it her goal to bring them to salvation.

Egyptians affectionately recognized her as "Mama Lillian" or "Mother of the Nile." She passed away on December 17, 1961, and the Egyptian government honored her for her dedication to social services, looking after some twenty thousand children and widows at the orphanage for over fifty years in Assiout, Egypt.²⁵ The orphanage has continued its work even after her passing, providing new life to countless children. Many children were trained in Christian education throughout the orphanage's one hundred years of operation. Presently, it is one of the largest orphanages in the world.

2. HIV/AIDS Intervention and Care and Lazarus Project Care for Street Children in Zambia

Since 1992, Joshua Banda, the senior pastor of Northmead Assembly of God Church in Lusaka, Zambia, has been involved in a holistic ministry providing care for HIV/AIDS patients and their families. He was very aware that the church's response to this pandemic had to be holistic, "encompassing spiritual, medical, educational, social, and community care."²⁶

---

23. Janet Benge and Geoff Benge, *Lillian Trasher: The Greatest Wonder in Egypt* (Seattle, WA: YWAM, 2004), 93–94.
24. Christie Florence, *Called to Egypt* (Wichita Falls, TX: Western Christian Foundation, 1997), 44.
25. Benge and Benge, *Lillian Trasher*, 103.
26. Joshua Banda, "Engaging with the Community, the Fight against AIDS," in *Good News from Africa: Community Transformation through the Church*, ed. Brian Woolnough (Oxford: Regnum Book International, 2013), 41.

As a nation, Zambia's future was bleak due to the rise of AIDS infections. "According to a 2011 UNICEF report, AIDS patients in Zambia consisted of 337,316 adults and 43,625 children."[27] It became an urgent concern for the government and social sectors.

The Circle of Hope was created in September 2005 to provide Christian-based deterrence and holistic care for HIV/AIDS patients, offering free anti-retroviral treatment and education to their families.[28] A willingness to be tested is the most essential and hardest first step for AIDS intervention, and Christian clinics such as the Circle of Hope (COH) achieved a high test rate. With their genuine spirit of care and compassion, more came for testing and consultation. The clinic's performance became extraordinary.[29]

> To date, COH has counseled and tested over 7,429 people, of whom 5,326 are HIV+ and have been enrolled in care. Of the number that is positive, 2,310 are currently on full ART, of which 516 are children. A group in excess of 200 community adherence personnel, caregivers, and counselors have sensitized, educated, and monitored clients on treatment in their homes. Approximately 80 people visit the COH Clinic per day, while 120 patients are enrolled monthly.[30]

The Health Care Association of Zambia, to which Banda's Northmead Assembly's program belongs, accounts for over 50 percent of healthcare provision in the nation. Christian involvement in the HIV/AIDS epidemic by local congregations has left a considerable influence on society. As a consequence, Banda was invited to lead the National AIDS Council in 2007.[31]

In 1999, Banda began a program to care for street children, most of whom were AIDS orphans. Other works also followed. The Lazarus

---

27. UNICEF, "HIV&AIDS: Key Statistics," www.unicef.org/zambia/5109_8459.html.
28. Banda, "Engaging with the Community," 41.
29. Banda, "Engaging with the Community," 49.
30. Banda, "Engaging with the Community," 49.
31. Wonsuk Ma, "A Pentecostal Reflection on Christian Unity in the New Christian Millennium," (paper presented at the Global Forum for the Future of World Christianity, Jeju, Korea, May, 2015), 2. See also "'A Changing Africa' Joshua Banda 1/1" (www.youtube.com/watch?v=p3cB63qmoew).

Project is a new social-care program of the church. It runs holistic care for orphaned and vulnerable children.[32] As time passed, the Lazarus Project advanced into a community of seventy former street children, providing its own housing with a forty-acre farm. To date, almost a thousand orphaned and vulnerable children have gone through its training, with astonishing stories of transformation.[33] Besides running the Lazarus Project, Banda never neglects to share the gospel:

> Through all these programs, the power of the gospel occupies the center. Banda, his church, and various ministries are all inspired and motivated by the gospel mandate. They also regularly share the good news of Jesus with HIV/AIDS patients, their families, and children under their care. In fact, the proclamation of the gospel and responding to the immediate needs of the vulnerable have been going hand-in-hand from the very beginning.[34]

Biblical Texts

This section presents several main tenets of Pentecostalism by studying two passages from Acts, one from a Gospel, and one from Paul's letters. They have also been popular passages among Pentecostal believers.

1. The Baptism of the Spirit to Be Witness (Acts 1:8; 2:1-12)

There is a close connection between Acts 1:8 and 2:1–12. The book of Acts reveals the expectation and experience of the early church with the Holy Spirit: "But you will receive power when the Holy Spirit comes upon you, and you will be my witnesses in Jerusalem and in all Judea and Samaria, and to the ends of the earth" (Acts 1:8 NRSV). This declaration is both a "command and a promise." The disciples have to wait to receive power through the Holy Spirit to accomplish their calling as witnesses to the "risen Messiah."[35] The calling of Christ and the calling of the disciples are inseparably related by means of the Holy Spirit,

---

32. Banda, "Engaging with the Community," 44.
33. Banda, "Engaging with the Community," 45. Numerous similar accounts are found in Miller and Yamamori, *Global Pentecostalism*.
34. Joshua Banda, "A Request" (an email message to the author, Sept. 9, 2015).
35. Craig S. Keener, *Acts: An Exegetical Commentary*, vol. 1 (Grand Rapids: Baker Academic, 2012), 675.

as the "anointing upon Christ is to be transferred to the disciples and the *ecclesia*" (1:4).[36] Acts 1:8 clarifies that the coming of the Holy Spirit is for missional empowerment in terms of being witnesses, which I will illustrate later. In Luke 24:47–48, Jesus specifies that "repentance for the forgiveness of sins will be preached in his name to all nations, beginning at Jerusalem. You are witnesses of these things."

The setting of the event is essential in understanding the significance of the Spirit's advent:

> This event occurs during the Jewish Feast of Weeks, held on the fiftieth day after the first Sabbath of the Passover. It was originally a harvest festival of the first fruits at which the first sheaf of the wheat harvest was dedicated to God (Exod. 23:16; 34:22). As such, it was an occasion when diaspora Jews would flock to Jerusalem to celebrate the goodness of God. One tradition has associated it with the giving of the Law on Sinai and the theophany associated with that event (Exod. 19:16–19) although this is disputed within scholarship because Luke does not clearly link it with Mount Sinai.[37]

Acts 2:1 indicates that the 120 disciples were all together (*pantes homou epi to auto*) in one place, expecting the fulfillment of the Lord's promise in 1:8.[38] It is not certain if this is the identical location as the "upper room" in which the Last Supper was eaten.[39] "It might have been in the upper city next to the temple."[40]

Verse 2 presents the Spirit coming like a powerful wind from heaven and covering the house. Luke starts to use a sequence of analogies to delineate what is occurring (wind, fire, and tongues). It is the sound that permeates the house, "not the wind as such."[41] The Spirit's presence is increased in the gathering place. Noticeably the idea of "coming from

---

36. Clark H. Pinnock, *Flame of Love: A Theology of the Holy Spirit* (Downers Grove, IL: InterVarsity Press, 1966), 113.
37. Keener, *Acts*, 787.
38. Daniela C. Augustine, *Pentecost, Hospitality, and Transformation* (Cleveland, TN: CPT Press, 2012), 17.
39. Witherington, *Acts*, 131.
40. Keener, *Acts*, 797.
41. Keener, *Acts*, 796.

heaven" means a "transcendent, and by implication divine origin, but the statement also uses the notion of space: from up there to down here."[42] The Spirit comes upon people from outside [external] of them, and yet the Spirit is also "immanent within them," breathing life and vivacity into them.[43] "There are echoes of earlier biblical texts where the Spirit of God is related to the breath of life (Gen. 2:7), as well as theophanies where God's presence is understood to have come down from heaven, the place where God dwells in his majesty and splendor."[44]

Verse 4 reports that all of them are "filled with the Holy Spirit," which is the indwelling Spirit. The verb used here is an aorist passive form of *pinplēmi* ("they were filled"), using a variety of "liquid-type metaphors to describe the Spirit coming upon people—filling, baptizing, and pouring." Witherington observes that Luke uses them interchangeably, although he avoids the verb "to baptize" for the subsequent narratives of the Spirit's advents.[45]

When the Holy Spirit comes upon them, they all speak in tongues of diverse languages. God supernaturally empowered them through the Holy Spirit to speak the languages without the necessity to acquire them first. The linking between the radical experience of tongues and mission is clear. Thus, the early Pentecostals thought of tongues as a missionary language, but this idea was soon abandoned.[46] Nonetheless, "Luke's narrative use of tongues was also mission-connected,"[47] and this is something that Pentecostals need to develop. Luke also pays attention to the Spirit's power for the mission, especially the "prophetic dimension of the Spirit's activity."[48] And this power for mission includes a "cross-cultural element."[49] At the core of Pentecostal theology is the empowerment of the Holy Spirit for mission and witnessing.

---

42. Keener, *Acts*, 796.
43. Keener, *Acts*, 800.
44. Mark J. Cartledge, *The Mediation of the Spirit: Interventions in Practical Theology*, Pentecostal Manifestos (Grand Rapids: Eerdmans, 2015), 93.
45. Ben Witherington, *The Acts of Apostles: A Socio-Rhetorical Commentary* (Grand Rapids: Eerdmans, 1997), 133.
46. Allan Anderson, *An Introduction to Pentecostalism* (Cambridge: Cambridge University Press, 2004), 33–34.
47. Craig S. Keener, *Spirit Hermeneutics: Reading Scripture in Light of Pentecost* (Grand Rapid: Eerdmans, 2016), 22–23.
48. Keener, *Spirit Hermeneutics*, 22–23.
49. Keener, *Spirit Hermeneutics*, 22–23.

2. Jesus's Ministry by Anointing of the Spirit (Luke 4:18-19)

Luke's Gospel stresses Jesus's unique relationship with the Holy Spirit by presenting him as the "Spirit-filled Messiah" equipped to "carry out God's plan for salvation."[50] Jesus's public declaration of the messianic mission takes place in his teaching upon the request of the leaders of the hometown synagogue. After the reading of a passage from Isaiah, the people in the synagogue exhibit strong expectations as they wait for additional construal.[51] "While some may speak of the ensuing moment as Jesus's inaugural speech, Luke does not record an official discourse, but simply the reading followed by Jesus's announcement that this Scripture finds its fulfillment at that very moment in the hearing of those in the synagogue (Lk. 4:21)."[52] He is the One promised in the prophecy that, through him, God will save his people; he will indeed be God's mediator of salvation through his ministry.[53]

In this compact example of early Christian hermeneutics, the Lukan Jesus announces the true understanding of his mission in the Nazareth synagogue through an explicit statement of what he has been sent to do.[54] With this pronouncement, Jesus emphatically invites the people to accept him as Israel's Messiah and to receive the salvation he is announcing.[55]

The declaration, "the Spirit of the Lord is on me, because he has anointed me" (Luke 4:18) is an unmistakable reference to Isaiah 61:1-2 and 58:6. By bringing these two prophecies together, he calls himself "anointed" with the Spirit of God and bravely declares his messiahship.[56] The Spirit is on Jesus, who will bring God's salvation in a fivefold

---

50. Robert L. Brawley, *Luke-Acts and the Jews: Conflict, Apology and Conciliation*, SBLMS 33 (Atlanta: Scholars Press, 1987), 29, 116.

51. Martin W. Mittelstadt, *The Spirit and Suffering in Luke-Acts: Implications for a Pentecostal Pneumatology* (London: T&T Clark, 2004), 51. According to Mittelstadt, it serves to "highlight the intense anticipation of how Jesus will interpret the Isaiah passage."

52. Mittelstadt, *Spirit and Suffering in Luke-Acts*, 51. He states that "the literal translation 'in your ears' is a strange figure for fulfillment of scripture, but they function as organs of reception of important truth."

53. I. Howard Marshall, *Luke: Historian and Theologian* (Exeter: Paternoster, 1970), 125.

54. Robert C. Tannehill, *Narrative Unity of Luke-Acts: A Literary Interpretation*, 2 vols. (Philadelphia: Fortress Press, 1990), 1:62–63.

55. Mittelstadt, *Spirit and Suffering in Luke-Acts*, 51.

56. Jack D. Kingsbury, *Conflict in Luke: Jesus, Authorities, Disciples* (Minneapolis: Fortress, 1991), 44. See also Roger Strongstad, *The Charismatic Theology of St. Luke* (Peabody, MA: Hendrickson, 1984), 42.

manner through God's anointing: (1) to preach good news to the poor; (2) to proclaim release to the prisoners; (3) to proclaim recovery of sight for the blind; (4) to set the oppressed free, and (5) to proclaim the year of the Lord's favor.

Luke anticipates in the account of Jesus's ministry hope for the poor, freedom for captives, sight for the blind, and deliverance for the oppressed.[57] The Spirit-led and empowered Jesus proclaims this prophetic promise and brings it into realization.

3. Gifts of the Spirit (1 Corinthians 12:7-9)

First Corinthians 12:7 presumes that every believer has varied gifts. "Each member of the church has a gift; none is excluded."[58] In verses 7–9 Paul uses three prepositions to explain the role of the Spirit in the operation of the gifts:

> The word of wisdom is exercised *through* (*dia*, διά), the Spirit; the word of knowledge *according to* (*kata*, κατά) the Spirit; both faith and healing *by* (*en*, ἐν) the Spirit. . . . The prepositions do not divide the gifts into categories; all three apply to each of the gifts. Each of the manifestations are "through," "according to," and "in" the Spirit. Although each preposition has its own special nuances, they sometimes overlap in meaning as well. Here, the main thought is that the presence and activity of the Spirit is absolutely essential to the existence and operation of the gifts.[59]

Specifically, Paul states in verse 8, "To one there is given through the Spirit a message [word, *logos*] of wisdom [*sophias*]." The purpose of giving this gift is to build up the body of Christ and to spread the gospel to the world. Gee considers the word of wisdom as the enthused sharing of the gospel.[60] The work of the Spirit is apparent in the "gifted expression of wisdom."[61] Numerous scholars believe that the "content of

---

57. Tannehill, *Narrative Unity of Luke-Acts*, 1:62.
58. George M. Flattery, *Spiritual Persons, Gifts, and Church: A Commentary on 1 Corinthians 12–14* (Springfield, MO: Network211, 2015), 35.
59. Flattery, *Spiritual Persons, Gifts, and Church*, 38–39.
60. Donald Gee, *Concerning Spiritual Gifts* (Springfield: Radiant Books, 1980), 35.
61. Flattery, *Spiritual Persons, Gifts, and Church*, 39.

the word of wisdom is the gospel."[62] However, it is also probable that the Holy Spirit may make known wisdom to each believer for their own specific situation.[63] Palma writes:

> Both with regard to this gift (word of wisdom) and the gift of a word of knowledge, it may be that the gift is not always meant to be vocalized. The Holy Spirit may give a word to a person for guidance or insight into a specific situation that faces him or her, but the Spirit may intend that the word not be expressed to others.[64]

The next gift is a message of knowledge. According to Fee, it is most likely "a Spirit utterance of some revelatory kind."[65] The frequently referenced occasion is God's disclosure to Peter that Ananias had lied about setting aside some of the property he sold (Acts 5:1–5). Flattery proposes that the word of knowledge can embrace "the expression of knowledge, how it is conveyed. As with all the Spirit's manifestations, the action of the Spirit is essential to the spiritual gift. Without it, there is no spiritual gift."[66]

Verse 9 introduces "faith and gifts of healing." Dunn acknowledges the connection between faith and the gifts of healing. He highlights the responsibility of faith in general for all the gifts when he writes that "in Rom. 12:3 Paul thinks of such faith in connection with charismata in general."[67] Presuming this view, faith is associated with a certain aspect in the practice of all the gifts. On certain occasions and activities, "faith stands out as the gift being exercised."[68]

Fee states, "The use of [*charisma*] itself in this case suggests that the 'manifestation' is given not to the person who is healed, but to the person God uses for the healing of another."[69] Frequently the gifts of healing

---

62. Flattery, *Spiritual Persons, Gifts, and Church*, 40.
63. Flattery, *Spiritual Persons, Gifts, and Church*, 41.
64. Anthony D. Palma, *The Holy Spirit: A Pentecostal Perspective* (Springfield, MO: Gospel, 2001), 223.
65. Gordon Fee, *God's Empowering Presence* (Peabody, MA: Hendrickson, 1994), 167.
66. Flattery, *Spiritual Persons, Gifts, and Church*, 43.
67. James D. G. Dunn, *Baptism in the Holy Spirit* (London: SCM, 1975), 211.
68. Flattery, *Spiritual Persons, Gifts, and Church*, 45–46.
69. Fee, *God's Empowering Presence*, 168–69.

are bestowed to those who experienced God's healing. Apparently, "the person healed receives the benefit of being healed, a definite gift in one sense of the word. But in the sense of the *charismata* of the Spirit, the gifts of healing are given to the people whom God is using."[70]

Response to the Gospel: Spirit Empowerment and Mission

The beginning decades of the Pentecostal movement were marked by dedicated and passionate mission activities. In 1906–1908, Pentecostal missionaries, after experiencing the Holy Spirit's baptism, believed that the Spirit empowered them for mission. Committed to the life of witnessing, they disposed of their possessions and left for the land of God's call. They reached far-flung corners of the earth to accomplish the Great Commission (Matt 28:18–20), and no sacrifice seemed too enormous for them to proclaim the gospel.[71] Also inspired by the eschatological urgency of the soon-returning Christ, many Pentecostals, clergy, and laypeople, both men and women, young and old, often not appropriately equipped, devoted their lives to bringing souls to Christ. Vinson Synan called them "missionaries of the one-way ticket" with a few valuable instances.[72] This army of fully dedicated missionaries did not expect to come back home in their lifetime, but to work "to end their lives" in mission fields.[73]

According to Gary McGee, by 1910, in four years of the ministry of the Azusa Street Mission, Pentecostal missionaries from Europe and North America were in over fifty nations.[74] He further argues that within five years of the Pentecostal revival in Los Angeles, at least two hundred Pentecostal missionaries from North America served in various parts of the world. From its beginning, Pentecostals have been champions of church planting. McGee also describes the first twenty years of Pentecostal missions as mostly "chaotic in operation."[75]

---

70. Flattery, *Spiritual Persons, Gifts, and Church*, 47.
71. Gary McGee, "The Lord's Pentecostal Missionary Movement," *Asian Journal of Pentecostal Studies* 8.1 (2005): 64.
72. Vinson Synan, *The Spirit Said "Grow": The Astounding Worldwide Expansion of Pentecostal and Charismatic Churches* (Monrovia, CA: MARC, 1992), 39–48.
73. Ma, "'When the Poor Are Fired Up,'" 3.
74. D. William Faupel, *The Everlasting Gospel: The Significance of Eschatology in the Development of Pentecostal Thought* (Sheffield: Sheffield Academic Press, 1996), 212–16.
75. Gary B. McGee, "Pentecostals and Their Various Strategies for Global Mission: A Historical Assessment," in *Called and Empowered: Global Mission in Pentecostal Perspective*, ed. M. Dempster, B. Klaus, and D. Peterson (Peabody, MA: Hendrickson, 1991), 201.

Clarke elaborates on the Pentecostal experience of being filled with the Spirit and the resultant empowerment for mission. This empowerment comprises offering resolutions to the world's issues, whether this is "spiritual salvation or social justice, or both."[76] The "spiritual and physical" features of life cannot be detached from each other in the Pentecostal worldview. It is also right that Pentecostals believe that "inner transformation is an essential priority for the transformation of society."[77]

Pentecostals likewise believe in sacrificial service, implying that all Pentecostal believers should be involved in serving God in some way. This is the drastic working of the "Reformation doctrine of the priesthood of all believers," where all members are involved in some form of mission work or service.[78]

Richard Shaull studied Brazilian Pentecostalism and concluded that Pentecostals are powerful agents of change: "[Although Pentecostals] have not made many efforts to develop a theology of social responsibility, [by] clearly integrating the personal and social, a number of things are happening in their communities in which this integration is a reality." As a result, they are "emerging as an important force for social transformation, especially among poor and marginal people."[79]

Pentecostals believe that Spirit baptism is an empowering for outstanding service to the world. It is the renewing work of the Spirit. Luke 3:16 notes that John the Baptist stated, "One who is more powerful than I will come, the straps of whose sandals I am not worthy to untie. He will baptize you with the Holy Spirit and fire," so that we are brought into "the light of faith in his gospel."[80]

"Live a Life Worthy of the Gospel": Transforming Life after Conversion

Many people who live in societies where practices of spiritism and shamanism are prevalent convert to Christ through healing experiences that

---

76. Matthew Clarke, "Friend or Foe? Finding Common Ground between Development and Pentecostalism," *PentecoStudies* 14.2 (2015): 164.
77. Allan Anderson, "Pentecostalism and Social, Political, and Economic Development," *Spiritus* 5.1 (2020): 129.
78. Clarke, "Friends or Foe," 168.
79. Richard Shaull and Waldo Cesar, *Pentecostalism and the Future of the Christian Churches: Promises, Limitations, Challenges* (Grand Rapids: Eerdmans, 2000), 214, 227.
80. Robert Menzies, *Pentecost: This Story Is Our Story* (Springfield, MO: Gospel, 2013), 43; see also John Calvin, *Institutes*, 3.1.4.

change their lives. Experiencing physical healing helps them realize that the power of the Christian God is greater than the gods whom they regularly worshiped and to whom they brought sacrifices, often for decades when they had a physical problem. The fact is that their gods couldn't heal the sick, but the Christian God healed when someone prayed. Since such experiences, their minds and thought were completely changed, and further their way of life was transformed, no longer seeking their gods' aid but drawing to the one true God for help. Dramatic physical healing assisted them to grow in their faith by leaps and bounds because they have seen the prominence of the true God with their own eyes.

A tribal group of people named Kankana-eys in the northern Philippines believed that keeping ancestor worship was crucial because the ancestor spirits were sources of healing and blessing in their lives. They were taught that ancestor worship should be passed from one generation to the next. Hence, they must retain and protect ancestor worship. At the same time, though, they have such a strong fear that if they don't worship the spirits of the ancestors any longer and discover a new god or spirit, the ancestor spirits will get angry and bring punishment upon them. However, after they converted to Christ through the supernatural experience of healing, they completely turned to Christ. They no longer lived in fear but found comfort and peace in God. There was a complete transformation of their minds and lives.

This transformed life also was evident when they were later willing to assist with a church building project when a missionary planned to build a new church. Since they did not have cash income, they contributed with physical labor, carrying lumber and other materials for the church building. Yet another case is that they enjoy coming to church for worship. The worship goes for hours and hours. It consists of preaching, singing, praying for any needs, and sharing testimonies. The tribal people are very reserved and shy, but when it comes to the time of sharing their testimonies, they are bold to stand up and share them. It implies that in daily life, they experience God's goodness and faithfulness. What is described in this section demonstrates the total transformation of the lives of the Kankana-eys people and the deep growth of their faith.

The life of the Kankana-ey tribe before their conversion to Christianity is closely associated with the ancestor spirits. They believe that the spirits exercise power for healing, blessing, and solving their life's problems. As animists, they assume that both animated and unanimated objects possess spirits. The ancestor spirits associate with other spirits, forming an active and densely populated spirit world. They closely interact and intermingle with people, constantly affecting the living, especially their descendants. According to their worldview, these spirits frequently converse with the living through dreams, omens, and mediums.[81] The Kankana-eys, like many tribes, actively seek to communicate with spirits by ritual performance. It often requires an animal sacrifice offered to the ancestor's spirit to obtain secrets of the spirit world. For the Kankana-eys, there are different mediums connecting the living with the spirit world: Manbunongs perform rituals, Mansi-oks interpret signs to determine the cause of illness, and Mankotom have the ability to interpret omens, signs, and dreams that other priests are unable to determine.[82] The people are literally in bondage to the endless demands of the spirits. In their substandard living conditions without roads, running water, electricity, or medical service, the religious burden worsens their lives. Although details of traditions may vary, most tribal communities in Asia and Africa share similar beliefs and dire living conditions.

Further Reflections

Pentecostals have a great passion for God's mission and for the fulfillment of the Great Commission after being empowered by the Spirit. Many missionaries went to the mission field by faith, believing that God would provide for their needs. Pentecostal cross-cultural workers proclaimed the gospel, and their work has been well accepted by non-Westerners due to their similar worldviews, especially in the spirit world. It is also noted that Pentecostals have excelled in proclaiming and demonstrating God's miraculous work of healing today as a vital component of mission. Signs and wonders can affirm the message of God's salvation.

Pentecostals have particularly appealed to the grassroots population, the poor and the marginalized in society. With the supernatural

---

81. Julie C. Ma, *When the Spirit Meets the Spirits: Pentecostal Ministry among the Kankana-ey Tribe in the Philippines*, 2nd rev. ed. (Frankfurt: Peter Lang, 2001), 103.
82. Ma, *When the Sprit Meets the Spirits*, 114–15.

power of God, on the one hand, they also practiced holistic ministry. As discussed in the earlier part of this paper, they started orphanages, provided education, built hospitals, and helped HIV/AIDS patients. Often their own roots of social marginalization makes them passionate about caring for the neglected, abandoned, and destitute. Such ministries are motivated by God's love and compassion. Through the demonstration of God's power and caring for the needy, the ultimate goal of Pentecostal mission has been spiritual conversion to bring people into God's kingdom.

Thus, it is imperative for Pentecostal believers and churches to continue to strengthen their inheritance, which distinguished itself as a movement for the extension of God's kingdom by bringing souls to Christ. While the advancement of Pentecostal scholarship is encouraging, it should also preserve and strengthen grassroots spirituality and mission empowerment on the level of daily life and engagement. This includes a passion for the poor and the marginalized. The combination of Pentecostals' spiritual empowerment and heart for the suffering make their gospel the "full gospel." And they are poised to influence and lead the Christian mission in the coming decades.

RESPONSE TO JULIE MA

SCOT MCKNIGHT

Julie Ma's approach to the gospel—that is, the Pentecostal Gospel, expands from the simple soterian or salvation gospel of a Billy Graham-like presentation into a healing gospel and then into a liberation gospel. Let me attempt to trace these expanding circles of the gospel in Ma's approach. She begins with a simple definition: "My understanding of the gospel is the good news of Jesus Christ to nonbelievers who are in darkness" (p. 157). This story of gospel expansion mirrors her own experience and witness to salvation. Her approach began in the combination of Buddhism, Shamanism, and Confucianism she inherited in her home. As a teen she had transcendent experiences that came to fruition in a Spirit-shaped conversion experience:

> As a teenager, this had such a strong influence on me that I later found myself in an empty local church in prayer. Even though I did not directly hear the gospel of salvation nor about the cross, death, and resurrection of Jesus, this event impacted me so profoundly that I started attending a church. In the fall of that year (1971), I attended a revival meeting where I experienced the baptism of the Holy Spirit. That was obviously my salvation experience. (p. 157)

The gospel that she articulates combines the image of God, the fall, the love of God in Christ's death that took on the punishment of God against sin, the power of restoration, and the need for repentance. The power of sin impacted humans in a comprehensive sense, and this sets Ma up for a more comprehensive sense of salvation with a soterian gospel:

"Pentecostals believe that all people have sinned, sin being defined as breaking God's law and also as offending or displeasing God" [Ma is quoting Keith Warrington here]. Sin affected human beings' rapport with God. It also affects people's relations with one another, and further it affects the entire creation as well. The Son of God came in human flesh to become an atoning sacrifice for the sins of the world. Jesus Christ was a sacrifice to pay that penalty, hence the relationship between God and humanity was reestablished through his blood. (p. 158)

This gospel, as it expands in her presentation, includes creation itself:

Critically, due to their exclusive position in creation and the extraordinary relationship with God before the fall, Adam and Eve were given the responsibility to be in charge of God's creation, and thus their sin affected not only humanity but the entire creation. (p. 159)

The greater impact of sin, the greater the redemption needed, and the greater the gospel that must be preached. She expands the Pentecostal Gospel yet again by appealing to Grace Milton: "Pentecostal soteriology is Christocentric only insofar as the work of Christ is interpreted through and extended by the work of the Holy Spirit" (p. 160). Here we find an unusually candid observation in which pneumatology reframes Christology. Anyone alert to charismatic and Pentecostal theology knows the Spirit becomes front and center. My grandparents were Holiness Pentecostals, and their faith was Spirit driven.

Ma's gospel, then, is a soterian gospel plus a creation-groaning gospel plus a Spirit-fronted gospel that then gets expanded into a healing gospel and a social-redemption gospel. With these gospel expansions, Ma's gospel approximates the experiential kingdom mission of Jesus in Galilee where these features are part of the experienced realities of Jesus's ministry. Her gospel approach now includes the Spirit's empowerment, healing, and social redemption:

Thus, the Pentecostal mission is holistic.

> Along with the stress on Spirit-empowered evangelism and healing, Pentecostals utilize a holistic mission in which the gospel is the remedy for social issues such as the plight of orphans and widows, the HIV/AIDS epidemic, and the like. (p. 161)

And,

> The assurance of good health and blessing reconstituted the understanding of Christian redemption to individuals, families, communities, and the here and now. This message is ready to tackle life's unrelenting problems, such as sickness, shortage, job loss, loneliness, and disaster. (p. 162)

She illustrates this expansive understanding of the gospel with an orphanage mission in Ethiopia and a Zambian care center for those with HIV/AIDS. At this point we have come to the fullness of her presentation of the gospel, and it has now become a version of a liberation gospel. All of this, however, is less concerned with economics as explicated in many of the liberation theologies on offer today, which have deep orientations to various forms of oppression, not least sexism, capitalism, and racism and ethnocentricities that become colonialism.

Because part of our assignment as authors in this volume is to explain how people are meant to respond to the gospel we articulate, Ma cites an earlier study of hers with Wonsuk Ma and explains that the proper response involves repentance and faith. Her expansive gospel appeals especially to the destitute of our world, and that in itself confirms Ma's expanded gospel.

> "The Pentecostal movement shares this soteriological driven mission as the evangelization of the lost" [Ma is quoting Ma and Ma here]. Through repentance, people believe that their sins are washed by the blood of Jesus, and they become the children of God. The Pentecostal gospel of salvation, along with hope and optimism, is particularly well accepted by people in destitute, socially marginalized situations, and the sick. (p. 158)

When it comes to a method for defining the gospel, Ma's approach to the Bible is narrowed to three texts, all three of which are (predictably)

Spirit fronting: Acts 1:8 and 2:1–12, Luke 4:18–19, and 1 Corinthians 12:7–9. Her gospel then is an expansive soteriological vision that forgives, heals, transforms, equips, empowers to mission, and encompasses holistic redemption.

This volume reveals that one's definition of the gospel can be driven by one's theology as much as by, if not more than, specific texts in the New Testament that actually define the gospel (1 Cor 15:1–8; 2 Tim 2:8; the sermons in the book of Acts; and the Gospels as the gospel). David deSilva's Wesleyan Gospel, Michael Horton's Reformation Gospel, and Julie Ma's Pentecostal Gospel are forms of one's theological worldview shaping one's understanding of the gospel. It is not unfair to say then that what shapes one's theology becomes a formative hermeneutical lens that results in determining one's understanding of the gospel. I want to say again that I'm not sure deSilva's Wesleyan Gospel is what deSilva's own framing of the gospel looks like because he's explaining his theological tradition's understanding of the gospel. It appears to me both Horton and Ma are explaining not only their tradition but their own perception of the gospel in that tradition, and the same is the case for Shively Smith when sketching a Liberation Gospel.

Back now to Ma's presentation of the gospel. There are two noticeable omissions that deserve prominent presence in any definition of the gospel, at least any definition shaped formatively by the gospel-defining texts of the New Testament. The first is the absence of an interest in the person and life and public ministry of Jesus. Apart from her admirable attention to Luke 4:18–19, which is undeniably a core gospel text for understanding Jesus, there is little attention to the life of Jesus, to the Gospels, to his teachings and preaching and miracles and parables and tension with Jewish and Roman leadership. If the Gospels are called gospels because they are the gospel, more attention needs to be given to the shape of the gospel found there. The form of each of the Gospels is a biography in which specific episodes in Jesus's life tell us about Jesus, and in so doing they "gospel" the reader or hearer of that episode. In particular, that means an attention to the story of Israel as coming to fulfillment in the story of Jesus as the crucible in which one can finally and fundamentally announce the arrival of the good news. That absence, as well, draws attention to any gospel that does not recognize the ongoing storied nature of the Bible's message—from

Israel to the church and from creation to redemption, new Jerusalem, and new creation.

Nor is sufficient attention, then, given to the most important hermeneutical term for Jesus: kingdom. At least it is important for the Synoptic Gospels, which becomes in the hand of the Fourth Gospel, life and eternal life. Kingdom appears in Ma's chapter twice, once each in the last two paragraphs of her essay. Not only is kingdom not defined, the lack of interest in the kingdom breaks away from the very term Jesus uses in the Gospels of Matthew, Mark, and Luke to explain what he was preaching. Matthew 4:17 reads, "From that time on Jesus began to preach, "Repent, for the kingdom of heaven has come near."

I plead with readers for a deeper discussion of method: let's define the gospel by texts in the New Testament that actually define the gospel. We can expand the gospel, as Ma does so admirably, from that basis. The apostle Paul tells us he is passing on the apostolic gospel when he writes these words to the Corinthians:

> Now, brothers and sisters, I want to remind you of the gospel I preached to you, which you received and on which you have taken your stand. By this gospel you are saved, if you hold firmly to the word I preached to you. Otherwise, you have believed in vain.
>
> For what I received I passed on to you as of first importance: that Christ died for our sins according to the Scriptures, that he was buried, that he was raised on the third day according to the Scriptures, and that he appeared to Cephas, and then to the Twelve. After that, he appeared to more than five hundred of the brothers and sisters at the same time, most of whom are still living, though some have fallen asleep. Then he appeared to James, then to all the apostles, and last of all he appeared to me also, as to one abnormally born. (1 Cor 15:1–8)

Paul gives his own version of that gospel to open the letter to the Romans, a letter by all accounts that has shaped Christian theology more than any New Testament text. He opens with his framing of the gospel:

> Paul, a servant of Christ Jesus, called to be an apostle and set apart for the gospel of God—the gospel he promised beforehand through his prophets in the Holy Scriptures regarding his Son, who as to his earthly life was a descendant of David, and who through the Spirit of holiness was appointed the Son of God in power by his resurrection from the dead: Jesus Christ our Lord. Through him we received grace and apostleship to call all the Gentiles to the obedience that comes from faith for his name's sake. (Rom 1:1–5)

The gospel, defined so clearly in each text, is the story about Jesus. The impact of that story is redemption. There is a difference between the story and the impact, between the gospel and its benefits.

RESPONSE TO JULIE MA

MICHAEL HORTON

I wondered, when Julie Ma refers to "the baptism of the Holy Spirit" as her "salvation experience," are these synonymous? Can one be saved without the experience described as "baptism of the Holy Spirit"? As with the sign gifts, the first question is not whether such experiences continue as normative in this era but what they were or are in the New Testament. Ma does that quite helpfully with tongues, following the view that this gift was a natural language known supernaturally and was tied to mission. Drawing on Craig Keener, she suggests that this was the original Pentecostal view that fell gradually out of favor in later Pentecostalism.[1] I could not agree more that this was the purpose of the gift of tongues. Passing over the complicated issues over whether Acts 2 and 1 Corinthians 14 refer to the same phenomenon, I simply register my agreement with Ma's (and Keener's) interpretation.[2]

Had this interpretation continued in Pentecostalism, it is hard to see how tongues itself could have become the wedge issue it has become among Christians. Surely, if the Lord still sends missionaries to an unreached people with a supernatural gift of understanding and interpreting languages, who could fail to rejoice? Even if tongues in 1 Corinthians 14 differs from this pattern, and even if it remains in effect, there are several things the apostle says here that seem to differ

---

1. "God supernaturally empowered them through the Holy Spirit to speak the languages without the necessity to acquire them first. The linking between the radical experience of tongues and mission is clear. Thus, the early Pentecostals thought of tongues as a missionary language, but this idea was soon abandoned" (Craig S. Keener, *Spirit Hermeneutics: Reading Scripture in Light of Pentecost* [Grand Rapids: Eerdmans, 2016], 22–23).

2. I engage these phenomena at length in *Rediscovering the Holy Spirit: God's Perfecting Presence in Creation, Redemption, and Everyday Life* (Grand Rapids: Zondervan Academic, 2017).

from widespread practice today. First, spiritual gifts are not for private benefit but the edification of the whole church and its mission. Therefore, it is secondary to prophesying (which I take to be preaching) in a common tongue (1 Cor 14:2). "The one who prophesies is greater than the one who speaks in tongues, unless someone interprets, so that the church may be built up" (v. 5 ESV). Whatever sounds are uttered, they must be intelligible to all. Otherwise, "you will be speaking into the air," he says (v. 9 ESV). "There are doubtless many different languages in the world, and none is without meaning, but if I do not know the meaning of the language, I will be a foreigner to the speaker and the speaker a foreigner to me. So with yourselves, since you are eager for manifestations of the Spirit, strive to excel in building up the church" (vv. 10–12 ESV).

The critique of unintelligibility extends to the liturgy: How will the congregation say its "amen" to thanksgiving? "For you may be giving thanks well enough, but the other person is not being built up" (1 Cor 14:17 ESV). Far from suspending his own intellectual activity, Paul refuses to pray or sing with his spirit apart from his mind (vv. 13–17). Whatever Paul's personal experience may be, "in church I would rather speak five words with my mind in order to instruct others, than ten thousand words in a tongue" (v. 19 ESV). Paul associates the practice he is criticizing with immaturity (v. 20). If there is no interpretation, "let each of them keep silent in church and speak to himself and to God. . . . For God is not a God of confusion but of peace. . . . If anyone thinks that he is a prophet, or spiritual, he should acknowledge that the things I am writing to you are a command of the Lord" (vv. 28, 33, 37 ESV). Once again, given that the gift was given for the rapid spread of the gospel, Paul's critique has visitors also in mind: if everyone is speaking in tongues, "will they not say that you are out of your minds?" (v. 23 ESV). But if the word is intelligible, the visitor will be convicted "and so, falling on his face, he will worship God and declare that God is really among you" (vv. 24–25 ESV). What is particularly intriguing is his statement that tongues is a sign of temporary judgment on Israel (in fulfillment of Isa 28:11); it is not meant as a sign for believers at all (1 Cor 14:21–22).

I agree that "baptism in the Spirit" is tied inextricably to the experience of salvation until the end of the age, but the crucial issue is definition. According to Reformed interpretation, the event itself is synonymous with regeneration, not with a subsequent gift granted only to some, and its evidence is nowhere identified as speaking in tongues (however defined) but as water baptism. Here we enter another minefield of historical interpretation. Here, I simply note that from Jesus's baptism onward, associations of the Spirit with baptism indicate (a) being anointed/approved and identified as "son" and (b) being baptized with water. The Spirit who hovered over the waters in creation to make them fruitful, and over the waters of Mary's womb, associates his ministry with creating life out of watery expanse that has no life-giving power of its own. The Spirit baptizes us not into himself but into Christ for new birth, forgiveness of sins, the gift of the indwelling Spirit, and all other gifts of our union with Christ. The Spirit also signifies and seals this visibly by water baptism.

Along with the sovereign freedom of the Spirit, emphasis is given by churches of the Reformation on the inseparable bond between the Spirit and the external word and sacraments. He is not bound, but ordinarily binds himself, to the means of grace. Thus, the church is always on the receiving end of its existence, "having cleansed her [the church] by the washing of water with the word" (Eph 5:26 ESV). The Spirit is always the active agent, but he employs physical instruments—water, bread, and wine—to signify and seal his word of promise.

I take the view of John R. W. Stott that baptism with the Spirit (into Christ) is regeneration but that there are many "fillings" with the Spirit that the believer not only experiences but seeks.[3] Instead of being intoxicated with wine, believers should constantly be drinking from the Living Water (Eph 5:18; cf. John 7:37–39). This is a metaphor, of course, but it points out the responsibility of those now *made alive* to live *as the living* and not as the dead.

Quoting Edmund Rybarczyk, Ma says, "The defeating of sin is not something that human beings can achieve by themselves, but rather God must enter into history and the individual believers' lives to provide 'atonement and to restore the broken relationships'" (p. 159). What an elegant way of putting it! At the same time, we are always wary of

---

3. John R. W. Stott, *Baptism and Fullness* (Downers Grove, IL: InterVarsity Press, 2006). I summarize my agreement with Stott's view in the foreword of this edition.

language about our not being able to do it *all* and God having to *help* us. According to the "Reformation Gospel," we are not merely those who have lost our way and need God to provide some remedies like atonement and restoration of broken relationships to help us get back on the right path. (This concern is pertinent also to the Wesleyan and Liberation Gospels.) We are spiritually dead, not backsliding in the far-off country but aliens and enemies of the good Father, hostile in mind to the things of God, condemned, helpless to lift a finger for our own salvation from sin's guilt and dominion. From beginning to end, "Salvation is of the Lord" (Jonah 2:9 KJV). It's rescue, not assistance. I'm not quibbling with Ma, who may well agree with everything I've just said, but with language that triggers our reaction!

After all, Ma mentions that Pentecostals favor "penal substitutionary atonement."[4] My concern, though, is that the meaning of the word "redemption" focuses on improving social conditions. What I appreciate about Pentecostalism's emphasis, summarized by Ma, is the individual and collective aspects of God's plan for ultimate restoration. However, my concern is that Wesley passed on to Pentecostalism (and the social gospel) an overrealized eschatology at both the personal and social levels. I'll talk about this more in the engagement with the "Liberation Gospel" below. As I read the New Testament, I find encouragement for those oppressed in body, mind, and soul, and for people to love their enemies, serve their persecutors, endure pain and infirmities, thus testifying to a new creation that has been won by Christ, inaugurated by his resurrection and ascension, and empowered by his Holy Spirit, but that will only be consummated *by Christ himself* when he returns. Lutheran and Reformed traditions have a long history of taking diaconal ministry very seriously. Yet whatever we can do to give material aid to those in distress can never redeem or restore creation. Yet the work testifies to the Lord who has done so and will complete it when he returns. We're like medics on a battlefield with what appears to be a sea of grief and pain, oppression and violence, injustice and evil. Yet we don't give up because we're not called to save but only to serve.

The labors of Pentecostals that Ma mentions, especially in HIV/AIDS treatment and orphanages—are a wonderful example to me of

---

4. Quoting the Church of God in Christ Statement of Faith (2018).

the whole *community* of believers taking up a *personal* interest in loving and serving their neighbor. Many of us, especially in the US, think that these are public (i.e., political) issues that need not concern us. We pay our taxes. We're not experts, anyway. And then we want to cut government funding for those who suffer, who are marginalized, and who have much to say but few who listen to them. I find Ma's examples bracing and convicting, as I do when I hear of similar stories from brothers and sisters of Lutheran, Reformed, and other ecclesial traditions who are extending Christ's love to orphans, HIV/AIDS victims, Dalits in Indian caste systems, indigenous peoples of the Americas, and many others. Every year, I visit some of these places, and I am always asked by fellow believers: "Why is this normal for Christians here but not in the US?" It shouldn't be controversial. It is one thing to be on the *giving* end without any fear of being unprivileged and quite another when sharing power with "others" is seen as a threat. What does it mean to love people anywhere, not only recipients of our charity but as equal claimants to justice? Sisters like Ma can help us to answer that question.

I also appreciate the link Pentecostals maintain between the evil powers "in heavenly places" and their torment on the earth. Sometimes the way we talk about spiritual warfare sounds a little abstract, occurring in some remote location *above us* that corresponds to threats *within us*. But Ma reminds us that Satan and his hosts inflict harm *all around us* as well. Several years ago, I stood on the steps of the Ganges River in Varanasi, the capital of Hinduism. As the high priests called down gods (demons, the apostles would have called them) to their sacrifices, the dead were set on fire and sent out into the water, while about thirty very young women sat to one side. Sacred prostitutes for the priests, they looked as though they were dead inside. A man came toward me, covered in white paint it seemed to me, wanting to have a conversation. Immediately, my Indian pastor-friend warned me not to let him engage me. He wasn't covered in paint but in the bone ash of humans. My friend told me that the last time he brought a pastor from America here, this same shaman told the visitor details about his family—their names and characteristics—and the pastor fell on the steps in a heap of sweat, crying inconsolably. I experienced this myself over two days.

Especially as it reached into the gentile world, the context of the New Testament was very similar, and we should expect that where the war in the heavens touches ground so palpably, good and evil signs accompany. Ma's narrative of the fear of demons and ancestors being broken by the news of Christ's triumph cheers the heart.

At the same time, the very success of Christianity in providing an alternative society, as it were, contributes—as it always has—to an unintended secularization. Ma says, "In Latin America, the Pentecostal faith has produced social upward mobility among its followers, and this has attracted many to its faith" (p. 162). The so-called prosperity gospel is one of the most dangerous heresies in the world today, particularly because so many have adopted it as if it were authentic Christianity. I'm sure Ma would agree that when the gospel is tied to prosperity, people find that they don't need Christ for this—which is evident in the rapid decline of Korean Christianity among younger generations.

Finally, the remarkable growth immediately of Pentecostal missions from the Azusa Street revival (however "chaotic," as Ma notes) reminds those of us from different traditions of that truth expressed well by Emil Brunner: "The church exists by mission, just as a fire exists by burning."[5] The challenge, it seems to me, is to proclaim the gospel with Christ's life, death, resurrection, ascension, and return as the content rather than the transformation of individuals and societies. That is not because we do not want to see the latter but because only the good news of what happened long ago *outside of us* can bring genuine renewal *within us* and, *through us*, to others.

---

5. Emil Brunner, *The Word and the World* (Lexington: American Theological Library Association, 1965), 108.

RESPONSE TO JULIE MA

DAVID A. DESILVA

The Wesleyan roots of Pentecostalism are apparent at many points in Julie Ma's contribution. We find this first in her acknowledgment of the "inclination to sin" (or, in Charles Wesley's hymnic language, "our bent to sinning") as a part of the fundamental problem with human beings needing a divine cure. We see it all the more in her emphasis on working to relieve human suffering, particularly among the poor and marginalized, as an integral part of the church's evangelistic mission—not just telling good news, but *bringing* good news. Ma's testimonies in regard to the latter are particularly moving, but perhaps ought not to surprise us since the same Spirit that can be named "the Spirit of Christ" or "the Spirit of [God's] Son" (Rom 8:9; Gal 4:6) moves believers to invest themselves in the same integrated work of healing, restoring lives, and proclaiming the kingdom that characterized Jesus's life and ministry. The overlap here with the liberation gospel is quite remarkable, down to the shared awareness of the importance of Isaiah 61:1–2 as (Luke's presentation of) Jesus's own mission statement and therefore a statement concerning the nature of the work that Jesus's followers must also be about (see Luke 4:16–20). I leave with the impression, however, that those who approach this work in the power of the Holy Spirit, who are open to the supernatural gifting that the Spirit brings, are better equipped to carry it out.

I agree with Ma that it is supremely important to expand the "soteriological narrative" beyond the cross and even resurrection to the outpouring of the Holy Spirit on Jesus's followers (p. 160). I whole-heartedly affirm a soteriology that regards it as essential to affirm that "the work of Christ is . . . extended by the work of the Holy

Spirit."[1] I realize that there is a certain rhetorical exaggeration at work in the five celebrated *solas* of the Reformation, but I particularly find problematic any focus on "Christ alone" that fails also to make room for the Holy Spirit and the Spirit's essential contribution to the full salvation that God intends for human beings to experience.

Ma foregrounds the Spirit and his activity in empowering effective witness and accompanying that witness with acts of healing, rightly noting the importance of this activity in the context of evangelism in the Majority World.[2] Her analysis of Acts 1–2 shows such an emphasis to be entirely scriptural (and we could also look to the testimonies concerning the Pauline mission in 1 Cor 2:1–5; cf. Heb 2:3–4). I would have wished *also* to see an emphasis placed on the Spirit's role in our sanctification, though one can admittedly only cover so much in a single essay. This is certainly not absent from the Pentecostal Gospel as, for example, the "Statement of Fundamental Truths" issued by the General Council of the Assemblies of God (the largest single denominational body within the Pentecostal tradition) makes clear: "by the power of the Holy Spirit we are able to obey the command: 'Be ye holy, for I am holy' (1 Peter 1:15, 16)," which happens as we offer "every faculty continually to the dominion of the Holy Spirit (Romans 6:1–11, 13; 8:1, 2, 13)."[3] The Holy Spirit is the content of the promised blessing conferred upon all the nations through Abraham, granted to all who exhibit trust in God's promise, secured for Jew and gentile alike by Christ's redemptive death (Gal 3:8–9, 13–14). The Holy Spirit is the God-given cure for "our bent to sinning," for those who "walk by the Spirit" are assured that they

---

1. See Ma's quotation of Grace Milton, "Salvation: Participating in the Story Where Earth and Heaven Meet," in *The Routledge Handbook of Pentecostal Theology*, ed. Wolfgang Vondey (Abingdon: Routledge, 220), 228.
2. I have often been critical of Western theologians and biblical scholars whose assumptions about miracles and manifestations of spiritual power in the scriptural narratives reflect our modern, anti-supernaturalistic worldview in the West and betray an almost willful ignorance concerning these phenomena throughout the Majority World (as well as admittedly less frequent reports of the same in the West). See the important and magisterial work by Craig Keener on this subject: *Miracles: The Credibility of the New Testament Accounts*, 2 vols. (Grand Rapids: Baker Academic, 2011). Also idem, *Miracles Today: The Supernatural Work of God in the Modern World* (Grand Rapids: Baker Academic, 2021).
3. The General Council of the Assemblies of God, "Statement of Fundamental Truths," 3–4, https://ag.org/-/media/AGORG/Beliefs/Fundamental-Truths/Statement-of-Fundamental-Truths.pdf.

"will surely not bring to consummation what the flesh craves" (Gal 5:16, author's translation). They will thus escape the reward that the flesh promises—namely, the decay that befalls all flesh in the grave—and receive, instead, the gift of eternal life promised to those who "keep sowing to the Spirit" (Gal 6:7–8; cf. Rom 6:20–23; 8:2–13).

I also appreciate the emphasis placed by Ma, as indeed by Pentecostal Christians generally, on each believer's gifting by the Holy Spirit for—and, therewith, each believer's responsibility to *contribute* to—the edification of the church and the execution of its mission in the world. Such an awareness of the gifts of the Spirit and the purposes for the same positions believers to fulfill the responsibilities of the "priesthood of all believers," perhaps better than one sees in many other denominations. I do not have enough personal experience of Pentecostal churches in the United States to know whether they are able to maintain the emphases on mutual service and on witness and service to the people outside the body of Christ as far as these spiritual gifts are concerned. I can, however, bear witness to this in regard to one particular, charismatic Episcopal church with which I was privileged to be associated for a number of years during my undergraduate and seminary studies.

My reservations in regard to Ma's presentation are twofold, and they admittedly arise in connection with matters that she certainly does not foreground, and so might be considered peripheral concerns.

First, I confess that I have grown less comfortable with the model of "penal substitutionary atonement," as typically articulated, as an adequate representation of the significance of the cross of Christ. I refer here to the portion of the Church of God in Christ's statement of faith quoted in this essay: "God required a penalty to be paid for sin, and Jesus Christ, God's pure and sinless Son, acted as a sacrifice to pay that penalty" that, by right, we owed on account of our disobedience (p. 159). This idea of how we entered into a restored relationship with God is of course rooted firmly in the Scriptures, but it is not the whole picture. I have come to feel the need, whenever making such a statement, however, also to affirm that Jesus's death on the cross was, at the same time, the supreme manifestation of divine love for fallen humanity (1 John 4:9–11). In the cross we do not see Jesus placating an angry and alienated God; we see the Godhead expressing the degree of God's love for, and desire to restore, alienated humanity. It is precisely because "God was in Christ reconciling the world to himself" (2 Cor 5:19, author's translation) that Jesus's death on the cross is, at the same time, an act of a loving rather than a vindictive God.

My second moment of unease comes as I read about mission "inspired by the eschatological urgency of the soon-returning Christ" (p. 171). I hope never to be counted among the scoffers who say, "Where is this promised coming, for ever since the fathers died all things remain as they have been since the beginning of creation?" (2 Pet 3:4, author's translation). Nevertheless, I have to confess to having come to a place where speaking of "eschatological urgency" feels somewhat contrived. Granted that God can experience a thousand years as a day and a day as a thousand years, that very fact renders the idea of "soon" somewhat meaningless for us. With the passing of two millennia, I wonder if scriptural expressions of imminence might not be better interpreted as expressions of "ultimate priority demanding our attention *now*" rather than some *chronological* "eschatological urgency"—though I readily grant that, where the latter can be established as a realistic mood and expectation, the former is also achieved. Nevertheless, I am personally motivated for mission by the fact that "we must all appear before the judgment seat of Christ" (2 Cor 5:10)—and we all have merely the brief span of this life to make use of God's provisions to stand before him with confident trust rather than shame—and not by any sense that the second coming is necessarily imminent. I fear that the long history of our insistence on the "soon-ness" of this coming (that is, the fact there has been a *long* history of this expectation!) undermines the credibility of the rest of what we have to proclaim. The fact that Christ's judgment seat is never further away from me than my own death seems to lend sufficient urgency to mission and to making full use of the grace divine.

RESPONSE TO JULIE MA

SHIVELY T. J. SMITH

I found Ma's opening story productively introspective and the broader essay galvanizing. It arouses a particularly Pentecostal moment for readers ... and for me. Defined by the guidance of loving relationships, Ma casts the Pentecostal Gospel as a message believers experience and encounter before they understand it in doctrinal terms or according to biblical story points about the cross, death, and resurrection of Jesus. She narrates her conversion story and describes the interreligious experiences of her Korean heritage in which Buddhism, shamanism, Confucianism, and Christianity interact. Ma's conversion story intertwines with the stories of her grandmother and high school teacher as she joins the Christian siblinghood in faith.

The personal story opening the essay created the environment for me to reflect on my Pentecostal heritage. Yes, I am an African Methodist Episcopal elder in my adult age, but as a college student I was a member of African American Pentecostal connectional churches. One of the details I remember most from my Pentecostal gospel experiences was how families—particularly my church families—mattered to my Christian journey and my gospel-reading experiences. I loved gospel reading and interpretation while participating in home-based Bible studies and church-family dinners. Remembering the Christian communities of my youth and young adulthood, I now understand that those faithful gatherings represented our commitment to live out Jesus's many "table talk" moments as cast in the Gospel of Luke (7:36; 8:55; 9:10–17). The subject of our table fellowship was the Bible, and those conversations formed my sensibilities about the gospel and its Pentecostal leanings in ways that accompany me even now.

Casting the Pentecostal Gospel as a storied way of being, Ma accomplishes several tasks that prove insightful. First, by starting with her own story, she identifies as an insider of the Pentecostal Gospel view and orientation. She has a story of conversion, salvation, biblical interpretation, and prayer that belongs to the witness of the Pentecostal Gospel experience. Her story, in turn, aligns and supports her working description of the gospel as a form of individual repentance and salvation. According to Ma, the Pentecostal Gospel empowers believers to involve themselves in missional endeavors that care for others, especially those less fortunate. She says, "Through the demonstration of God's power and caring for the needy, the ultimate goal of Pentecostal mission has been spiritual conversion to bring people into God's kingdom" (p. 175).

But Ma describes the Pentecostal Gospel with more than just her personal story. Her essay treats the gospel message as a series of event-based moments occurring in both the biblical and contemporary worlds. In terms of modern contexts, Ma explains the aims of the Pentecostal Gospel view as focused on a mission to care for the holistic person. She illuminates this understanding by highlighting various approaches to "the poor and the marginalized" world contexts. From orphaned children in Ethiopia to HIV/AIDS intervention and care that has unfolded in Zambia for decades, Ma describes the Pentecostal Gospel as attentive to the spiritual and bodily needs of those the world has left unattended and uncared for.

To their credit, as Ma points out, Pentecostal Gospel missionaries have functioned in capacities that provided presence, provision, community, and affirmation unfilled by geopolitical systems and human societies. The focus on doing something with one's gospel faith resonated with me. What is the value of our gospel belief if it does not awaken us to those imprisoned by the dangerous situations and struggles this world produces? Moreover, Ma's essay relocates US American Christians like me in Majority World Christian spaces. Starting in Asia and moving to Africa, Ma's essay shifts the map of the contemporary Christian confession. She signals a worldwide Christian siblinghood often left unacknowledged by American (and some European) Christian interpretations of the gospel.

The gospel starts with the individual, according to Ma's elucidation, but it does not stay fixed to the person. Rather, as her personal story demonstrates, individual Christian conversion turns public and communal rather quickly. In the lives of Pentecostal believers, the activity of the Spirit compels them to get involved in expanding the account of salvation beyond themselves, into the ends of the world (Acts 1:8). As such, contemporary believers, guided by God's Spirit, extend the gospel accounts as found in passages like Luke 4:18–19, Acts 2:1–4, and 1 Corinthains 12:7–9. In this way, the Spirit of the Pentecostal view is like the Spirit and commitments of the Liberation Gospel view. The gospel message compels believers to attend to the physical and social aspects of humanity, near and far, Christian and non-Christian. The gospel is a driving force to go into the world and do something for more than just oneself—to do something for God's kin-dom. Indeed, reading Ma's essay was at times a bit like reading a gospel testimony. She penned a literary witness to what the gospel does in the lives of believers who follow the Spirit's lead of proclamation.

One is left to wonder, however, is there more the Pentecostal Gospel should offer from *inside* the communities it attends? In his iconic book, *Jesus and the Disinherited*, Howard Thurman warns readers about the Christian impulse to "share with others what one has found meaningful" enough to elevate to the height of a faithful and moral imperative.[1] Thurman critiques interpretations of the gospel that understand it to primarily involve attending to "others" rather than understanding the gospel as arising from the lived resources of those designated "other." Ma's descriptions of the Pentecostal Gospel frequently appear to arise from outside cultural communities. It is recognizable by the faith-based actions of the missionaries and care tenders, rather than the actions of those in need of such care in the first place. Consequently, the Pentecostal Gospel is not described as arising from *within* the communities of the orphaned, the ill, the disenfranchised, and the marginal.

In this pattern of handing over, the gospel becomes an object that is brought, implemented, and deployed rather than a subject that lives—is even "enfleshed"—within cultural contexts. Such a mode of gospel sharing runs the risk of enacting a diminished, even corrupted version of Paul's proud creedal declaration of his gospel message as one received and passed on, and not one he created: "For I handed on to you as of first importance what I in turn had received: that Christ died for our sins in accordance with the scriptures" (1 Cor 15:3 NRSV). The Pentecostal gospel can be decontextualized and recontextualized by the missionary's

---

1. Howard Thurman, *Jesus and the Disinherited* (1949; repr., Boston: Beacon Press, 1996), 2.

"calling" endeavor and thus become an instrument and a tool rather than an embodiment. This concerns me.

Once Ma moves away from the contemporary mission-based description of the Pentecostal Gospel, she attends to the authority of the Bible. I found this movement refreshing. Ma traces a pattern of Spirit-led activities in community creation and care running through the New Testament. In particular, she enacts the experience of Christian "retellings" notable in places like the book of Acts. Soon after the Pentecost moment, for example, gospel readers repeatedly note Peter recounting his Spirit-led missions to the Jerusalem church (Acts 11:1–18) or Barnabas and Paul rehearsing their experience of God performing "signs and wonders" through them "among the gentiles" (15:12 NRSVue). Ma's essay creates a literary environment that invites Christian memory, storytelling, and consideration. Such a practice is not only Pentecostal in nature, but gospel-like in form.

Similarly, her treatment of the workings of the Spirit looks familiar to my Africana Pentecostal sensibilities. The Spirit's activities, more than the agents activated by the Spirit, are what matters in Ma's view. The Holy Spirit is the animating force of the Pentecostal Gospel, which is missionally driven. Witnessing is the act of "bringing to" people what they do not have. Framed in this way, the Pentecostal Gospel appears to move in a clear direction—it discerns divine imperatives to move *toward* communities and people.

There is, however, a subtle but dangerous shortfall in this reading. In some ways, the Spirit's caricature in the Pentecostal view appears to carry a colonizing tendency. It can lead to the erasure of a people's ancestral resources and family stories in which God has already been a part. The Holy Spirit empowers people *to speak to* and *to go to* others, instead of the Spirit empowering people *to speak from* their "othered" classes and *to speak from within* their locations. One can quickly find themselves restating Thurman's inquiry: "The masses of men live with their backs constantly against the wall. They are the poor, the disinherited, the dispossessed. What does our religion say to them? The issue is not what it counsels them to do for others whose need may be greater, but what religion offers to meet their own needs."[2]

---

2. Thurman, *Jesus and the Disinherited*, 3.

At times, Ma's description of biblical texts supporting the Pentecostal Gospel indicates a theological position that emphasizes the fallenness or sinfulness of humanity to such a degree it glosses over the creative "made in God's image" resources that our human stories, contexts, and communities already possess. For example, the first chapter and verse of the New Testament, Matthew 1:1, begins by situating Jesus in the testimonies and peoplehood of Israel: "An account of the genealogy of Jesus the Messiah, the son of David, the son of Abraham" (NRSVue). Reading Ma's view, I wondered what is lost in the Pentecostal Gospel's accounting of the Spirit's movements when it overlooks the accounts of the Spirit's activities *before* the Pentecost moment or even before Jesus's birth? The stories of Zechariah and Elizabeth or Mary and Joseph, or even Mary and Elizabeth together, who are pregnant with attestations of the Spirit's movement before Jesus's birth, death, resurrection, and Pentecost experience of Acts. Before Jesus was born, if we follow the pattern of Luke-Acts, all was not sin-filled, fallen, or lost to the point that the Spirit was not yet active. The Pentecostal Gospel frame as deployed hides this nuance. It misses that the Spirit-led impulse is not to create witnesses from nothing. Rather, the Spirit amplifies the work of witnesses from among the people with whom God has always been involved—even if the people did not know it was God or even know the name of God and God's agents at the time.

The Pentecostal Gospel, according to Ma, is a "soteriological driven mission," that travels across time, space, and human hearts. Using compelling anecdotes, she describes the Pentecostal Gospel as not simply a matter of biblical passages but as a lived confession of Christian fellowships and endeavors. The Pentecostal Gospel's embrace of the spirit world as present in this world aligns to the beliefs of many non-Western believers. It becomes a site of symmetry and continuity to cultural and indigenous beliefs tied to the land. But on a more personal note, Ma's Pentecostal Gospel essay reminds me of the faith communities who prayed for me and with me as I followed the leading of the Spirit on my vocational path of a biblical scholar and teacher. Her essay reminds me of the sacred work involved in Christian recollection and testimony. I join her witness to the power of the Pentecostal Gospel to reset the lives of individuals, families, and communities. Thank you for this reminder.

CHAPTER FIVE
A LIBERATION GOSPEL VIEW

SHIVELY T. J. SMITH

Introduction

The iconic mural painted by Aaron Douglas in 1934 titled *Aspects of Negro Life: From Slavery through Reconstruction* supplies visual representation for a liberation gospel view of the New Testament and its interpretive approach.[1] The mural is one of four panels that the 135th Street Branch of the New York Public Library (now the Schomburg Center for Research in Black Culture) commissioned Douglas to paint in the 1930s. His visual rendering traced the history of African Americans through enslavement, emancipation, the emergence of a voting African American citizenry, and the backlash of white America that ensued.

Douglas divided the mural into three sections, which flow from right to left. The far right depicts silhouettes symbolizing the transformation of doubt into celebration at the jubilant announcement of emancipation. The middle section focuses on the power of the dispossessed in claiming their collective voice through voting rights. The far-left section depicts the withdrawal of the Union soldiers and the emergence of Christian white supremacist groups to stamp out African American agency and

---

1. Aaron Douglas, "Aspects of Negro Life: From Slavery to Reconstruction," 1934, Schomburg Center for Research in Black Culture, Art and Artifacts Division, The New York Public Library, New York, New York, New York Public Library Digital Collections (https://digitalcollections.nypl.org/items/634ad849-7832-309e-e040-e00a180639bb).

197

full inclusion in society as citizens. Douglas's signature style used sharp lines and flat colors to create dramatic silhouetted forms. This panel reflects his use of both warm and bright colors. Depending on where one looks in the mural, the scene appears noisy and chaotic or quiet and peaceful. "Read" as a single work of art—not a composite of three different pieces—Douglas's mural interprets the American story from the location of a disenfranchised population—forcefully displaced Americans of African descent.

Douglas detailed a comprehensive record of African American life in this mural and across his corpus of silhouette visual renderings from the 1930s to his death in 1979. Drawing from the social fringes of dominant American culture and experience, he liberated the American story from misrepresentation and oversight by tracing its history from the underside. His works interpret American history in the bodily silhouettes and aesthetics of its oppressed and targeted citizens. Such creative, interpretive endeavors brought the experiences of the dispossessed, the poor, the subjugated, and the overlooked forward, rendering their stories current and central to the present context.

Douglas's creative approach to the visual arts in the early twentieth century is a precursor and parallel to the approach of Christian biblical interpreters and theologians like Howard Washington Thurman with his 1949 publication of *Jesus and the Disinherited* or Gustavo Gutiérrez and his 1973 publication of *A Theology of Liberation*.[2] They understood the gospel message to reflect God's predilection for the oppressed and poor. Their reading strategy looked for those interpretive signposts in the Gospels and the book of Acts as they pioneered liberation gospel theology from the social location of populations exposed to discrimination, subjugation, and displacement. For both Thurman and Gutiérrez, the social locations of the poor and oppressed are diverse. No single form exists, and the notion of "the poor" as limited to a particular social class is ahistorical. Gutiérrez asserts that "any interpretation of poverty that reduces the poor and the option for the poor to the purely economic and political level is therefore mistaken and can claim no support

---

2. Howard Thurman, *Jesus and the Disinherited* (1949; repr., Boston: Beacon Press, 1996); Gustavo Gutiérrez, *A Theology of Liberation: History, Politics, and Salvation*, rev. ed. (Maryknoll, NY: Orbis Books, 1988).

from our [liberation theology] thinking."³ The endeavor of liberation interpretation, therefore, is to yield thick descriptions of the various struggles, realities, and forms of human oppression and suppression while illuminating the gospel message of salvation that frees the body, head, *and* heart.

A liberation gospel view approaches the New Testament writings from the assumption that spiritual and social matters are interrelated. The social problems that separate human beings into the haves and have-nots, the rich and the poor, the dignified and the derided, and the free and the censured are problems plaguing human institutions and systems. Still, they are also problems of the human spirit. A common trend threaded through liberation interpretations of the fourfold Gospel, Acts, and the New Testament letters is the articulation of where the social and spiritual coalesce in ways affirming God's idiom in human beings.

Viewing the gospel as liberatory also highlights texts where the social and spiritual are destroyed in the story or by biblical readers. Gospel interpreters can exercise a selective literalism that favors individual salvation while looking past the social critiques levied at oppressive institutions that benefit some human classes and disadvantage others. From this perspective, a liberation gospel view cannot gloss over the repeated instances of social care and redress on full display in the Gospels. Liberation-focused interpreters seek to understand how Jesus addressed social issues of neglect, oversight, and exclusion, and they identify Jesus as one of the excluded himself. Liberation readings approach the writings of the New Testament as testimonies of "good news" that speak in the contexts of poverty, illness, ethnic and racial discrimination, gender bias, social-class stratification, and religious difference.

What Is the Gospel?

A Liberation Gospel perspective testifies to God's present voice and actions in the lives of those on the margins. Born in poverty yet free, Jesus died the death of an enslaved person. A liberation perspective of the gospel marks Jesus's social status as one among the oppressed and reads with other "non-persons."

---

3. Gustavo Gutiérrez, *The Truth Shall Make You Free: Confrontations* (Maryknoll, NY: Orbis Books, 1990), 10.

Expanded Summary Definition

The gospel from a liberation perspective testifies to God's present voice and actions in the lives of those situated on the margins. It begins where Jesus began as a child born into subsistence-level poverty (Luke 2:7, 22–24), and it follows him to his state-sanctioned death as an innocently crucified person (Luke 23:47; cf. Matt 27:19).[4] Born free, Jesus died the death of an enslaved person.[5] A Liberation Gospel view marks Jesus's social status as one among the oppressed. It also looks for the other "non-persons" of the gospel—namely, "those who are not considered to be human beings with full rights, beginning with the right to life and to freedom."[6] In conversation with the life, deeds, and actions of Jesus, this approach expresses an unwavering commitment to human dignity, equality, and relatedness signified by the treatment and recognition of marginalized communities rather than the experiences of dominant and normative classes. The calibration in a liberation gospel view is decisive: to interpret the gospel is to read for "what the teachings and the life of Jesus have to say to those who stand, at a moment in human history, with their backs against the wall."[7]

Martin Luther King Jr.'s description of the gospel, informed by his reworking of social-gospel theology from the early mid-twentieth century, exemplifies a reading strategy that casts liberation as both a spiritual and social matter. King wrote in his 1963 book *Strength to Love* that "the gospel at its best deals with the whole man, not only

---

4. It is worth noting that the Greek word behind the NRSV translation decision of "innocence" is *dikaios* (mostly translated as righteous, right, or fair in English translations) as opposed to the Greek term *athōos*, which occurs only twice in the NT, specifically in Jesus's trial proceedings described in Matt 27 (see vv. 4, 27). More can be said about this intriguing translation history, but it exceeds the focus of this essay.

5. In Roman sources, crucifixion is often referred to in short form as an enslaved person's punishment. Three classes of people were the primary candidates: (1) runaway enslaved people; (2) traitors to the state; and (3) political revolutionaries. See Cicero's account of "The Persecution of Verres" in Jo-Ann Shelton, *As the Romans Did: A Sourcebook in Roman Social History* (Oxford: Oxford University Press, 1998), 284; Richard A. Horsley, *Jesus and the Empire: The Kingdom of God and the New World Disorder* (Minneapolis: Fortress, 2003), 28–29.

6. Gutiérrez, *Theology of Liberation*, 18–19. Also, see Shively T. J. Smith, "Witnessing Jesus Hang: Reading Mary Magdalene's View of Crucifixion through Ida B. Wells's Chronicles of Lynching," in *Stony the Road We Trod: African American Biblical Interpretation*, Thirtieth Anniversary Expanded Edition, ed. Cain Hope Felder (Minneapolis: Fortress, 2021), 296–323.

7. Thurman, *Jesus and the Disinherited*, 1.

his soul but also his body, not only his spiritual well-being but also his material well-being."[8] King's description of the gospel is not only a statement about the content of the gospel message but the objective for reading the gospel in the first place. To what end does one interpret the gospel message? A liberation reading of the gospels as stories of faith and social transformation emphasizes that the social problems are Christian moral problems. To separate them as separate matters is to miss the point of Jesus's story, pronouncements, and implications, which leads to misreading and misappropriating the gospel witness. Reading the gospel stories can sensitize interpreters to the interconnectedness between faith and society. It can awaken those who follow its storylines to their current contexts and galvanize them to be more present in the world, not less. Instead of retreating from the world and withdrawing into a faith experience disconnected and inattentive to struggling communities, a liberation gospel view exercises the alternative impulse. It intertwines spiritual and social transformation. This view interprets the Gospels to deepen the collective sense of God-endowed human responsibility for one another across the boundaries people construct to separate themselves.

What Context?

A liberation reading of the New Testament locates interpretation within biblical people's historical, social, and theological struggles, and later Bible interpreting communities. An interpretation of liberation describes the positive—namely, where liberation occurs in gospel accounts—and it also describes the negative—where oppression, censure, and violence against the liberated and those struggling under subjugation manifest. Liberation readings expose the imposition of dominant classes upon the oppressed inscribed in the content of the gospel stories or recorded in the social histories of interpretive communities that derive meaning and significance from those stories. For example, liberation readings trace the imperial context of the gospel world with its emperors, kings, governors, and religious leaders (Luke 1:5; 2:1–2; 3:1–2; Acts 5:21; 25:1–2, 13). It also highlights when local community life harms people by placing

---

8. Quoted in Vanessa Cook, "Martin Luther King, Jr., and the Long Social Gospel Movement," *Religion and American Culture* 26.1 (2016): 80. The primary source is Martin Luther King Jr., *Strength to Love* (Philadelphia: Fortress, 1963), 150.

them in chains (chained Gerasene man, Mark 5:1–20), denying people benevolence (feeding the masses, Mark 8:1–9; cf. Matt 25:42–45), or dismissing petitions for mercy (the Canaanite woman, Matt 15:21–28; blind Bartimaeus, Mark 10:46–52; cf. Matt 23:23). It follows social, political, and cultural life as conveyed in biblical texts while noticing how it impacts the contexts of readers, both ancient and contemporary. Liberation gospel readings acknowledge that no reading of the gospel is value neutral. Sprinkled throughout every understanding of the gospel are its interpreters' values and socially conditioned vantage points. Thus, its starting point takes a decisive side—that of the historically marginalized, oppressed, disinherited, erased, and silenced. It fashions a vision of liberation and provides a trenchant critique of oppressive arrangements, taking its cues from Jesus himself.

Generally, a liberation view of the gospel identifies Jesus as a free Galilean peasant man, born into subsistence-level poverty (Luke 2:22–24). As a country-dweller and Roman noncitizen, he acted on behalf of the other masses of Jewish people living in and around Galilee and Judea at subsistence-level poverty. Jesus is a son and brother (Matt 13:55–56; Mark 3:31–35) and an itinerant teacher and healer (Mark 1:32–34; 3:10; 4:1). He traversed the regions of Galilee and Judea in the tradition of the Jewish prophets (Mark 6:4; Luke 13:33; 24:19). He was literate, reading Jewish scrolls in synagogue spaces where he observed his people's religious and social customs (Luke 4:16–20).

Across the four Gospel accounts of Jesus's short-lived public ministry, he functions as an ancient version of a community organizer, galvanizing ordinary working people like Galilean fishermen (Peter and John), tax collectors (Levi), and women (Mary and Martha). His followers shared the everyday challenges of poverty, illness, hunger, isolation, and disenfranchisement. Nevertheless, as followers of Jesus, they formed communities who acted together in the self-interests of the whole (e.g., four men carry the paralytic man, Mark 2:1–12; Samaritan woman proclaims to her village, John 4:39–42). Consequently, a liberation view of the gospel is as interested in the communities constituted around Jesus as it is with the man himself. The people and experiences that share the narrative stage with Jesus in the stories, however brief, are important points for interrogating the nature of freedom, inclusion, and acceptance at work in the proclamation of good news. Liberation readings attend to the social signposts of biblical passages and their attestation of access to God's "kin-dom" as salvific and necessary.

A liberation gospel view does more than attend to the stories and sayings of Jesus cataloged across the four narratives about his life, death, and resurrection. It is also a particular kind of reading strategy born from the experiences and stories of those who encounter the gospel accounts as disinherited people in their contexts. A liberation focus on the Bible reads from and toward a place of dispossession, disinheritance, and marginality. It resources the gospel stories as counterresponses to contemporary social realities of struggle and inequity. Read from this angle, the gospel is both affirmation and critique. It affirms the existence and equality of all human beings, while critiquing those stakeholders and systems that wield power in a way that keeps their own status intact. This view is not merely a lens through which someone reads the gospel message, but a liberation perspective is a location from which and to which one understands the message of "good news."

Which Texts?

As briefly demonstrated, a liberation view of the gospel is a content-driven interpretive approach. It mines the Gospels, Acts, Paul, and other New Testament letters for messages and stories of freedom, access, care, hospitality, and inclusion. For example, liberation interpretation highlights Luke's inaugural moment of Jesus's ministry when he stands in the Galilean synagogue and characterizes his ministerial message for the poor, prisoners, infirmed, and oppressed on the literary authority of the prophet Isaiah (Luke 4:16–21). A liberation view draws meaning from this passage and deploys it to understand other passages. It uses Jesus's declaration in the synagogue as a cipher to identify when the gospel depicts the experience of freedom occurring in other parts of the story. From the prison release of Peter, Paul, and Silas (Acts 12:6–11; 16:19–34) to the measures four companions took to lower a sick person from a roof to secure the care and healing Jesus provided (Mark 2:1–12; Luke 5:17–26)—liberation reading strategies hunt for the traces of freedom, humanity, and social change threaded throughout the gospel witness.

As a content-driven approach, two other texts are valuable examples for considering a liberation vantage point: the stories of the good

Samaritan (Luke 10:25–37) and of the communal ethic of sharing in the book of Acts (2:42, 44; 4:32).

Reading the Good Samaritan as Liberation

The story of the good Samaritan is a familiar parable to Christian and non-Christian alike. Jesus shares the parable in Luke's extended travel narrative as he and his disciples journey to Jerusalem (Luke 9:51–19:27). The parable is a teaching moment (10:29–37) surrounded by other teaching moments, like the necessity of love for God and other human beings in scriptural interpretation (10:25–28), the importance of women's agency and leadership in faith matters (10:38–42), and models for how to pray (11:1–13). The entire teaching cycle in which Luke sets the good Samaritan story occurs in Jesus's description of the behaviors and attitudes of God's kingdom in the current moment (10:8–11). The parable captures an incident when an innocent person is robbed and abandoned on the side of the road. Two different religious and political leaders—a priest and a temple functionary (Levite), people who are expected to care for the communities they serve—avoided interaction, leaving a "stranger," a Samaritan, to supply care and kindness (cf. Luke 17:11–19; also Matt 10:5; John 4:9). A popular reading of this parable discusses the quality of neighborliness—particularly among people in the same community and sharing similar proximities. However, the parable of the good Samaritan is not only about local neighborhood relations; it is a story that highlights the necessity for crossing ethnic-racial and social-cultural boundaries as an imperative of Jesus's kingdom vision.

Martin Luther King Jr. and one of his spiritual advisors, Howard Washington Thurman, repeatedly appealed to the parable of the good Samaritan as an essential witness to understanding the work of liberation and inclusion. They interpreted the parable in service to their faith and social commitments, which saw American and global forms of racism and the multiplicity of other systemic prejudices as the corruption of Christian moral conscience. Exactly one year before his assassination, on April 4, 1967, King delivered a sermon to the Clergy and Concerned Laity meeting at Riverside Church in New York City, called "A Time to Break Silence." Linking his opposition to the Vietnam War to the global matter of civil rights, King said:

> We are called to play the good Samaritan on life's roadside, but that will be only an initial act. One day we must come to see that the whole Jericho road must be transformed so that men and women will not be constantly beaten and robbed as they make their journey on life's highway. True compassion is more than flinging a coin to a beggar; it is not haphazard and superficial. It comes to see that an edifice which produces beggars needs restructuring.[9]

King interpreted the parable as fundamentally a critique of oppressive social systems that endanger its people, subjecting them to violence, scarcity, and death. For King, Jesus's parable depicts both sides—namely, non-liberatory and liberatory behaviors and attitudes.

A little over a decade earlier, on November 25, 1956, Thurman preached a sermon titled "Who is My Neighbor?" at Boston University's Marsh Chapel. He, too, understood a significant implication of the parable as one that challenged assumptions about "community relatedness." He said, "When the members of this primary social unit begin to put at the center of their behavior toward each other a deliberate intent to love, to trust, to be kind, to be gracious, to recognize no boundaries to the community—that's what Jesus is talking about."[10] A liberation reading of the good Samaritan casts boundary-crossing action as necessary. Although the priest and the Levite crossed the Jericho road to move away from the abandoned stranger (Luke 10:31–32), King and Thurman deploy this parable to enjoin their hearers and readers to cross the road in the opposite direction. For them, the parabolic liberating witness of the good Samaritan encourages a road crossing *toward* another person, not away from them. They locate liberation in the directional movement a stranger makes toward their disenfranchised human being.

Thurman and King interpret the parable as an emancipatory action in human relatedness whereby one "comes alongside" another. One scholar describes the value King (and Thurman) assigned to interpret the parable in service to both spiritual and social commitments by noting:

---

9. Martin Luther King Jr., *A Testament of Hope: The Essential Writings and Speeches*, ed. James M. Washington (New York: HarperOne, 1986), 241.
10. Howard Thurman, *Sermons on the Parables*, ed. David B. Gowler and Kipton E. Jensen (Maryknoll, NY: Orbis Books, 2018), 124, 129.

Christian activists, King believed, needed to emulate the actions of the Good Samaritan on Jericho Road. Though the Good Samaritan was "a man of another race," he "got down from his beast, decided not to be compassionate by proxy," and, instead, administered aid from a position of equality at the side of the man in need. "Jesus ended up saying this was the good man," King concluded, "because he had the capacity to project the 'I' into the 'thou,' and to be concerned about his brother." The Good Samaritan's concern was expressed in true solidarity and compassion, not paternalistic charity. This particular point, popular among liberation theologians, was known as accompaniment, the responsibility of one human being to struggle alongside another in times of trouble, as equals. King considered it the only way to build the Kingdom of God and the brotherhood of man on earth.[11]

From this view, the good Samaritan parable supplies a biblical model for flattening power relations instead of goodness flowing from a top-down or insider-to-outsider power dynamic. It implies that the person needing support and the one giving support are equals. The one with resources in the account extends help as a proverbial gesture of "crossing the aisle" rather than an act of handing down.

The good Samaritan parable is an essential text in a Liberation Gospel view because it emphasizes human dignity and accompaniment as a necessity for resolving human misery, exploitation, and struggle. The "good" Christian act transgresses national and ethnic allegiances and chooses international partnerships. It models a resolve toward true brotherhood, sisterhood, and human relatedness that values the care of the other as more important than personal conveniences and the expenditures of material possessions and time. In this way, a liberation perspective looks for the creation of human connection and responsibility. It reads the gospel to overlay spiritual matters with social responsibility, measured by the quality of human treatment for the "least of these" in local, national, and global societies (Matt 25:30–45). In turn, the experiences of those historically susceptible to diminished

---

11. Cook, "Martin Luther King, Jr. and the Long Social Gospel Movement," 92.

forms of human dignity measure the quality of the kingdom of God actualized in the present moment. The manifestation of the kingdom of God is only as good as how "the least of these" experience human relations, particularly among those proclaiming their status as "children of God."

Reading Liberation as the Sharing of Common Ground

A text from the book of Acts that extends the story of accompaniment and equality is that of the communities sharing "all things in common" (Acts 2:44; 4:32–35). The book of Acts extends a Liberation Gospel view through its narrative about the expansion of Christian communities, following a prophetic tradition (2:16–18, 24; 3:13–18; 15:32). Liberation gospel readings trace the Spirit's movements through key figures and communities as they repeatedly transgress social boundaries of ethnicity, religious regulations, gender, and class (1:2, 5, 8; 2:4, 17–18). Justo L. González links the events, mission, and resistance of the expanding Christian fellowship to the example Jesus embodied, especially as encountered in the Gospel of Luke. While designating the Holy Spirit as the leading actor in Luke-Acts, González writes, "The first part is a Gospel in which it is clear that Jesus, although not a revolutionary after the manner of the Zealots, clashed with those in authority both among his own Jewish people and among the Romans. The second part shows that the same was true with reference to the early disciples."[12] The church emerges in Acts as diverse and loosely connected assemblies whose very identity and orientation in the world are grounded in prophetic expectations nurtured and realized within the community (1:16; 3:18; 13:33). The story of the beginning of Christian mobilization, organization, and assembly extends Jesus's story, and it unfolds as a prophetic sequence of liberated people and their strivings in non-liberatory environments.

Acts 4:32–37 depicts the communal life of the growing movement as one characterized by sharing possessions (*koinon*, 2:42, 44; 4:32). Members contribute to the welfare of the community according to their means without differentiation. The pattern Acts 4 describes runs like

---

12. Justo L. González, *Acts: The Gospel of the Spirit* (Maryknoll, NY: Orbis Books, 2001), 7–8.

a silver lining throughout the larger plotline. For example, Barnabas, Ananias, and Sapphira could afford to sell their property and donate money for the greater good of the entire community. Lydia in Philippi (16:40) and Philip (21:8) made their homes available to the community as hospitality and reverence for God. The storyline of Acts depicts the common ground shared between members in the form of disciples constantly in the company of disabled or impoverished people (3:1–11), the tormented and the sick (5:14–16), the widows (6:1–7), and foreigners from other countries and regions (Ethiopian eunuch, 8:26–39; Apollos, 18:24–28). The community of Acts engages its tormenters (Saul, Acts 9:10–19a), offers asylum to the unjustly persecuted (Peter, 12:12–17), and fellowships with the rich and powerful (the centurion Cornelius, 10:23–48; the proconsul, 13:4–12). It even hosts impromptu interreligious dialogues (Simon the magician, 8:9–13; Paul's Areopagus speech, 17:22–34). A liberation view of Acts traces its prophetic message as a call for radical inclusion, interaction and dialogue, and unparalleled equality. Groups and individuals who typically do not cross paths in the Roman world are thrown together and labeled "Christian" in Acts (11:26). Spirit-led liberation that is salvific and godly emerges as a vision of authentic, boundary-crossing social interaction.

A liberation perspective also acknowledges how Christian idealism constantly clashes with the realities of social context. The vision for a new social arrangement in the book of Acts unfolds in a world that responds with hostility. Resistance to social change and new patterns of human fellowship takes on many forms in the story, and a liberation reading tracks those distinctions. It attends to the aggressive responses as much as it highlights the emancipatory actions on display in Acts. The former ranges from religious and political backlash (Acts 4:1–22), deception and complicity (5:1–11), profiling and violent attacks (5:17–42; 19:29–41), and even assassination (7:54–8:3; 12:1–2). Although a prophetic unfolding of human fellowship and acceptance recur in the book, the storyline also portrays the biases and evils of the world within which believers live. As Peter's hopeful vision of a new social politic develops after Pentecost in Acts 2, the radical social program diminishes as much as it manifests in the rest of the story.

The writer of Acts captures the distance between the expanding gospel witness that persistently transgresses social boundaries and the human obstacles erected to oppose the continuing realization of human freedom and mutuality. A liberation reading notes the discrepancy between the ideal Spirit-led fellowship of God's people and the contentious resistance they face from within and outside the community. For instance, Luke-Acts has numerous references to women, named and unnamed, who do not surface anywhere else in the New Testament literature (Joanna, Susanna, and "many others," Luke 8:1–4; Dorcas, Acts 9:36–43; Rhoda, Acts 12:6–17; Lydia, Acts 16:11–15). These figures remain secondary to the book's marquee male figures, leaving the Roman world's patriarchal interests and caste systems intact. Similarly, ethnic distinctions and stigmas, and cultural differences remain an ongoing conflict in Acts (cf. Mark 7:24–30). For example, Acts 16 follows the Jerusalem Council's decree of Acts 15 that non-Jewish believers share the same rights as Jewish believers in the community without the requirement of circumcision (Acts 15:22–39). Paul, however, still compels his Greek companion, Timothy, to be circumcised (Acts 16:3). Acts fails not only to resolve the disparity of power in the case of women and men but also fails to resolve ethnic conflict and variance in religious observances. Internal conflicts regarding the disparities of power and affluence repeatedly arise in the book of Acts (6:1–6; 9:26–30; 11:1–18; 18:24–28). From a liberation view, the book of Acts conveys the complexity of changing human relatedness. When communities follow the gospel witness of inclusion, equality, and freedom, they face mounting social resistance to their fellowships.

Biblical readings focused on liberation understand the story of Christian beginnings as new modes for human fellowship blended with divine encounters. It attends to how new human relationships are forged from unexpected and unconventional human communion. To read the book of Acts from a Liberation Gospel view is to take up the pursuit for community. According to the mystic theologian and biblical interpreter Howard Thurman, an emancipatory impulse articulates "that community cannot feed for long on itself; it can only flourish where always the boundaries are giving way to the coming of others from beyond them—unknown and undiscovered brothers [and sisters and human beings]."[13]

---

13. Howard Thurman, *The Search for Common Ground* (Richmond: Friends United Press, 1986), 104.

A liberation view of Acts embraces its vision of a boundary-transgressing communion in the real world of human avarice, complicity, destruction, and indifference. Liberation-focused readers notice that the barriers facing the radical strivings portrayed in Acts are unavoidable in the birth of the gospel and its present unfolding in the world.

A Mixed Reception of Paul

The letters of the New Testament, particularly Paul's writings, have mixed reception in liberation views of the gospel. Just as 2 Peter 3:15–16 notes the uneven reception of Paul's letters among early Christian communions, that trend has persisted in liberation and social readings of Paul for communities historically located on the underside or labeled "other" than the normative social conventions. In addition to understanding the Christian message in the Gospel accounts and Acts, Thurman and King are also instructive for considering the mixed reception of Paul's writings among liberation gospel reading communities.

One of Thurman's first understandings of Paul's letters and their use in African American communities derives from his grandmother's position that, as Scripture, it bore no authority in her life. A formerly enslaved woman and the primary caregiver for Thurman, Nancy Ambrose instructed her grandson to never read Paul's letters to her because those were the preferred texts her enslaver would require preachers to proclaim to the enslaved on his plantations. Recounting that experience, Thurman reflects:

> During much of my boyhood I was cared for by my grandmother, who was born a slave and lived until the Civil War on a plantation near Madison, Florida. My regular chore was to do all of the reading for my grandmother—she could neither read nor write. Two or three times a week I read the Bible aloud to her. I was deeply impressed by the fact that she was most particular about the choice of Scripture. For instance, I might read many of the more devotional Psalms, some of Isaiah, the Gospels again and again. But the Pauline epistles, never—except, at long intervals, the thirteenth chapter of First Corinthians. . . . I asked her one day why it was that she would not let me read any of the Pauline letters. What she told me I shall never forget. "During the days

of slavery," she said, "the master's minister would occasionally hold services for the slaves. Old man McGhee was so mean that he would not let a Negro minister preach to his slaves. Always the white minister used as his text something from Paul. At least three or four times a year he used as a text: 'Slaves, be obedient to them that are your masters . . . , as unto Christ.' Then he would go on to show how it was God's will that we were slaves and how, if we were good and happy slaves, God would bless us. I promised my Maker that if I ever learned to read and if freedom ever came, I would not read that part of the Bible."[14]

Nancy Ambrose's approach to reading (or, in her case, hearing) Pauline letters as Scripture carries the markings of its complex history. On the one hand, certain classes of interpreters have used the Pauline letters as tools for control. They wielded Paul's canonical voice to authorize power differentials that established some people as those who "lord over" and other people as those who are "lorded"—such as enslaved people, women, children, and the host of "othered" classes based on age, nationality, language, and more. On the other hand, Nancy Ambrose's critique of Paul is not about Paul but his interpreters. She chooses to silence Paul's voice and influence in her gospel encounter because of how dominant communities historically used Paul to create a community for some while destroying human dignity and stealing the rights of freedom and inclusion of others. She reads Paul's letters as biblical texts weaponized against her oppressed community. As such, she exercises "choice" in where she hears the gospel message articulated in the New Testament. In this way, the gospel message is not self-evident but requires sifting and sourcing, even in the Bible, in conversation with the experiences of the oppressed.

In contrast, Thurman himself designates Paul "the first great creative interpreter of Christianity" by emphasizing that his letters are the oldest early Christian writings.[15] For Thurman, the letters carry both an emancipatory and non-emancipatory message conditioned by Paul's status as "a minority but with majority privileges."[16] Paul's writings,

---

14. Thurman, *Jesus and the Disinherited*, 19–20.
15. Thurman, *Jesus and the Disinherited*, 21.
16. Thurman, *Jesus and the Disinherited*, 21.

particularly their insistence on fidelity to overlords, state oversight, and caste systems, reflect Paul's privileged status and the security he found in the social and political institutions and processes of his time. At times, Paul's particularly privileged minority setting gets in the way of his liberatory statements, such as "there is no longer Jew or Greek, there is no longer slave or free, there is no longer male and female; for all of you are one in Christ Jesus" (Gal 3:28 NRSV) or "now faith, hope, and love abide, these three; and the greatest of these is love" (1 Cor 13:13 NRSV). Thurman views Paul's letters as containing a Christian message of freedom and radical transformation of human relations. From his perspective, it records concerns about civil arrangements and magistrates that lend themselves to those "who wish to use the weight of the Christian message to oppress and humiliate their fellows."[17] From this perspective, liberation views of the gospel separate Paul's regard for social arrangements and the security of law from Jesus's critique of inequitable and harmful social arrangements. Liberation interpreters prioritize Jesus's model and story as the gospel message for matters of human tolerance, care, and civil responsibilities and responses, not Paul.

The liberation gospel in Paul's writings exists in its structure as situational correspondences that address the present quality of Christian fellowship and ethics while referencing the past as authoritative resources. For example, in response to the Corinthian's ongoing threat of fracture, Paul resources the tradition. He rehearses an early creedal formulation to calibrate the community to its collective gospel attitude and behavior (1 Cor 15:1–11). Liberation views of the gospel highlight Paul's strategy of retrieving cultural traditions and blending them with ethical imperatives. Such approaches resource the traditions and experiences of historically oppressed people alongside the gospel traditions as another form of accompaniment and attestation of the ongoing activity of God's Spirit in the life of believing communities, past and present.

The literary form of Paul's letters has also served as exemplars for more contemporary forms of Christian epistolary addresses keyed toward liberation and the affirmation of all humanity. For example, in 1956 Martin Luther King Jr. delivered a sermonic address at Dexter Avenue Baptist Church in Montgomery, Alabama, inspired by Paul's

---

17. Thurman, *Jesus and the Disinherited*, 22.

letter-writing enterprise in both form and message. King states, "It is miraculous, indeed, that the Apostle Paul should be writing a letter to you and to me nearly 1900 years after his last letter appeared in the New Testament. . . . I can imagine the Apostle Paul writing a letter to American Christians in 1956 A.D."[18] King employed Paul's letter-writing form and message as a source of intervention into the American social experiment, defined at the time by segregation and separation. The literary form of Christian correspondence and dialogue that Paul pioneers, liberation interpreters like King and Thurman seize upon as instructive for the spiritual and social strivings of Christian fellowship and accompaniment set out in the Gospels and Acts. From a liberation view of the gospel, letters are a literary site for prophetic intermediaries to reenact Paul's gospel message of Christian hospitality, communion, and union in the name of Jesus instead of deepening social distances and cultural differences with the same name.

Response and Benefits

A Liberation Gospel reading approaches the Gospels, Acts, and letters as living documents testifying to God's actions for the oppressed, disinherited, marginalized, and minoritized in the present moment. This perspective expects interpreters to "see what is at stake in the present stage of history," and not just in ancient biblical history and story forms.[19] A liberation focus views existential realities of struggle as the problem plaguing the faithful interpreter of the gospel message. It marries the transformation of souls to the change of societies. Caring for others and dismantling systems that harm people and God's creation is never another's problem. Consequently, liberation gospel readers refuse to interpret the gospel as a retreat from current social challenges.

To this end, an essential benefit of the Liberation Gospel view is the starting assumption that all people are morally equal and responsible to one another. It holds human relatedness and social arrangements

---

18. I am grateful for a conversation with my colleague Margaret Mitchell about the significance of King as an interpreter. For a version of text, see Martin Luther King Jr., "Paul's Letter to American Christians," in *A Knock at Midnight: Inspiration from the Great Sermons of Reverend Martin Luther King, Jr.*, ed. Clayborne Carson and Peter Holleran (New York: Warren Books, 1998), 25.

19. Gutiérrez, "Introduction to the Revised Edition: Expanding the View," in *Theology of Liberation*.

accountable when they espouse domination under the guise of "faith." Resistance to such a view often comes from those committed to maintaining the bifurcation of faith and society, sacred and secular, human and spirit, holy and unholy. But a liberation reading sees those as complementary dimensions of the same reality in which Thurman states, "God speaks in many tongues, but one voice."[20]

Further Reflections

Reading the Gospels, Acts, and letters for the proclamation about Jesus Christ and freedom is like walking through an art museum and viewing an exhibit called "Jesus in Retrospect." You pause to consider each portrait of Jesus produced by different artists who captured their model as they remembered him *after* he left the studio, not as they observed him in the actual posing moment. No two portraits are the same in color selection and shading, angle and shape, or size and frame. The backgrounds depicted and the media used vary, with one artist employing acrylic paint, while another chooses to carve their portrait from clay. Even when they share a common subject—as in the figure of Jesus and the communities of faith that proclaim him—a group of artists can produce an incredible variety of portraits, perspectives, and impressions from that observation. When it comes to Jesus and liberation, we encounter diverse interpretive artists. Still, they fundamentally share a common priority, which is to depict the work of faithful followers of Jesus who proclaims "good news to the poor," "release to the captives," "recovery of sight to the blind," and who demands that "the oppressed go free" (Luke 4:18 NRSV).

---

20. Howard Thurman, "Black Pentecost #2: Reflections on the Black Experience," audio recording in Boston University's Howard Gottlieb Archival Research Center's Howard Thurman and Sue Baily Thurman Collections (address delivered at the Black Ecumenical Commission of Massachusetts, Eliot Congregational Church, Roxbury, Massachusetts, May 30, 1972).

RESPONSE TO SHIVELY T. J. SMITH

SCOT MCKNIGHT

Shively Smith presents an exquisite, consistent, and thick case for the Liberation Gospel as she demonstrates a liberationist hermeneutic at every turn. In the context of this book, Smith offers a refreshing closer reading of the Gospels when far more turn to the soteriology of Paul, at least as understood in the Reformation, to define gospel. Because she attends to the social context into which gospel liberation took root, she routinely demonstrates the power of the gospel to establish various dimensions of justice.

To Jesus she goes to define the gospel, not to his message but to him as a person and as a social reality:

> Born in poverty yet free, Jesus died the death of an enslaved person. A liberation perspective of the gospel marks Jesus's social status as one among the oppressed and reads with other "non-persons." (pp. 199–200)

She says further that "a Liberation Gospel view marks Jesus's social status as one among the oppressed" (p. 200). The implications of locating Jesus in a marginalized context are enormous for understanding Jesus and his mission but also for a liberation gospel today. Such an approach offers a way forward as well as a prophetic critique of a present, hegemonic theological context that silences voices and diminishes human experiences of oppression at the hand of those in power:

> In conversation with the life, deeds, and actions of Jesus, this approach expresses an unwavering commitment to human dignity, equality, and relatedness signified by the treatment

and recognition of marginalized communities rather than the experiences of dominant and normative classes. (p. 200)

No other author in this volume (including me) has made the point that every hermeneutic emerges from a social location, and it is one that only with disciplined effort (and never completely) can transcend that culture. Smith joins a host of liberationists not only acknowledging location for liberationist readings but affirming it as its advantage. Thus,

Liberation gospel readings acknowledge that no reading of the gospel is value neutral. Sprinkled throughout every understanding of the gospel are its interpreters' values and socially conditioned vantage points. Thus, [the liberation reading's] starting point takes a decisive side—that of the historically marginalized, oppressed, disinherited, erased, and silenced. It fashions a vision of liberation and provides a trenchant critique of oppressive arrangements, taking its cues from Jesus himself. (p. 202)

Honoring location and intention, the gospel itself comes to a singular expression that is

both affirmation and critique. It affirms the existence and equality of all human beings while critiquing those stakeholders and systems that wield power in a way that keeps their own status intact. (p. 203)

Over and over, I have observed in this book an insufficient interest in Jesus and in the Gospels. Over and over the gospel becomes something seemingly not known or preached until post-Pentecost, if not centuries later. Over and over the incarnate Jesus and the gospel are divorced. Until Shively Smith says the following and the whole of these two paragraphs must be reread with care, though I would quibble here and there while affirming the general direction of her sketches:

Generally, a liberation view of the gospel identifies Jesus as a free Galilean peasant man, born into subsistence-level poverty

(Luke 2:22–24). As a country-dweller and Roman noncitizen, he acted on behalf of the other masses of Jewish people living in and around Galilee and Judea at subsistence-level poverty. Jesus is a son and brother (Matt 13:55–56; Mark 3:31–35) and an itinerant teacher and healer (Mark 1:32–34; 3:10; 4:1). He traversed the regions of Galilee and Judea in the tradition of the Jewish prophets (Mark 6:4; Luke 13:33; 24:19). He was literate, reading Jewish scrolls in synagogue spaces where he observed his people's religious and social customs (Luke 4:16–20). (p. 202)

Across the four Gospel accounts of Jesus's short-lived public ministry, he functions as an ancient version of a community organizer, galvanizing ordinary working people like Galilean fishermen (Peter and John), tax collectors (Levi), and women (Mary and Martha). His followers shared the everyday challenges of poverty, illness, hunger, isolation, and disenfranchisement. Nevertheless, as followers of Jesus, they formed communities who acted together in the self-interests of the whole (e.g., four men carry the paralytic man, Mark 2:1–12; Samaritan woman proclaims to her village, John 4:39–42; cf. Acts 2:42–47). Consequently, a liberation view of the gospel is as interested in the communities constituted around Jesus as it is with the man himself. (p. 202)

Much is set in place for a fuller appreciation of the gospel, which in fact corrects abstruse articulations of the gospel using non-Jesus categories and vocabulary. Social context matters, and that context—once again—has enormous implications for the gospel today:

The endeavor of liberation interpretation, therefore, is to yield thick descriptions of the various struggles, realities, and forms of human oppression and suppression while illuminating the gospel message of salvation that frees the body, head, *and* heart. (p. 199)

A particular weakness of many approaches to the gospel has been the swallowing up of the gospel in individual soteriology and its intricate theological nuances, but Smith will not let the social context of Jesus go there, and so her essay becomes a healthy, steady admonishment of narrowed understandings of the gospel. Notice then that a

> liberation gospel view approaches the New Testament writings from the assumption that spiritual and social matters are interrelated. The social problems that separate human beings into the haves and have-nots, the rich and the poor, the dignified and the derided, and the free and the censured are problems plaguing human institutions and systems. Still, they are also problems of the human spirit. A common trend threaded through liberation interpretations of the fourfold Gospel, Acts, and the New Testament letters is the articulation of where the social and spiritual coalesce in ways affirming God's idiom in human beings. (p. 199)

Ignoring holistic redemption in favor of personal salvation fails the gospel Jesus preached and embodied. Thus, both an emphasis on the spiritual and the social extends to the sociopolitical realm for Smith. She "sees" what many other approaches to the gospel miss:

> For example, liberation readings trace the imperial context of the gospel world with its emperors, kings, governors, and religious leaders (Luke 1:5; 2:1–2; 3:1–2; Acts 5:21; 25:1–2, 13). It also highlights when local community life harms people by placing them in chains (chained Gerasene man, Mark 5:1–20), denying people benevolence (feeding the masses, Mark 8:1–9; cf. Matt 25:35–37), or dismissing petitions for mercy (the Canaanite woman, Matt 15:21–28; blind Bartimaeus, Mark 10:46–52; cf. Matt 23:23). It follows social, political, and cultural life as conveyed in biblical texts while noticing how it impacts the contexts of readers, both ancient and contemporary. (pp. 201–2)

When it comes to reading studies of the meaning of gospel, I have myself over the years read with care in order to discern which texts of the Bible become central for the appeal to biblical authority. Which text or texts one chooses will always reflect a person's location and theology, so much so that one can rightfully wonder if any of us have the ability to transcend our own location to hear Jesus again as if for the first time (to grab oft-repeated words of Marcus Borg).[1] Texts chosen matter.

Smith begins with some words about Luke 4:16–21 (no surprise there), but then drills down into the parable of the good Samaritan. (I'm no longer capable of saying "good" with "Samaritan" without realizing how diminishing the title is—all thanks to the work of Amy-Jill Levine in *Short Stories of Jesus*.)[2] A recent study of the Samaritan by Emerson Powery, *The Good Samaritan*, sketches the history of how this parable has been read and preached and implemented, and Smith, too, knows that scholarship and brings to the forefront the parable's fundamental vision and implications for faith communities today.[3] The parable tells "a story that highlights the necessity for crossing ethnic-racial and social-cultural boundaries as an imperative of Jesus's kingdom vision" (p. 204). She continues:

> From this view, the good Samaritan parable supplies a biblical model for flattening power relations instead of goodness flowing from a top-down or insider-to-outsider power dynamic. It implies that the person needing support and the one giving support are equals. (p. 206)

She turns then to the justice-shaping early church communities in the book of Acts, summarizing her stimulating sketch when she observes that a "liberation view of Acts traces its prophetic message as a call for radical inclusion, interaction and dialogue, and unparalleled equality" (p. 208). And: "A liberation view of Acts embraces its vision of a boundary-transgressing communion in the real world of human avarice, complicity, destruction, and indifference. Liberation-focused readers notice that the barriers facing the radical strivings portrayed in Acts are unavoidable in the birth of the gospel and its present unfolding in the world" (p. 210). It is noticeable that she both not only has less

---

1. Marcus Borg, *Meeting Jesus Again for the First Time: The Historical Jesus and the Heart of Contemporary Faith* (New York: HarperOne, 1994).
2. Amy-Jill Levine, *Short Stories by Jesus: The Enigmatic Parables of a Controversial Rabbi* (New York: Harper Collins, 2014).
3. Emerson B. Powery, *The Good Samaritan: Luke 10 for the Life of the Church* (Grand Rapids: Baker Academic, 2022).

attention to the gospel of Paul but that 1 Corinthians is not fronted in defining the gospel.

The Liberation Gospel that Smith articulates centers audience (marginalized), need (systemic injustice and oppression), and benefit (freedom, liberation, social justice). The first is ignored in almost all studies of the gospel, including my own, and one cannot be excused by dismissing her concern for audience by making the claim it is for all. It's not that simple. The connection of "need" and "benefit," however, ties Smith's gospel to the Wesleyan, the Reformed, and the Pentecostal Gospels. One cannot extract benefit from gospel, but one can distinguish the two. So vital, in my view, is the distinction between gospel and benefit that one must observe that most of the time benefit swallows the distinction so completely that the implication of the gospel becomes the gospel itself.

What I like most about Smith's presentation is its single-minded focus on Jesus in his social context, but at the same time one notices an absence of any attention to kingdom as a content summary of the gospel. The term itself is mentioned less than a half dozen times, yet it is for the Synoptic authors the heart of Jesus's message. Smith's focus, to be sure, is on the liberating mission and action of Jesus, but any articulation of the gospel of Jesus must land squarely on defining and expounding the meaning of kingdom and why he chose that term to express his message. The lack of emphasis on kingdom as a centering device for Jesus's mission correlates with two other gospel elements of the New Testament—namely, an articulation of the gospel statement in 1 Corinthians 15 as not only Paul's but the apostolic gospel of the earliest churches. Though many will devalue the historical importance of the sermons in Acts, at the least those are gospel sermons of the early church, and they do, as C. H. Dodd said long ago in *The Apostolic Preaching and Its Developments*, conform to the gospel statement of 1 Corinthians 15.[4]

For years, I have argued that the gospel is first of all a Christology and only then a soteriology, and this does not diminish the importance of soteriology (the gospel's benefit), but it does put it in its place. The

---

4. C. H. Dodd, *The Apostolic Preaching and Its Developments* (London: Hodder & Stoughton, 1970).

gospel statements of Paul, the sermons in the book of Acts, and the Gospels themselves make the person, the mission, the teachings, the life and death and burial and resurrection and ascension and return of Jesus the *irreducible content* of the gospel. The gospel is a message about Jesus before it is the implication of Jesus for redemption and liberation. The gospel, which is after all a public announcement of good news, was a statement that Jesus is here and that he is Israel's Messiah, and thus any gospel can only make sense in the social context of Jesus if the story of Israel and its hope become the foundation for the gospel.

RESPONSE TO SHIVELY T. J. SMITH

MICHAEL HORTON

Shively Smith relates a moving story about Howard Thurman's grandmother, who could not accept Pauline texts because of their repeated use by the enslaver's pastor. "As such, she exercises 'choice' in where she hears the gospel message articulated in the New Testament. In this way, the gospel message is not self-evident but requires sifting and sourcing, even in the Bible, in conversation with the experiences of the oppressed" (p. 211).

Dismissing the visceral reaction of this woman to Paul reflects the extent to which people of white privilege such as myself fail still to acknowledge the unique experience of Africans *of enslaved and excluded heritage*. Our first response, I believe, is to pause and acknowledge that we all hear God's word from our own location.

I have a very different history of hearing God's word than Thurman's grandmother. It's a history of privilege, convinced that America is a land of opportunity and freedom, where one's children could have a life that parents could only imagine. When I say "privileged," I do not mean that my parents were wealthy Ivy League alumni. My dad's final year of schooling was the eighth grade. My parents, coming to California from dust-bowl ravaged Oklahoma and Texas not long before I was born, lived in a house with a dirt floor. But they believed in the American Dream because it was their birthright. Failure or success lay in their hands. America is a "melting pot" united by its democratic ideals rather than by blood and soil. Yet the experience of my Black friends (confirmed by the daily news) is quite different from this inclusion narrative: a history of exclusion, dashed hopes, yet a powerful determination to overcome perpetual setbacks.

As he approached Los Angeles, my dad stopped in a diner and, finding a Black man sitting at the counter, slugged him off his stool. Nobody told my dad that here such freedom was tolerated. Though poor, he was privileged, and he knew that if he worked hard, then he could make it. The Black man on the stool was a measure of his sense of privilege—and his determination to protect whatever scraps he could from it. My dad would have resisted or at least tuned out to Paul's teaching about ethnic divisions being overcome through unity in Christ. But the gospel changed my dad. Late in his life, he was helping John Perkins and Dolphus Weary build houses for disadvantaged African Americans in Mississippi. There is no saving power in the law, even in the true and good imperatives of loving our neighbor as ourselves, pursuing justice and equality for all God's image bearers. But the good news of Christ's saving work even for a sinner like him transformed my father. A new community of genuine inclusion (e.g., Rev 5:9) no longer grated against his sensibilities. Now, the imperatives made sense because his whole horizon of meaning had changed. Something *alien* to his experience created its own pathway into his hard heart. He came to see that he had been formed in even a church community that was beholden to the secular narrative precisely because the parts of God's word that were used to reinforce prejudice (and were once heard in this way), understood properly, conquered his heart.

We see prosperity evangelists explaining away offensive passages, such as Jesus siding with the poor and outcasts. Reading the Bible as though it were a manual for get-rich-quick schemes, their experiential location is hardly normative. The only way of challenging such distortions, in fact, is to appeal to a canon that judges our autonomous experience and subordinates our familiar (contextual) interpretations to "that Word above all earthly powers," as Luther's hymn has it.

I am not in any way comparing Thurman's grandmother to my father, much less to prosperity preachers. Moreover, in her understandable reaction to the uses to which these passages were put, it is at least salutary that she did find the gospel in other parts of Scripture. My concern is less with her response than in turning it into a hermeneutic that raises "exercising choice" in what we find authoritative in Scripture and "sifting and sourcing, even in the Bible," according to our experience. The enslaver's preacher was doing this, suppressing the truth in unrighteousness. Why should Thurman's grandmother remain a victim of this man's Scripture twisting and have the Pauline corpus stolen from her canon because of it?

Smith relates, "Thurman himself designates Paul 'the first great creative interpreter of Christianity' by emphasizing the letters are the oldest early Christian writings. For Thurman, the letters carry both an emancipatory and non-emancipatory message conditioned by Paul's status as 'a minority but with majority privileges'" (pp. 211–12). We all "shift and source," subordinating troubling passages to our agency, experience, and assumptions. But when we stand over God's word in this way, even subconsciously, we rob ourselves of opportunities to be liberated both as victims and victimizers. There were pro-slavery preachers who were powerfully converted precisely by the word that they had abused. Not only the oppressed but oppressors can be saved and reconciled to God and each other when God has the first and last word. There is no canon within a canon determined by our experience. We must have confidence in God's word—all of it—to address us. Where it has been misinterpreted and exploited for ungodly ends, it must be properly interpreted and allowed to interrogate our tacit as well as explicit corruptions.

To say that "the gospel message is not self-evident" (p. 211) in Scripture is not just to question the clarity of the gospel from Genesis to Revelation but is to foreclose the possibility that we will hear the good news in passages that have been abused to tyrannize us. Dr. King, for example, spoke directly of the gospel message being self-evident. In his sermon, "Man's Sin and God's Grace," he emphasized not only the clarity of original sin and redemption through Christ as doctrines too easily dismissed by liberals but saw these truths as a powerful diagnosis and cure in the present struggle.[1] One hears in the Old Spirituals an astonishing confidence in the clarity of the gospel. It was white liberals who taught that the Bible is an opaque testimony to human experience rather than God's judging and saving speech through the agency of weak and sinful human beings. If there is no transcendent criterion of our speech, then the church becomes a club constituted by the collective experiences of various groups, enabling (even ensuring) the perpetuation of the dreary war of all against all.

---

1. Martin Luther King Jr., "Man's Sin and God's Grace," exact date unknown, https://kinginstitute.stanford.edu/king-papers/documents/mans-sin-and-gods-grace.

There is a sense in which Thurman's grandmother was right to reject "Paul," because it was not an authentic application or even interpretation of his teaching. I am reminded of George Lindbeck's contrast between saying "Christ is Lord" on one's knees, receiving his mercy, and making it a war cry as a crusader cleaves the skull of an infidel. The *use* of the phrase to some extent determines its meaning—at least its connotation. Consequently, we must ask first about the context of the relevant passages before applying them to our own. To make our own context normative is to engage in the type of violence exhibited by the enslaver's preacher.

Of course, I agree that biblical interpretation is never value neutral. Words such as "liberation" and "emancipatory" are not value neutral either. Yet they seem to function in liberation theology as a "final vocabulary" for a metanarrative that is different from the grand narrative of Scripture.[2] Rather than enter the world created by God's powerful word, we tend to assimilate it to the very patterns of this present evil age that hold us in bondage. I would suspect that Howard Thurman's grandmother—or at least her generation—would have been far more in tune with the Bible's exodus narrative than the post-Enlightenment metanarrative of emancipation. How much of our discourse, among progressives and conservatives alike, *uses* the Bible as a quarry of metaphors for a more fundamental outlook shaped by white Europeans since the eighteenth century? And how much is our experience determined by an immanent eschatology determined by the powers of this age that is far from what we find in the old Spirituals?

In defining the gospel, McKnight's primary question is whether Jesus taught it. For Smith, however, "The calibration in a liberation gospel view is decisive: to interpret the gospel is to read for 'what the teachings and the life of Jesus have to say to those who stand, at a moment in human history, with their backs against the wall'" (p. 200,

---

2. I am appealing to Richard Rorty's notion of "final vocabulary" here: words we use because of their social resonance (see his *Contingency, Irony, and Solidarity* [Cambridge: Cambridge University Press, 1989], 73). These words typically justify other parts of our vocabulary, even though they cannot themselves be justified objectively. I also draw here on Lyotard's concept of "metanarrative": a story that behaves like it's not a story but just an explanation of the real world (Jean-François Lyotard, *The Postmodern Condition: A Report on Knowledge* [Minneapolis: University of Minnesota Press, 1979], xxiv–xxv). I take the Bible to be a "grand narrative," but not a metanarrative according to Lyotard's definition.

quoting Thurman in part here). I agree that the Bible exhibits a preferential option for the oppressed. At the same time, human beings remain, in any moment of history, recipients of a word they cannot speak to themselves. It is the word of the Other who addresses all people in judgment and grace. Smith adds, "Liberation interpreters prioritize Jesus's model and story as the gospel message for matters of human tolerance, care, and civil responsibilities and responses, not Paul" (p. 212). If "Jesus's model" *is* "the gospel message," all of us are without hope. Jesus *lived* the law, summarized in the Great Commandment, *for* those who have not lived it, and he bore their curse, rising again *for* them. He did all of this *in our place* as God-in-flesh, the Last Adam. Jesus is, of course, our model for loving God and neighbor, but to turn the law into the gospel leads to either self-righteousness or despair. As I have tried to show briefly, this is as much the teaching of Jesus as it is of Paul.

So much of the exegesis now is "moralistic therapeutic deism."[3] There are privatized versions of this, where individuals try to remain sexually pure and virtuous. And there are more socially sensitive versions that imagine that the "Great Society" can be created in this present age by the realization of the extraordinary exceptionalism of American ideals. But there are also African American versions that see America as the eschatological location of the "city on a hill" if only the nation will renounce its racism. Dr. King, for example, moralized and domesticated many New Testament narratives and parables into a story of American exceptionalism, as much as any Christian nationalist in our midst. But human beings are inherently vicious, not by created nature but because of the fall. We will never repent of our narcissism until there is a better story than these insipid versions that I know are preached in Black as well as White churches. It's all about us: moralistic, self-righteous, banal. Nothing can penetrate us from outside our autonomous constructions of reality.

An example of this is Smith's reprise of a typical American Protestant recital of the good Samaritan parable: "A popular reading of this parable," she says,

---

3. Christian Smith with Melina Lundquist Denton, *Soul Searching: The Religious and Spiritual Lives of American Teenagers* (New York: Oxford University Press, 2005); cf. Christian Smith, "On 'Moralistic Therapeutic Deism' as US Teenagers' Actual, Tacit, de Facto Religious Faith" in *Religion and Youth*, ed. Sylvia Collins-Mayo and Pink Dandelion (Farnham: Ashgate, 2010), 41–46.

discusses the equality of neighborliness—particularly among people in the same community and sharing similar proximities. However, the parable of the good Samaritan is not only about local neighborhood relations; it is a story that highlights the necessity for crossing ethnic-racial and social-cultural boundaries as an imperative of Jesus's kingdom vision.

She cites King: "We are called to play the role of the good Samaritan on life's roadside, but that will be only an initial act. One day we must come to see that the whole Jericho road must be transformed so that men and women will not be constantly beaten and robbed as they make their journey on life's highway'" (p. 205). Similarly, Smith appeals to Vanessa Cook: "King considered it [the good Samaritan] the only way to build the Kingdom of God and the brotherhood of man on earth" (p. 206).

This is better than an individualistic interpretation that relieves me of my burden to care for the excluded. Yet it remains in the ambit of moralism. Christ is the good Samaritan in this passage, I believe, not as a model but as the actual caregiver who takes me to a hostel to recover. Instead, in both the White and Black versions of moralism, I'm supposed to be the good Samaritan. Evidently, Shively does not have much experience in white evangelicalism. Until I started hearing preaching that raised my eyes to Christ, the sermons I heard were quite similar to what Dr. King and Dr. Smith present here. *I* am the good Samaritan, according to these narratives; Jesus is merely the model. Once again, I escape the courtroom. I'm the victim, not the one who turns the other way. This is terrible news, because it keeps me from realizing that I am the problem: "And I said: 'Woe is me! For I am lost; for I am a man of unclean lips, and I dwell in the midst of a people of unclean lips; for my eyes have seen the King, the Lord of hosts!'" (Isa 6:5 ESV).

Peter has a similar experience in a fishing expedition with Jesus. The consummate fisherman had failed in his efforts, yet Jesus summoned the fish he had created into the nets. "But when Simon Peter saw it, he fell down at Jesus's knees, saying, 'Depart from me, for I am a sinful man, O Lord'" (Luke 5:8 ESV). It is the experience of Paul after encountering the glorified Jesus on the Damascus road: "Wretched man that I am! Who will deliver me from this body of death?" (Rom 7:24 ESV).

What if we all shed our appeals to our unique experiences supposedly justifying us as the "righteous" and took the place of the wicked tax collector and the apostles themselves, in order to be put on the receiving end of redemption? Is there a good Samaritan who saves *people like me* from the ditch? Theology is reflection on practice, but *God's* practice, not ours. I just don't hear this interpretation very frequently in many settings across the denominational and political divide.

Suffering the general effects of living in a fallen world is difficult enough; suffering systemic hatred and violence over centuries is crippling not only to victims but to perpetrators. Yet there is a danger of turning suffering into a new badge of righteousness, of transforming a theology of the cross into another theology of glory. Given the direction of our hearts—all of our hearts, self-justification is our default setting. "The Pharisee, standing by himself, prayed thus: 'God, I thank you that I am not like other men, extortioners, unjust, adulterers, or even like this tax collector'" (Luke 18:11 ESV). The tax collector was of course unjust, exploiting his own fellow Jews. Rather than taking our place with the ungodly race of Adam, we all fill in the blank in our own way: "I thank you, Lord, that I am not an oppressor," a slogan like that can become another way of self-justification. Smith says, "Across the four gospel accounts of Jesus's short-lived public ministry, he functions as an ancient version of a community organizer, galvanizing ordinary working people like Galilean fishermen (Peter and John), tax collectors (Levi), and women (Mary and Martha). . . . It resources the gospel stories as counterresponses to contemporary social realities of struggle and inequity" (pp. 202–3). I'm all for community organizers who seek justice. But to imagine that the Word became flesh so that America could become the Beloved Community or "Great Again" is sacrilege.

Across the board, it appears, religion is about us. It's about our privileged or non-privileged experience and the works we do to transform ourselves and society. There are conservative Pharisees, but there are also progressive Pharisees. I am not suggesting that Smith is one of them, but only that the framework of moralistic (white European) liberalism to which she appeals inevitably transforms "Who is Jesus and what has he accomplished?" into "What would Jesus do and what can I accomplish based on his model?"

We all want to be "the righteous," whether by morality or sound doctrine or as the victim rather than the victimizer. But the fact is that in unequal degrees we are all sinners and sinned against. The poor are sinners, the rich are sinners. However much we compare and contrast ourselves with "the others," we have all fallen short of God's glory (Rom 3:23). Even the oppressed are children of Adam. We—you, I, all of us—*are* the ungodly. But that democracy of sin means that we can all be reconciled to God and to each other in Christ. Herein lies the victory that overcomes the world.

My final point relates to eschatology. As soon as Christ becomes a theory, something we can use to criticize not only the world but the Bible itself, we have begun to accommodate to secularization. The blasphemous use of Jesus to support not only the worst but the best of human values is destroying Christianity far more than any external ideologies or movements.

There was no pope or even bishops, no external organization at all, much less state support, that could account for the unity of the ancient church. It was *only* the gospel that held the early Christians together, as they were mocked for the simplicity of their message of "Christ and him crucified." We have no other anchor. Ironically, that's what I have heard most from my Black friends and especially their parents. To turn the gospel into another version of "emancipation" that leaves people in the grip of sin's guilt and power is to surrender the real power the Black Church has had in the broader witness of American society.

Concluding her discussion of Acts, Smith writes, "Biblical readings focused on liberation understand the story of Christian beginnings as new modes for human fellowship blended with divine encounters" (p. 209). Maybe I just don't understand this language, but my inclination is to disagree. The new social life described in the book of Acts is not a "new mode" of the dreary carcasses of social projects; it is an eschatological beginning of a totally new human fellowship based on divine intervention.

Yet no eschatological society can emerge without the beginning of an eschaton, and that is the resurrection of Jesus. Not a single word in Smith's essay told me what difference Jesus of Nazareth made in human history aside from being a moral example. There is nothing about his incarnation. Nothing about his "fulfilling all righteousness" in my place. Nothing about his sin-bearing or bodily resurrection. If this is a representative essay on the Liberation Gospel, then there is no liberation in it.

Let me conclude with a brief reflection on my own experience. I have delved deeply into liberation theology and learned much from it, not only in books but among brothers and sisters in Nicaragua, India, Africa, Asia, and the Middle East. I listened to late-night recitals by eyewitnesses of atrocities committed in the name of democracy and freedom at the International Institute of Human Rights. Conservatives tend to spiritualize crucial biblical texts. There is a deep Platonizing of the gospel over many centuries that has transformed the good news of the salvation *of* the world into salvation *from* it. John the Baptizer was not off base in his question. The prophets told of a new covenant mediated by the Messiah who would bring not only the forgiveness of sins and a new heart but heaven on earth. At last, the king would dwell in the midst of his people as the source of consummate blessing. To spiritualize these promises—the meek inheriting the earth, a worldwide feast with rich meats and the best wines, the liberation of the oppressed with everlasting peace, righteousness, and justice—is to relocate biblical eschatology to a completely gentile frame.

But the question is *when*? What if, as John expected, perfect justice had been consummated at Christ's first advent? "For the wrath of God is revealed from heaven against all ungodliness and unrighteousness of men, who by their unrighteousness suppress the truth" (Rom 1:18 ESV). Who among those living then, much less since, could have survived that judgment? Only by substituting himself, becoming the risen head of his universal body, could a salvation appear that is far greater than the transformation of any geopolitical nation or empire. Only by delaying the judgment could there have been an intermission for Christ's kingdom of grace before his return in glory. Only through such a patient reprieve could he send the Holy Spirit to unite sinners to himself through the gospel proclaimed throughout the world.

The Messiah does bring all of these benefits—spiritual resurrection *and* bodily resurrection, justification *and* justice, peace with God *and* peace among nations and peoples, healing in soul *and* body. The signs Jesus and his apostles performed certified this in-breaking of the kingdom. But for now, they are *signs*, not yet the consummated reality. The whole earth *will* be full of the glory of God, but now it is filled with the grace of God through the gospel proclaimed in word and administered in baptism and the Supper. Wherever these are present, there is a church, the kingdom of God, a tree spreading its living branches across the world.

For now, we seek relative justice in a fallen world preserved by God's common grace. Perfect justice now would leave us all outside the wedding feast "where there will be weeping and gnashing of teeth" (Matt 13:42). Anyone familiar with Dickens's *A Christmas Carole*, however convoluted it is, can identify with a rich person being converted. The gospel is for Pharisees and CEOs and fascists too.

When the Spirit has united those chosen from all nations to the Son, justified sinners will be able to stand in the final judgment; those formerly alienated from the people of God will be adopted as coheirs with Christ; the regeneration of all things begun in human hearts will be completed. "And this gospel of the kingdom will be proclaimed throughout the whole world as a testimony to all nations, and then the end will come" (Matt 24:14 ESV). When he has showered the earth with his grace, then the Son of Man will appear "with power and great glory. And he will send out his angels with a loud trumpet call, and they will gather his elect from the four winds, from one end of heaven to the other" (Matt 24:30–31 ESV). What were merely signs of the consummated kingdom will become the normal condition of the whole earth as it shares in the resurrection of the children of God (Rom 8:18–25). Indeed, there will no longer be any distinction between heaven and earth (Rev 21). I long for that. In the meantime, this hope orients me away from Platonizing and yet also resisting any utopian dream. Human beings—including sinful Christians—will *never* be righteous in this life, not the way God intended. The worst systems are selfish ones that wear priestly garb. Jesus knows. He intercedes. He will return. The meek *will* inherit the earth.

RESPONSE TO SHIVELY T. J. SMITH

DAVID A. DESILVA

This essay is valuable—immensely so—as a corrective to deficient understandings of the scope of God's call to disciples in the gospel to be certain to work both for people's temporal as well as their spiritual flourishing. In some traditions, believers are led to focus too much on the kingdom of God that lies off on the eschatological horizon or in postmortem existence and too little on the transformed attitudes and practices that realize Jesus's pronouncement in the here and now: "The kingdom of God is among you [pl.]" (Luke 17:21 NRSV). Shively Smith rightly challenges all disciples to reckon with the prophetic text that Jesus selected, as it were, as his mission statement in Luke 4:18–21 and to examine the degree to which their own (and their congregations') mission aligns with that of the Lord they claim to follow. She rightly, even salvifically, holds the vision of Matthew 25:31–46 before us and reminds us that those who do not attend to the physical and relational needs of those "whose backs are against the wall" will face a grim reckoning when they meet the Lord they thought to serve. She rightly challenges disciples to cross boundaries and break barriers, in league with Paul, who understood Jesus's death to have had such goals particularly in mind (Gal 3:28; Eph 2:11–22).

John Wesley was himself a great ally for a liberationist gospel that calls disciples to "be more present in the world, not less" (p. 201). The practice that he adopted, and that led to the formation of the "General Rules" for his earliest Methodist societies, foregrounded "doing good; by being in every kind merciful after their power; as they have opportunity, doing good of every possible sort, and, as far as possible, to all men: To their bodies, of the ability which God giveth, by giving food to the hungry, by clothing the naked, by visiting or helping them that are sick or in prison; to their souls, by instructing, reproving, or exhorting all we have any intercourse with."[1] In this he stood firmly in the Catholic and Anglican tradition of the twin sets of "works of mercy"—the temporal and the spiritual. He would have agreed that it was insufficient merely to attend to the injuries of the victims of unjust systems and that the systems themselves needed to be addressed. He and the movement that became his legacy were active in systemic reform, particularly in the creation of *alternative systems*, putting new educational and health-care institutions in place that would end the unequal access to these services in eighteenth-century Britain.[2]

While the Liberation Gospel as presented here offers an essential *corrective*, it seems insufficient as an *independent* statement of the gospel. For one thing, an articulation of the gospel that includes only a single reference to resurrection—and one that essentially sets it off to the side—strikes me as incomplete. Indeed, I would expect that a gospel focused on liberation stood to derive significant power and encouragement from God's vindication of Jesus and grant of new life beyond the reach of the oppressive powers that sought to crush him. Similarly, Jesus's enthronement as Lord, calling for his followers' loyal commitment to a new and Christ-defined political and economic order in the here-and-now of embodied discipleship, and Jesus's coming again in judgment of the kingdoms ordered by the world's exploitative wisdom and in vindication of his faithful ones, might advantageously play a larger role in the exposition of God's "good news" for the marginalized, exploited, and victimized. The historic gospel as summed up in what liturgical traditions call "the mystery of faith"—Christ has died; Christ is risen; Christ will come again—offers more in the way of good news for the work of liberation than I read here.

I was also surprised to find so little reference to the Holy Spirit, and only in connection with the work of Justo González's attention to the Spirit, essentially, as a character in the *narrative* world of Acts rather than a living and empowering presence in and among Christian disciples and Christian community. Christians in Southeast Asia, Africa,

---

1. "The General Rules of the Methodist Church," in *The Book of Discipline of the United Methodist Church 2016* (Nashville: The United Methodist Publishing House, 2016), 77–80, quote from 79.
2. This is not to say that Wesley did all that he could in the matter of social justice, particularly in regard to slavery, against which he was reticent to speak until quite late in his life. See the critique in Sean McGever, *Ownership: The Evangelical Legacy in Edwards, Wesley, and Whitefield* (Downers Grove, IL: IVP, 2024).

and South America rely explicitly and immanently on the power of the Holy Spirit as they hold one another erect and on their feet in the face of waves of oppression and persecution. Again, there is more to the "good news" that God brings to the unempowered in this world, particularly in regard to the empowerment of the Spirit for work, witness, and bold investment in an alternative community.

There are a number of points at which I found myself wishing I could persuade the author to reconsider her stance.

1. I have an ongoing problem with the notion of God's "option" or "preference" or, as here, "predilection" for the oppressed and poor. I would be reluctant to attribute *bias* to God. God's absolute, essential commitment to justice ("essential" as central to the very *essence* of God's character as revealed in the Scriptures of both testaments) puts God *on the side of* the oppressed and poor. This, however, is a function of God's *justice*, and bias corrupts justice wherever bias encroaches upon it.
2. I think that Smith's tweet sells the Liberation Gospel short. Would it have been better to foreground the liberating effects that result where people actually live by Jesus's word and example, building their lives upon a fresh foundation? And would it be both truer and more helpful to consider Jesus, not to have "died the death of an enslaved person" (p. 200), but rather the death of a revolutionary who proclaimed an upside-down kingdom? This, it seems to me, would be a truer liberationist perspective on Jesus's proclamation and practice—and one that helps explain why Judean leaders and Roman overlords conspired to remove such a challenge to the systems that perpetuated their own status, power, and privilege.
3. We have no basis for believing that Paul *compelled* Timothy to undergo circumcision. Acts is silent on the matter of the nature of Timothy's motivation and consent. Why assume the worst? This seems to me a symptom of the unfair treatment that Paul often receives at the hands of liberationist interpreters, hence:
4. I would have wanted to see Thurman's claims about "Paul's privileged status and the security he found" nuanced considerably (p. 212). The catalog of hardships in 2 Corinthians 11:23–33

suggests that Paul persisted, rather, very much in the status-quo-challenging proclamation of the gospel in the face of great opposition by those who *did* enjoy privileged status and security. Being beaten with rods—a Roman punishment—three times is a testimony to how little Paul's Roman citizenship availed him as well as how committed he remained to his mission of calling all people to a higher allegiance and, as a corollary, a different way of living in community. There are readings of Romans 13 that call into question the claim that Paul's writings evidence an "insistence on fidelity to overlords" and "state oversight" (p. 212), teasing out the subtle subversion of the public discourse concerning imperial power and providence (more akin to "Rome, right or wrong!") that we find in Paul's demythologized version of Roman domination.

I wonder if liberation theologians approach Paul with too heavily weighted a hermeneutic of suspicion to acknowledge what Paul actually accomplishes; for example, in the revolutionary transformation of the dynamics and lived experiences of patriarchy and slavery in believing households, where the wife's submission is embedded in the mutual submission expected of all believers toward each other, where the husband's love must be expressed in the self-denying, other-serving manner of Christ, and where masters are told to "do the same" for their slaves as their slaves do for them (Eph 5:21–6:9).[3] And does not Paul back Philemon into a corner when he confronts him with Onesimus and summons him, none too gently, to dismiss the caste-system relationship he has with Onesimus in favor of his new and equal relationship to Onesimus as "a beloved brother . . . both in the flesh and in the Lord" (Phlm 16)? I would challenge liberation interpreters not to create a canon within the canon that looks primarily to Jesus and expects less from, or even dismisses, Paul.[4]

These concerns, of course, should not be heard to diminish my heartfelt appreciation for what Dr. Smith's essay brings to this collection as an indispensable facet of the whole of the good news.

---

3. See my *Ephesians*, NCBC (Cambridge: Cambridge University Press, 2022), 274–312.
4. Revelation, of course, also has a great deal to offer liberationist interpreters, as Allan Boesak demonstrated so well in his *Comfort and Protest: The Apocalypse from a South African Perspective* (Louisville: Westminster John Knox, 1987).

RESPONSE TO SHIVELY T. J. SMITH

JULIE MA

Shively Smith's description of the Liberation Gospel is both confronting and inspiring. She carefully uses art, literature, and history that describes the plight of African American slaves as her pathway into the topic of explaining the gospel as good news of liberation from oppression. Smith is clearly influenced by Howard Washington Thurman's book *Jesus and the Disinherited* and Gustavo Gutiérrez's volume *A Theology of Liberation*. She shares their view of the gospel message as a reflection of God's preference for the weak and the afflicted. As an Asian Christian, I share Smith's concern for the marginalized, oppressed, those without access to healthcare, or who simply have a poor standard of living. I agree the gospel speaks about this and looks for our redemption from it. Any holistic gospel, such as the one I champion in my Asian Pentecostal tradition, is going to have the same concerns, even if we do not always adopt the same methods or come precisely to the same goals.

I understand how Smith wants to read the parable of the good Samaritan as an expression of the Liberation Gospel because, in her view, it emphasizes human dignity and resolving the injustice of human misery, exploitation, and struggle. The "good" Christian act transgresses national and ethnic allegiances and chooses international partnerships. Such a position models a resolve toward true brotherhood, sisterhood, and human relatedness that values the care of the other as more important than personal conveniences and the expenditures of material possessions and time. I'd join Smith by also adding to the mix John 4:1–42, the story of the encounter between Jesus and the Samaritan woman. This, too, is a story of liberation! But note that the issues discussed are not just the woman's marginal status and the various sneers and shame that she has faced. Jesus's conversation with her begins with water and leads her to a deeper level of confessing her sinful life through tactfully engaging talk, to the point of one-to-one counseling. Even in the midst of injustice there is still a spiritual reality that needs to be addressed; even the poor have sins that need to be forgiven even if they are not the same sins as the rich or the sins of the perverse and powerful. The woman's needs are jointly physical and spiritual. The concept of "living water" is brought to this woman as an invitation to enter God's salvation. It is not only the Samaritan woman's experience of salvation that is pointed out, but it is also extended to the entire Samaritan village through her being a passionate witness. The story of the Samaritan woman is an example of our need for both physical justice as well as for spiritual wholeness.

Smith notes the various types of injustice in the world, including illness, ethnic and racial discrimination, gender bias, social-class stratification, and religious discrimination. These are all true and I, as an Asian American woman, an immigrant, am fully aware of the injustices of sexism, racism, and xenophobia. Yet, as bad as many types of discrimination are, to be brutally honest they do not compete with the intense suffering and misery created by the injustice of crushing poverty. Liberation theology was, mostly, a religious manifestation of class warfare against globalist companies and corrupt governments who "fattened" their hearts "in the day of slaughter" (Jas 5:5). It is this poverty I have seen as a missionary all over Asia. I would stress that of the world's 736 million extremely poor in 2015, 368 million, half of the total, live in just five countries: India, Nigeria, the Democratic Republic of the Congo, Ethiopia, and Bangladesh. They also happen to be the most populous countries of South Asia and sub-Saharan Africa, the two regions that together account for 85 percent (629 million) of the world's poor.

The poorest in the world are frequently starving, going to bed with a hungry stomach, have low opportunities for education, often have no light at night, and suffer from poor health. Making progress against poverty is therefore one of the most urgent global goals for any liberation theology. My point is that while all injustices are bad, some injustices are worse than others, and liberation theology should retain its focus on liberation from poverty above all things.

On this score, I think Smith might agree with me because she is aware of the continual conflict between Christian concern for what is good and holy and the social realities of our world. I concur with Smith in her reading of Acts that anything evangelical must be emancipatory for those who experience alienation and oppression, whether in poverty, in discrimination, or in demonic strongholds. Whether you want to call it liberation, holistic, or just plain biblical, the gospel of the apostles describes God's deliverance against manifestations of oppression, discrimination, and violence. Liberation readings like those of Smith reveal the imposition of dominating classes on the downtrodden. A liberation will be ideally holistic as it also includes the transformation of souls to the change of societies. Caring for others and dismantling systems that harm people and God's creation is never another's problem. It is a world problem, a government problem, a global business problem, a church problem, a human problem. And the gospel offers the divine solution! On this, Smith and I walk in lockstep. I only wish to add, as I suspect Smith herself would support, that the spiritual lives of people are connected to their contexts, plight, and disempowerment. We need good Samaritans as much as we need the living waters that Jesus offers.

CONCLUSION

JASON MASTON

The fundamental question that this book has explored is "What is the Gospel?" The gospel, as set out in the introduction and each of the contributor's essays and responses, is basic to the Christian faith. Having some clarity about it—to say nothing of getting it right—is important to all aspects of the Christian faith. Our views of the triune God and his activity, of the purpose of the church and its practices, of our individual identities and actions: these and so much more are impacted by how we define the gospel. The "gospel," however defined, is what unites all the different expressions of Christianity, and also what typically divides us.

This book arose out of a desire to help each of us who claim to believe and follow the gospel to have a better understanding of it. Indeed, the book's origin is specifically located in a dispute that arose in 2020 when Greg Gilbert delivered a sermon titled "What Is (and Isn't) the Gospel?"[1] At a time when the world was collapsing around us and we were all locked in our homes, this sermon opened a floodgate of responses. Authors from all sides and throughout the world offered their opinions.[2] As with so many of these internet debates, the fire died almost as quickly as it arose.

---

1. Greg Gilbert, "What Is (and Isn't) the Gospel?," Together for the Gospel (T4G), 2020, https://t4g.org/resources/greg-gilbert/what-is-and-isnt-the-gospel; idem, "A T4G 2020 Sermon: What Is and Isn't the Gospel," 9Marks, April 15, 2020, www.9marks.org/article/a-t4g-2020-sermon-what-is-and-isnt-the-gospel.

2. The primary exchanges were between Gilbert, Matthew Bates, and Scot McKnight. References to others are made in these exchanges. See Matthew Bates, "Good News? Are T4G/TGC Leaders Starting To Change Their Gospel?," Jesus Creed | A Blog by Scot McKnight, 2020, https://web.archive.org/web/20240417174435/https://www.christianitytoday.com/scot-mcknight/2020/april/good-news-are-t4g-tgc-leaders-starting-to-change-their-gosp.html; Scot McKnight, "King Jesus Gospel: Mere Kingship? No," *Jesus Creed | A Blog by Scot McKnight*,

Yet, as one sitting on the sidelines watching the exchanges, the thought occurred to me: How is a person unfamiliar with the scholarly contexts of this debate supposed to understand what is going on? How will the typical pastor process this? Will anything in their sermons change? What would the businessmen and women, engineers, schoolteachers, and policemen in my Sunday School class make of this? These are Jesus-loving people trying to navigate how to be a Christian in a complex world. Would they just say that this is a typical academic debate—professors and pastors who live in their ivory towers? Or would they see something fundamental at stake in this debate? Thus, this book was born out of a desire to bring clarity to an important topic for those who might wonder what all the brouhaha is about.

At the end, has any clarity been achieved? I think it is clear that our authors do not see eye to eye. There are differences, even fundamental differences. But clarity does not have to mean uniformity. Thus, here in the conclusion, I want to draw attention to some elements in this debate that stand out to me. These elements arise from my own reflections on the essays and responses and at times are points made by our contributors that I think deserve greater attention.

1. So often the gospel is reduced to an event involving the Father and Son. In crass versions, it is an act of a son placating the wrath of a father. In biblical and more theologically accurate accounts, it is an act of the Father and Son working together to redeem humanity. Either way, the Spirit is sometimes nowhere to be found. Yet, I wonder, does the focus on the Son or Father and Son reflect the Trinitarian identity of God that lies at the heart of the Christian faith? Shouldn't our understanding of the gospel reflect God's own triune identity? Is the good news only about Jesus or

---

2020, https://web.archive.org/web/20240519082846/https://www.christianitytoday.com/scot-mcknight/2020/april/king-jesus-gospel-mere-kingship-no.html; Greg Gilbert, "A Response to Scot McKnight and Matthew Bates," 9Marks, April 22, 2020, www.9marks.org/article/a-response-to-scot-mcknight-and-matthew-bates; Matthew Bates, "Why T4G/TGC Leaders Must Fix Their Gospel," *Jesus Creed | A Blog by Scot McKnight*, 2020, https://web.archive.org/web/20240725234831/https://www.christianitytoday.com/scot-mcknight/2020/april/why-t4gtgc-leaders-must-fix-their-gospel.html; Greg Gilbert, "A Final Reply to Scot McKnight and Matthew Bates," 9Marks, May 4, 2020, www.9marks.org/article/a-final-reply-to-scot-mcknight-and-matthew-bates.

really a statement of good news about the identity and work of the triune God? Is the good news we proclaim truly Christian if it is not Trinitarian? Several contributors offer accounts of the gospel that incorporate the Trinity. In the Wesleyan Gospel, as deSilva explains, the empowerment of the Spirit to sanctification is part of the gospel. The power of the Spirit to overcome evil beings and evident in spiritual giftings is part of the Pentecostal Gospel described by Ma. Whether one incorporates the Spirit into their view of the gospel in the same manner as some of the contributors to this book do, I think the place of the Spirit in our definitions of the gospel is worth pondering.

2. So often definitions of the gospel mention only the cross. It is easy to understand why: Paul, after all, claimed "I resolved to know nothing while I was with you except Jesus Christ and him crucified" (1 Cor 2:2). Christ crucified: this is the gospel. I'm often struck, however, by how Paul can begin 1 Corinthians with the assertion to know nothing but Christ crucified and yet at the end of the letter give his most detailed argument for the resurrection of the body (1 Cor 15). Christ crucified does not, for Paul, mean only the cross. Christ crucified highlights a single event in a series of events that together make up the story of Christ. To declare Christ crucified without also declaring the resurrection is actually to fail to declare the true story of Christ crucified. Contributor after contributor has argued that the gospel cannot be reduced to the event of the cross. For example, McKnight emphasizes the arrival of the kingdom of God in the story of Jesus—his life, death, burial, resurrection, and ascension—as the fulfillment of Israel's hopes. Smith focuses on Jesus's social location among the disadvantaged of society. Horton provides a moving quotation from Calvin that draws out connections between events in Jesus's life and redemption. It is not any single event in the life of Jesus that is the gospel, but the entirety of that life. We might choose to highlight one event over others for particular rhetorical or argumentative purposes, but we cannot reduce the gospel of Jesus to anything less than the full account of the life of the Incarnate One.

3. In many ways, the tension that promoted the exchanges that led to this book can be summed up in this question: What is the

relationship between Christology and soteriology in the gospel? To give a little more precision to the question: Does the gospel center on the person of Jesus or the saving work of Jesus? While none of the contributors advocates a strict either-or approach, they do order the relationship differently. McKnight emphasizes the person of Jesus by focusing on the claim that Jesus is king as seen in his proclamation of the kingdom of God and other statements about his royal activity. Smith centers her account on the person of Jesus as an outcast. Horton, deSilva, and Ma, in different ways, stress the saving work of Christ, the concepts of justification or forgiveness of sins being especially prominent. Being clear about whether we prioritize the person or the saving work can help us better understand from where others are coming. Seeking an approach that balances these two may also help us move forward.

4. Every one of us approaches life through a specific set of lenses. Our lenses are determined by our ethnicity, social context, upbringings, experiences in life, and so on. Because we come to the biblical text from these different contexts—with these different lenses—certain features of the text will stand out to each of us in different ways. McKnight raises the pressing question of how our social contexts influence the way that we define the gospel. As he observed, the gospel definitions offered by each contributor are in some way or other a reflection of their social and theological context. At one level, we should not be surprised by this. But we might also wonder if this prevents us from being able to unite around a single definition of the gospel. While there is a danger that our social contexts will lead us to distort the meaning of the Bible, it is equally possible that our different social contexts will enable us to see things that others overlook. In other words, our different contexts are not necessarily oppositions to a united faith but may actually be opportunities to see the depth of the gospel in greater detail. Perhaps the real danger is when we conclude, "I'm right, you're not," rather than asking how the other person can help us better understand the good news.

5. One final observation: so often gospel presentations make the whole thing about the individual: my sins and my need for redemption. Such a claim has a precedent in Scripture: "I have

been crucified with Christ and I no longer live, but Christ lives in me. The life I now live in the body, I live by faith in the Son of God, *who loved me and gave himself for me*" (Gal 2:20; emphasis added). Yet several of our contributors remind us that the gospel is about more than just me, myself, and I. The gospel is cosmic: Jesus is declared king over the heavens and the earth. As Smith and Ma point out, the gospel aims to transform communities. Their reference to Luke 4 is important:

> "The Spirit of the Lord is on me,
>   because he has anointed me
>   to proclaim good news to the poor.
> He has sent me to proclaim freedom for the prisoners
>   and recovery of sight for the blind,
>   to set the oppressed free,
> to proclaim the year of the Lord's favor." (Luke 4:18–19)

At a time in history that stresses individualism, the gospel stands in opposition. The gospel pulls us out of our narrow, often self-centered, views to see the world around us. Getting the balance between the individual and corporate is difficult in our definitions of the gospel, and I suspect that this tension is part of what underlies current debates. In the end, though, it may be that both are needed to fully account for the truth of the gospel.[3]

There is always a danger when debating theological matters that battle lines will be drawn and the wagons circled tighter. I hope, however, that the result of reading this book for you is not that. I hope, instead, that you go away with a better understanding of the various views on offer and of the issues involved. If reading these positions forces us to think more deeply about the triune God—who he is and what he has accomplished for us—then we are all better off.

---

3. My thoughts turn to the Eucharist at this point. I suggest that there is no greater symbol of the corporate and individual aspects of the gospel than in the act of giving the bread and wine to one's neighbor: "This is Christ's body broken for you"; "This is Christ's blood shed for you."

FOR FURTHER READING

Bates, Matthew. *Gospel Allegiance: What Faith in Jesus Misses for Salvation in Christ*. Grand Rapids: Brazos, 2019.
———. *The Gospel Precisely: Surprisingly Good News about Jesus Christ the King*. Middletown, DE: Renew Resource, 2021.
———. *Why the Gospel? Living the Good News of King Jesus with Purpose*. Grand Rapids: Eerdmans, 2023.
Bird, Michael F. *Evangelical Theology: A Biblical and Systematic Introduction*. 2nd ed. Grand Rapids: Zondervan Academic, 2020. Pages 30–38.
Bock, Darrell L. *Recovering the Real Lost Gospel of Jesus*. Nashville: Broadman & Holman, 2010.
Campbell, Ted A. *The Gospel in Christian Traditions*. Oxford: Oxford University Press, 2009.
Cannon, Mae Elise, and Andrea Smith, eds. *Evangelical Theologies of Liberation and Justice*. Downers Grove, IL: InterVarsity Press, 2019.
Carson, D. A. "The Biblical Gospel." Pages 75–85 in *For Such a Time as This: Perspectives on Evangelicalism, Past, Present, and Future*. Edited by S. Brady and H. Rowdon. London: Evangelical Alliance, 1996.
Carson, D. A., and Timothy Keller, eds. *The Gospel as Center: Renewing our Faith and Reforming our Ministry Practices*. Wheaton, IL: Crossway, 2012.
Dickson, John. *The Best Kept Secret of Christian Mission: Promoting the Gospel with More Than Our Lips*. Grand Rapids: Zondervan, 2010. Pages 111–40.
Gilbert, Greg. *What Is the Gospel?* Wheaton, IL: Crossway, 2010.
Gupta, Nijay, Tara Beth Leach, Matthew Bates, and Drew J. Strait, eds. *Living the King Jesus Gospel: Discipleship and Ministry, Then and Now*. Eugene, OR: Cascade, 2021.
Mason, Eric, ed. *Urban Apologetics: Restoring Black Dignity with the Gospel*. Grand Rapids: Zondervan, 2021.
McKnight, Scot. *The King Jesus Gospel: The Original Good News Revisited*. Grand Rapids: Zondervan, 2011.
Packer, J. I., and Thomas C. Oden. *One Faith: The Evangelical Consensus*. Downers Grove, IL: InterVarsity Press, 1999. Pages 187–91.
Snodgrass, Klyne. *You Need a Better Gospel: Reclaiming the Good News of Participation with Christ*. Grand Rapids: Baker, 2022.
Taylor, Iain, ed. *Not Evangelical Enough: The Gospel at the Centre*. Carlisle, UK: Paternoster, 2003.
Treat, Jeremy R. "Gospel and Doctrine in the Life of the Church." *Scottish Bulletin of Evangelical Theology* 32 (2014): 180–94.
Wax, Trevin. *Counterfeit Gospels: Rediscovering the Good News in a World of False Hope*. Chicago: Moody, 2011.
Wilson-Hartgrove, Jonathan. *Reconstructing the Gospel: Finding Freedom from Slaveholder Religion*. Downers Grove, IL: InterVarsity Press, 2020.
Wright, N. T. *Simply Good News: Why the Gospel Is News and What Makes It Good*. New York: HarperOne, 2017.

SCRIPTURE INDEX

Genesis
1:26–27 ... 109, 146, 153
2:7 167
3. .... 28, 71
3:15 ..... 69, 71, 72, 85, 87, 115
5:3 .... 110, 138, 146
12. 39
15. .... 39, 72, 76
15:2, 8 99
15:6 .... 78, 91
17:5 99

Exodus
16:22–30 105
19:8 .... 80, 87
19:16–19 166
23:16 166
24:7–8 72
33:16 70

Leviticus
19:18 126

Deuteronomy
6:5 .... 126, 135
7:1 61
30:6 .... 73, 125

1 Samuel
8. 28

2 Samuel
4:10 31
7. 73
7:18–19 99
7:19 99
18:20, 22, 25, 27 31

Job
9:2 70

Psalms
39:10 31
40:9 31
51:4–5 143
67:12 31
68:11 31
96:2 31
95:2 31
103:1–13 22

Isaiah
4:16–30, 18–19 31
6:5 227
28:11 183
40:3 .... 20, 33
40:9 31
49:6 149
52:7 31
53:4–5 22
53:11–12 68
58. 105
58:3–10 105
58:6 168
58:6–7 105
61. 31
61:1 31
61:1–2 .... 168, 188

Jeremiah
20:15 31
31. 75
31:32 76
34:18 76

Ezekiel
36:25–27 126

Hosea
6:7 .... 69, 71, 88

Joel
2. 41

2:32 31
3:5 31

Jonah
2:9 185

Nahum
1:15 31
2:1 31

Malachi
4:1–6 69

Matthew
1:1 196
1:3, 5 61
1:21 42
1:23 61
4:17 180
5:13 30
5:14 49
5:17–48 30
5:22, 28 116
5:48 .... 125, 149
7:21–27 52
7:28–29 43
8:25 42
9:15 105
9:21–22 42
10:5 204
10:22 42
11:3–6 50
11:28–30 73
12:46–50 60
13:42 231
13:55 59
13:55–56 ..... 202, 217
14:30 42
15:21–28 ... 61, 202, 218
15:22 61
15:26 61
16:25 42

SCRIPTURE INDEX

19:25 42
20:28 52
22:37–40 . . . . . . 126, 135
23:23 . . . . 202, 218
24:13, 22 42
24:14 231
24:30–31 231
25:30–45 206
25:31 232
25:35–37 218
25:42–45 202
26:28 41
26:48–54 60
27:19 200
27:29, 37, 42 58
27:40, 42, 49 42
28:18–20 . . . . . . 69, 171
28:20 61

Mark

1:1 33
1:4 41
1:14 60
1:14–15 59
1:15 . . . . . . 20, 33, 52, 92
1:16–17 59
1:32–34 . . . . 202, 217
2:1–12 . . . . 202, 203, 217
2:19–20 105
3:10 . . . . 202, 217
3:31–35 . . . . 202, 217
4:1 . . . . 202, 217
5:1–20 . . . . 202, 218
6:3 59
6:4 . . . . 202, 217
7:24–30 . . . . 61, 209
7:27 61
8 34
8:1–9 . . . . 202, 218
10:45 52
10:46–52 . . . . . . 202, 218
12:17 47
12:29–31 . . . . . . 126, 135
15:2, 26 58

Luke

1 58
1:5 218
1:8–23 58
1:77 41
2:1–2 . . . . 201, 218
2:7, 22–24 200
2:22–24 . . . . 202, 217
2:24 59
3:1–2 . . . . . . 58, 201, 218
3:3 41
3:10–14 41
3:16 172
4 243
4:16–20 . . . 188, 202, 217
4:16–21 . . . . 203, 219
4:16–30 32
4:16–31 16
4:18 . . . . 168, 214
4:18–19 . . . 21, 103, 168,
          179, 194, 243
4:18–21 232
4:19 41
4:21 168
5:8 227
5:17–26 203
5:34–35 105
6:46–49 52
7:22 49
7:32 78
7:36 192
7:48–50 73
8:1–4 209
8:55 192
9:10–17 192
9:31 69
9:51–19:27 204
10:8–11 204
10:25–28 204
10:25–37 . . . . . . 21, 204
10:29–37 204
10:31–32 205
10:38–42 204
11:1–13 204
13:33 . . . . 202, 217
17:11–19 204
17:21 232
18 92
18:9–14 . . . . . 77, 91, 103
18:9–16 20
18:11 228
18:11, 13 104
18:13 84
18:14 . . . . 78, 91
18:18 . . . . 70, 78
22:19–20 76
23:1–56 16
23:2 58
23:37 58
23:47 200
24:13–53 69
24:19 . . . . 202, 217
24:27 66
24:47 41
24:47–48 166
24:50–53 37

John

1:5–2:2 16
1:14–18 61
1:17 73
1:29 68
1:49 58
3:3 . . . . 21, 113, 146, 153
3:3–8 . . . . 113, 146
3:16 17
3:16–17 22
4:1–42 236
4:9 204
4:39–42 . . . . 202, 217
5:39 66
6 50
6:15 58
7:37–39 184
14:26 46
18:33 58
18:36 . . . . 47, 69
19:15 47
19:25–27 60

Acts

1–2 189
1:6–8 69
1:8 . . . . 15, 21, 148, 158,
       160, 165, 179, 194
1:9–11 37

Reference	Page(s)
2.	41, 182, 208
2:1	166
2:1–4	194
2:1–12	21, 165, 179
2:14–39	34
2:36	35
2:36, 38	20
2:38	35, 40, 41, 160
2:38–39	35, 49
2:42, 44	204
2:42–47	217
2:44	207
3:12–26	34
3:19–21	35
4.	207
4:1–22	208
4:8–12	34
4:32	204
4:32–35	207
4:32–37	207
5:1–5	170
5:21	201, 218
5:31	41
6:1–6	209
7:2–53	34
7:59–60	37
8–28	39
8:35	35
9:10–19a	208
9:26–30	209
9:36–43	209
10:34–43	16, 34
10:43	35, 40, 41, 56
10:44–47	42, 49
11:1–18	60, 209
11:4–18	34
11:16–18	42, 49
11:17	40, 56
11:20	35
11:26	208
12:6–11	203
12:6–17	209
13:16–41	34
13:38	41
13:38–39	20, 35, 40, 42, 49, 56
13:47	149
14:15–17	34
15.	78, 90, 209
15:8–11	20, 79
15:22–39	209
16.	209
16:3	209
16:11–15	209
16:19–34	203
17:18	35
17:22–31	16, 34
17:24–31	35
18:5	35
18:24–28	209
18:28	35
19:13	36
20:20–21	36
25:1–2, 13	201, 218
26:18	41
28:23	36
28:31	36

Romans

Reference	Page(s)
1–3	73
1:1–5	181
1:2–4	16
1:16	107, 135, 145
1:18	110, 230
1:18–32	54, 110
2:4	120
2:5, 8	110
3.	28
3:21–26	16
3:21–28	81
3:23	229
3:23–25	112, 150
3:24	73
4.	71, 73, 79
4:3–6	20, 79
4:6–8	112, 139
4:25	63, 67, 88, 89, 90
5.	73
5:1	16, 85
5:11	42, 49
5:12–21	86, 110, 138, 146
5:19	113
6.	141
6:1	116
6:1–11	21
6:1–11, 13	189
6:1–23	115
6:4, 6	129
6:5–6	116
6:12–14	116, 150
6:12–14, 17–23	54
6:13	116
6:20–23	190
6:22	118
6:23	117
7.	141
7:7–10	81
7:12, 22	143
7:24	227
8:1	50, 140
8:1, 2, 13	189
8:1–3	16
8:1–4	44
8:2–13	190
8:4	94
8:9	120, 188
8:18–25	231
8:29–30	137
8:30	82, 85
8:31	84
10.	50
10:17	74
11:15	42, 49
12:1–2	49
12:3	170
13.	235
13:8–10	97
13:11	21, 108

1 Corinthians

Reference	Page(s)
2:1–5	189
2:2	241
2:9	66
3:16–17	31
6:19	31
12:7	169
12:7–9	21, 169, 179
13:13	212
14.	182

14:2 183
14:17 183
14:21–22 183
15. . . . . . 37, 90, 220, 241
15:1–5 22
15:1–8 . . . 37, 38, 52, 90, 179, 180
15:1–10 59
15:1–11 212
15:1–28 136
15:3 . . . . 22, 194
15:3–4 . . . . 67, 88, 92
15:3–5 20
15:24–25 37
15:56 68

2 Corinthians
3:18 . . . . 40, 42
4:5 85
4:6 . . . . 114, 154
5:10 191
5:15 . . . . 54, 93, 119, 127
5:18–19 . . . . 42, 49
5:19 . . . . 49, 191
9:13 23
10–13 134
11:23–33 234

Galatians
2:11–14 134
2:20 . . . . 126, 243
3:2–5, 13–14 . . . . 95, 119
3:5–6 74
3:6–9 39
3:7–14 74
3:8 99
3:8–9, 13–14 189
3:12 80
3:13–14 . . . . 54, 94
3:15–25 39
3:16 75
3:21–22 72
3:26–29 99
3:28 . . . . 39, 212, 232
3:28–29 76
4:6 188
4:24 . . . . 80, 87

5:5 95
5:6 . . . . 80, 95, 119
5:13–15 97
5:14 . . . . 126, 135
5:16 . . . . 94, 120, 190
5:22–23 . . . . 117, 120
5:22–26 44
5:24 120
5:25 144
6:7–8 . . . . 121, 190
6:10 130
6:15 95

Ephesians
1:3 . . . . 43, 138
1:3–10 99
1:17 24
2:1 84
2:1–5 83
2:5 143
2:8 119
2:8–9 . . . . 124, 153
2:10 130
2:11–22 232
2:13–15 76
2:21–22 31
4:15 . . . . 114, 147
4:22 116
4:22–24 127
4:24 . . 110, 116, 146, 153
5:2 126
5:18 184
5:21–6:9 235
5:26 184

Philippians
1:27 . . . . . 23, 49, 84, 129
2:1–11 94
2:3–5 . . . . 117, 130
2:5 . . . . 120, 129
2:6–11 44
2:12–13 123
2:13 . . . . 108, 146
3 74
3:8b–9 74
3:8–11 93
3:10–11 94

Colossians
1:15 129
2:14–15 . . . . 68, 98
3:1 37
3:12–14 49
3:13 100

1 Thessalonians
1:3 120
5:23 127

2 Timothy
2:8 . . . . 90, 136, 179
2:8–13 . . . . 38, 44

Titus
2:14 130

Philemon
16 235

Hebrews
1:8 37
2:3–4 189
2:8–9 66
4:14–16 37
6:13–18 75
8:6–7 75
12:14 . . . . 21, 67, 95, 117, 147

James
1:4 130
5:5 237

1 Peter
1:15, 16 189
2:1–10 16
3:21–22 . . . . 37, 372

2 Peter
1:4 17
3:4 191

1 John
1:5–2:2 16
1:8–9 142

2:6 120	**2 John**	4:2, 9–10 37
3:6, 9 114	1:49 58	5:6, 13 37
3:8 115	18:33 58	5:9 223
4:8 . . . . 110, 146, 153	**Revelation**	5:9–10 63
4:9–11 190	1:13 37	21 231
4:18 142	3:12 31	21–22 31
		22:21 85

SUBJECT/AUTHOR INDEX

Abraham
   covenant with, 71, 72, 75–76, 77.
      See also covenants
   faith of, 39, 54, 73–74
Abraham, William, 127, 144
African Methodist Episcopal Church
   (AME), 150, 151, 192
Africana Wesleyan communities, 151–52, 155
Allison, Dale, 30
Ambrose, Nancy, 211
Anglican Church in North America
   (ACNA), 22, 109
atonement, 158–59
apostolic gospel, 37, 63, 88, 95, 101, 180, 220

Barclay, John M. G., 87
Bates, Matthew W., 48
Bird, Michael F., 9, 15–24
Borg, Marcus, 219
Brunner, Emil, 187
Bucer, 64, 83, 88

Calvin, John, 22, 23, 64, 83, 88, 89, 137–39, 143–44, 241
Calvinistic. *See* Reformation Gospel
Campbell, Douglas, 82
Catholic, 93, 95–96
Celsus, 70–71
Christ. *See also* Jesus
   ascension, 27, 36, 64, 67, 69, 82, 98
   cross of, 50, 98, 190–91, 241
   gospel and, 39, 40, 47, 50, 136. See also gospel
   resurrection, 67, 98, 241
   righteousness of, 144
   salvation alone, 64–65, 78–79
   triumph of, 68, 98
Christian perfection, 124–29
Christocracy, 28, 29, 54, 60
Christoformity, 20, 38, 43

Christology, 26, 29, 43–45, 49, 57, 89, 90, 135, 136, 177, 220, 242
Clarke, Matthew, 172
covenants
   Abrahamic, 71–72, 75, 77, 99, 104
   Davidic, 71, 73, 99–100
   Mosaic, 72, 99
   grace, 71–72, 87, 100, 117
   Sinaitic, 72–77, 80, 81
Cremer, Hermann, 80
cross-cultural view, 61–62, 167, 174

deSilva, David A., 9, 20–21, 86, 107–30, 179, 242
   Horton's response to, 137–44
   Ma's response to, 145–49
   McKnight's response to, 131–36
   response to Horton, 93–97
   response to Ma, 188–91
   response to McKnight, 51–54
   response to Smith, 232–35
   Smith's response to, 150–55
discipleship, 21, 31, 44, 52, 84, 129, 233
Dodd, C. H., 220
Douglas, Aaron, 197–98
Dunn, James D. G., 69, 86, 89, 170

faith
   Abrahams's, 39, 54, 73–74
   alone, 39, 67, 73, 95
   in Christ, 26, 39, 67, 74, 80, 82, 99
   justification and, 26, 48, 73–74, 85
   living, 118–19, 148
   saving, 82–84, 94, 98, 107
   vs. law, 80
   works and, 79, 123–24
fasting, 105–106
Fee, Gordon, 170–71
Flattery, George M., 171
forgiveness
   justification and, 49, 77–78, 85, 98

of sins, 41–42, 48–49, 96, 127, 144, 184, 230

gifts, spiritual, 84, 169–71
Gilbert, Greg, 239
God
    character of, 68, 147, 234
    grace of, 71–72, 82–85, 100
    image of, 122, 138–39
    kingdom of, 28, 42, 60–61, 77
    promises of. *See* covenants
    righteousness of, 81
    submission to, 43–45, 56
    triune, 85, 239, 240–41, 243
good news. *See also* gospel, the
    beneficiaries of, 49, 51, 53, 67–68, 93–94
    biblical summary, 63
    Holy Spirit and, 119–20, 126–27
    interpretation of, 69–70, 157
gospel, the. *See also* specific gospels
    Africana Wesleyan view, 151–53
    contrast with law, 72–76
    defining, 15–17, 22–24, 90, 239, 240–41
    goal of, 21, 45, 49
    holistic, 56, 162–65, 178. *See also* Liberation Gospel
    importance of, 22–24
    location advantage, 202, 216–18
    obedience to, 53, 84–85, 137–38
    personal salvation, 25–26, 69–70, 82, 110–11
    perspectives of, 18–22, 66–67, 93
    politics and, 32–33, 46–47
    power of, 56, 82
    summaries of, 20–22
    surrender to, 43–45, 48–49
    testing, 29, 46
grace
    alone, 76
    covenant of, 72
    God's, 21, 83, 123
    of Christ, 100
Graham, Billy, 25–26, 55, 176
Gutiérrez, Gustavo, 198–99

healing, 172–74
Heidelberg Catechism, 139–40, 141, 142

Holy Spirit. *See also* Wesleyan Gospel
    empowerment of, 119–22, 130, 133, 148–49, 160, 165–68, 241
    gifts of, 169–71
    Jesus and, 168–69
    unifying, 66
    work of, 119–21
Horton, Michael S., 9, 20, 63–85, 179, 241, 242
deSilva's response to, 93–97
    Ma's response to, 98–100
    McKnight's response to, 86–92
    response to deSilva, 137–44
    response to Ma, 182–91
    response to McKnight, 46–50
    response to Smith, 222–31
    Smith's response to, 101–6

Israel. *See also* covenants
    guilt of, 69–71, 88, 95
    hope of, 221, 241
    promises to, 27, 35, 37
Irenaeus, 22–23, 66

Jesus
    covenant servant, 76
    gospel and, 37, 44–45, 50, 56–57, 90–92, 96–97, 102, 241
    Holy Spirit and, 168–69
    Israel and, 30, 37, 196. *See also* Messiah
    kingdom of, 28–31, 56
    liberation view of, 201–3
    Messiah, 20, 27, 28, 35, 36, 40–41, 168, 230
    Savior, 138, 160
    solution to problem, 27, 58–59, 66, 111, 129
    Syrophoenician woman and, 61–62
    transforming lives, 43–45, 50, 100, 108–9
justification, 89, 139–41. *See also* Reformation Gospel

Keener, Craig, 182
King, Martin Luther, Jr., 200, 204, 212–13, 224, 226, 227
kingdom
    five elements of, 30–31

gospel and, 34, 36, 45, 52, 55, 92
King Jesus Gospel
  biblically grounded, 33–39
  Christocracy, 28–29
  context, 18, 31–33, 45
  definition, 27, 29, 36
  gospeling, 26–27, 29
  kingdom of, 28–30
  life shaping, 43–45, 49, 52–53
  personal: response, 39–43; salvation, 25–26
  problem, 28, 54
  solution, 27, 54

law-gospel contrast, 72–76
Levenson, Jon, 69
Levine, Amy-Jill, 91, 219
Liberation Gospel
  Acts, book of, 207–10
  benefits of, 213–14
  biblical texts, 203–13
  context, 199, 201–203
  definition, 199, 200–201
  Good Samaritan, 204–7
  location advantage, 202, 216
  Paul's writings, 210–13
  problem, 199, 201–2, 220
  solution, 199, 206, 208
  visual representation, 197–98
Luther, Martin, 48, 64, 70, 83, 95, 98

Ma, Julie C., 21, 157–75, 179, 242
  deSilva's response to, 188–91
  Horton's response to, 182–87
  McKnight's response to, 176–81
  response to deSilva, 145–49
  response to Horton, 98–100
  response to McKnight, 55–56
  response to Smith, 236–38
  Smith's response to, 192–96
Macchia, Frank, 160
Maddox, Randy, 110, 138, 146
Maston, Jason, 10, 239–41
McKnight, Scot, 10, 20, 25–45, 225, 241, 242
  deSilva's response to, 51–54
  Horton's response to, 46–50
  Ma's response to, 55–56

response to deSilva, 131–36
response to Horton, 86–92
response to Ma, 176–81
response to Smith, 215–21
Smith's response to, 57–62
Melanchthon, 64, 83, 88
Messiah, 20, 27, 28, 35, 36, 40–41, 168, 230
Milton, Grace, 160, 177
missions, Pentecostal, 162–65
Murray, John, 144

new birth. *See* Wesleyan Gospel
Nouwen, Henri, 147

obedience, 53
O'Donovan, Oliver, 23
Old Testament
  gospel announced, 68, 71, 101, 125
  kingdom evidence, 30–31
Origen, 23, 46

Palma, Anthony D., 170
parables
  good Samaritan, 204–207, 219, 226–27, 236–37
  publican and Pharisee, 76–78, 91–92, 96, 103–105
  wedding guests, 105–106
Paul
  gospel and, 16, 22–23, 32–33, 44
  Holy Spirit, 94–95
  justification. *See* Reformation Gospel
  law and, 39, 72–79, 93–94
  liberation and, 210–13, 235
  rabbis teaching, 71, 96
  resurrection teaching, 35–39
Payne, Daniel A., 152
Pelagius, 143
Pennington, Jonathan, 28
Pentecostal Gospel
  context, 165–71
  definition, 157, 158–61
  holistic, 162–65, 177–78, 193
  Holy Spirit: baptism of, 165–67, 172, 183–84; empowerment of, 160, 171–72, 189–90; gifts of, 169–71, 183, 190; Jesus and, 168–69

lives transformed, 172–74
mission of, 157–58, 161, 167, 171–72, 174–75
problem, 158–58
salvation, 160
solution, 158–59, 162
spiritual warfare, 172–74, 186
Powery, Emerson, 219
Protestant Reformation, 98

Qumran, 32, 96

Reformation Gospel
biblical source, 80–81
context, 18, 68–76, 86, 95, 101–102
definition, 63, 67
deification, 65, 86, 89
justification, 48, 63–65, 67–68, 72–75, 77–78, 80, 83–85
law-gospel contrast, 72–76, 86–87
principal source, 80–82
problem, 65–66, 71, 91–92, 102, 138, 185
resurrection, 64, 89
sanctification, 65, 73, 83–85, 137–38
solution, 66, 69, 71, 78–79, 85
traditional view, 83–85
works of the law, 79–80
Reformers, 63–65, 70
soteriology and, 89
Rybarczyk, Edmund, 159, 184

salvation. *See also* soteriology
holistic, 132, 160
ongoing work of God, 107–109, 145
Pentecostal, 160–61
through faith, 98
sanctification. *See* Reformation Gospel, Wesleyan Gospel
Sanders, E. P., 69, 86, 89
Schweitzer, Albert, 50
Second Temple Judaism, 68–69, 76–77, 89–91, 96
Shaull, Richard, 172
Sievers, Joseph, 91
Smith, Shively T. J., 10–11, 21–22, 179, 197–214, 242
deSilva's response to, 232–35

Horton's response to, 222–31
Ma's response to, 236–38
McKnight's response to, 215–21
response to deSilva, 150–55
response to Horton, 101–106
response to Ma, 192–96
response to McKnight, 57–62
social
context, 61–62, 208, 215, 217–18, 220–21, 242
issues, 152, 154–55, 161–62, 199
soteria, 26, 28, 45, 51, 53, 176, 177
soteriology/-ical
Christology and, 43, 45, 49, 57
justification, 136
mission, 158, 178, 196
narrative, 160, 188
gospel, 86, 90, 134, 179
Reformed, 92
spiritual
gifts, 84, 169–71
warfare, 172–74, 186, 187
Stott, John R. W., 184
Stylianopoulos, Theodore, 29

Thurman, Howard Washington, 59–60, 150, 154, 194, 195, 198, 204–206, 209–14
Tidball, Derek, 23
tongues, gift of, 182–83
transformation
character, 27, 42, 49–50, 109, 122
Holy Spirit and, 121
social, 172, 201, 213, 230, 238

Vermigli, 64, 83, 88

Watts, Isaac, 66
Webster, John, 24
Wesley, Charles, 20, 127–28, 137, 168
Wesley, John, 23, 232–33. *See also* Wesleyan Gospel
Wesleyan Gospel
Christian perfection, 124–29
concerns regarding, 135–36
context, 109–11
core conviction, 108, 145–46
definition, 107

Holy Spirit empowerment, 119–22, 130, 133, 148–49, 241
justification, 112–13, 139–40
living faith, 118–19, 123–24
new birth, 113–15, 141–42, 146–47, 148
new life, 115–18
overview, 107–109, 131–32
problem, 108, 109–10
sanctification, 114, 116–18
solution, 110–11, 129, 132–33
Westminster tradition. *See* Reformation Gospel
Willimon, William, 137
works of the law, 39, 74, 79–81

www.ingramcontent.com/pod-product-compliance
Lightning Source LLC
Chambersburg PA
CBHW010929180426
43194CB00045B/2844